To Bill
Love Dad
Christmas
1990

ROBERT TRENT JONES

Golf's
Magnificent Challenge

with Larry Dennis Photography by **Tony Roberts**

Foreword by Peter Dobereiner

McGraw-Hill Publishing Company

New York St. Louis San Francisco Auckland Bogotá Hamburg
London Madrid Mexico Milan Montreal New Delhi Panama
Paris São Paulo Singapore Sydney Tokyo Toronto

Preceding pages: Page 1: *Mauna Kea, #3*. Pages 2-3: *Metedeconk, #7*. Pages 4-5: *Arrowhead, #10*. Pages 6-7: *Pebble Beach, #9*. Pages 8-9: *Innisbrook, #5 Copperhead*. Pages 10-11: *St. Andrews, #14 Old*. These pages: *Kananaskis, #2 Mount Lorette*. Following pages: *Royal County Down*.

1 2 3 4 5 6 7 8 9   9 2 1 0 9

ISBN 0-07-032816-1

TO IONE, MY BELOVED WIFE AND ANCHOR;
TO MY SONS, ROBERT JR. AND REES;
AND TO THE GAME WHICH HAS BEEN SO GOOD TO ME
AND TO ALL OF YOU

LIBRARY OF CONGRESS CATALOGING-IN-
PUBLICATION DATA

Jones, Robert Trent
   Golf's magnificent challenge by Robert Trent Jones with
Larry Dennis and Tony Roberts.

   ISBN 0-07-032816-1
   1. Golf courses—Design and construction. I. Dennis,
Larry. 1933-   . II. Roberts, Tony. III. Title.
OV975.J66   1989
712″-5—dc19   88-7792
                                         CIP

Prepared and produced by the
Sammis Publishing Corporation
Project editor: John Sammis
Book design by Allan Mogel
Production supervision by Layla Productions, Inc.
Typesetting by LCR Graphics, Inc.
Printed by Sagdos, Italy

Contents

Foreword
By Peter Dobereiner

Back in the days when professional golfers (with the exception of Jimmy Demaret) wore clothes of autumnal tints so that they would blend into the background and be rendered invisible to the galleries, I had the notion that these men were gods. It was a common delusion among innocent young golf writers and still is. After all, anyone who can nail a 1-iron out of a cuppy lie must possess supernatural powers, hence he must also be all-wise.

All the pros ever talked about was some malicious monster they called

Robert-Effing-Trent-Effing-Jones. Naturally, I accepted this received wisdom as the gospel truth. Even Ben Hogan, who I still believe to be a god, confirmed the perfidy of this Jones chap. There was the well-documented incident at the 1951 U.S. Open at Oakland Hills, which Jones had extensively remodeled or, as the pros insisted, turned into a monster. Ione, the architect's charming wife, was genuinely thrilled at Hogan's victory and duly offered her congratulations, only to be taken aback by Hogan's gruff reply: "If your husband had to play his own courses for a living, you'd starve." Incidentally, this is believed to be not only the rudest but also the longest sentence ever uttered by Hogan during his illustrious career.

I should have known better. The late Bernard Darwin, the father of golf writing or, at least, golf writing with a verb in every sentence and insight in every word, had fulminated: "My readers are not interested in what the pros say; they want to know what I thought of the golf." Oddly enough, Harry Vardon accepted that imperious judgment. When asked how he had played, he replied: "I never know how well I have played until I read Mr. Darwin's verdict in the next day's *Times*."

That was all very well for Darwin. I was expected to report what people did and said and to keep my own thoughts to myself. Not that I had many thoughts in those days; I was still skidding wildly through the learning curves of golf. Jones was a monster because the pros said so.

Then two things happened. In a locker room I overheard Peter Thomson and Billy Casper discussing some Trent Jones modifications. Most pros talk about courses in terms of clubs and lines: "It's a 2-iron on the line of the left hand bunker." Thomson and Casper spoke of arcs and landing areas and stroke values, and the tone of their conversation was of men seeking to unravel a mystery. They clearly had the utmost respect for the man who had set the mystery. I had never before perceived golf as a battle of wits between player and architect. The golf course as an intelligence test was a new concept altogether.

The next gleam of enlightenment came when I went to Sardinia to view a golf course that Jones had designed for the Aga Kahn. I knew that four architects had inspected the rocky cliffs and precipitous mountains covered with impenetrable bushes and proclaimed that it was impossible to build a golf course on the site. Trent Jones had undertaken the commission, and I wondered what manner of dog track had been created in this unlikely area.

The reality was an eye-opener, a gorgeous course that made you itch to grab some clubs and get out there. They told me that Jones had blasted the tops off the mountains to create areas for fairways through the narrow valleys. The obvious next move would have been to ship in thousands of tons of topsoil from mainland Italy, a hideously expensive undertaking. Jones shipped in a rock crusher, reduced the boulders to sand and grew grass on it. That master stroke saved the client hundreds of thousands of dollars.

Clearly I had to revise my views on the infallibility of the pros. Monster or not, the man was a genius. I began to question the omniscience of the pros, subjecting their utterances to the litmus test of logic and the evidence of my own eyes. I quickly reversed my ideas completely, deciding that most of them, most of the time, talked mindless rubbish. Their thought processes were governed by how well they had just played, and I even invented a new form of pronunciation to help the reader make due allowances for the speaker's state of mind. The U.S. Open of 1970 at Hazeltine, another Jones product, provides some examples. Tommy Bolt said: "Haven't you newspaper sons of bitches got something to do out on the golf course?" Jack Nicklaus said: "Excuse me while I go throw up." Dave Hill said: "They ruined a good farm when they built this course." Tony Jacklin, who won the Championship, said: "I liked playing out there."

On that particular occasion, Trent Jones was moved by the vitriolic criticism of his work to deliver a mild reproof: "If you built the kind of course the pros would really like, you would have dead flat greens and dead flat fairways, very little rough and very few traps. That kind of course wouldn't require an architect; you could order it from a Sears Roebuck catalog." How very true.

Soon afterward I met Trent, not an ogre at all but a Welsh pixie with laughing eyes and a heart the size of a bucket. Goodness knows how many instructive hours I have spent listening to him talk about design, tramping over sites with him and watching him paint greens and bunkers in his mind's eye. There is a lyrical quality about the man, the Welsh heritage no doubt, but the real key to his undoubted genius as an architect is the fact that first and foremost he is an artist. That is literally the case, for he is a watercolorist of some distinction, but his artistic sensibilities are seen to best advantage in his golf courses. His contours have a natural flow of point and counterpoint. Walk down a sweeping Trent Jones fairway and you can imagine that this was exactly the way a residing glacier left the land many millennia ago. That is his art that conceals art, because twelve months previously the land looked quite different. Those unfolding vistas, one of his greatest design strengths, have been meticulously planned and shaped.

At the same time there is nothing arty about his art; everything is harmonized to the strictly practical purpose of golf. Inspect a Trent Jones green and you will detect five suitable pin positions. They did not happen by accident, but they look as if they did. Like every good architect, he employs trickery in his designs, tempting the golfer to blast away with a hooking drive with a wide sward of fairway away to the left while creating a green better approached from tight down the right. If you cannot read a Trent Jones course, then you cannot hope to score on it. But if you can get inside his mind, the traps he has laid are plain enough to see. His golf is half chess, half archery.

The great problem with judging an architect's work is that you never know what budget was available to him, nor what constraints were placed upon him by the client. So we should be wary of condemning Buggins for making a rather humdrum job of Suchandsuch Country Club. The rule, therefore, is to judge an architect by his best work.

Trent has built many remarkable courses in many parts of the world, and it would be wildly impractical, though great fun, to play them all and attempt to place them in some kind of order of merit. How can you begin to compare the quality of a links course, for instance, with a forest course, or a heathland course, or a clifftop course, or a desert course? It would be like adjudicating between the merits of apples, oranges and bananas. But at least I am prepared to select Trent's greatest masterpiece, and I suspect that as I climb out onto that precarious limb I shall find Trent perched there as well. By coincidence, I was in on this project from the start, even before the start, because for years I had looked across the site and speculated on what manner of course it could provide. The original Ballybunion course on the Atlantic coast of Ireland is wild enough for most tastes, but its dunes were bland and puny compared with the majestic proportions of the neighboring dunesland wilderness.

Eventually the club acquired the land and invited Trent to breathe his genius into a site that nature had already created as a golf course waiting to happen. You might think that after designing more than four hundred courses, and being in his advanced years, a man might become blasé about yet another project. Trent was as excited as a teenager on his first date, so overwhelmed by the challenge that he so far forgot his professional obligations as to waive his fee. This must be a labor of love because, he decided, Ballybunion New would be his monument, the ultimate statement of his golfing philosophy.

Controversy raged from the moment play was permitted on the new course. Some people enthused, none more vigorously than I. Others branded it an unplayable monster, the epithet that has dogged Trent from the earliest days. The course, I should add, was far from ready, and it is still not finished by any means. Trent planned a multiplicity of tees for every hole, as many as five in some cases, to create maximum flexibility and accommodate the changing conditions. Some of the comments about playing a 580-yard uphill hole into the prevailing wind are best not repeated, proof of the old saying that you should never show something half-finished to fools or children. Gradually the sheer excellence of the course, and the exhilaration of playing through an Andes of dunes, won over the critics, or most of them. Today the people who know it best, the members, rate it better than the old Ballybunion by a considerable majority. And that means, quite simply, that it is the greatest links course in the world.

This book is also a monument to Trent. I hope it adequately reflects the scale of the man and his achievements. He is the father of modern golf course architecture, the inspiration of an entire school of imaginative and innovative designers including his two sons, Rees and Bobby Jr. Some contemporary design is spectacular, or vulgar, or grotesque, which has drawn some of the flak from Trent, who has finally inherited his rightful reputation as the master of his art. Some of it is superb. But I see nothing that surpasses the best work of Trent Jones and, frankly, I doubt if I ever will.

Introduction

The toughest part of writing a book with Robert Trent Jones is finding him. At eighty-two, Jones remains indefatigable. He is usually on an airplane, flying somewhere in the world to look at a golf course. When he is home in Montclair, New Jersey, or Fort Lauderdale, Florida, which is seldom, he usually has a telephone in his ear, talking about a golf course.

I don't know how many phones Trent has in his Montclair home (I do know there are two within eight feet of each other in his breakfast nook, one on either side of the table), but telephone company stock may drop precipitously when he retires.

At this point, retirement isn't likely. He seems inclined to do forever what he has done for almost sixty years, which is build more golf courses in more places than any man ever. And, I might add, marvelous golf courses. There may be better individual golf courses around the globe than Trent Jones has built, but nobody has designed more good and great layouts than he.

Courses that Jones has designed or remodeled have been the site of twenty-seven U.S. Open or PGA Championships. This is not to mention Augusta National Golf Club, home of the Masters, on which Jones has done extensive remodeling that includes the construction of the famed 11th and 16th holes. Firestone Country Club in Akron, Ohio, a complete Jones redesign, is the home of the annual World Series of Golf. His courses have hosted seven World Cup Matches. And a number of Tour events are played annually on Jones' layouts. In all, thirty-six of his courses have been the sites of national or international tournaments, a staggering total when you consider the relative paucity of such events.

The latest *Golf Digest* list of the 100 Greatest Courses in America included fourteen by Jones, plus two others he has extensively redesigned. His total on that list and others used to be much larger until the explosion, in the last decade or so, of fine architects and fine courses for which Jones, through his influence on the craft, has been responsible.

Let us not put too much emphasis on such lists, which almost always are predicated on how well the professionals and top amateurs can play the courses. Jones obviously holds his own in this category, but he never has lost sight of the intrinsic challenge of the game for players of all levels of skill or the beauty that is inherent in the game and is perhaps its most siren-like attraction.

He is the most significant golf course architect in history. His firm has designed or redesigned some four-hundred-fifty courses in forty-three states and thirty-four countries. Of course his sons and his associates—Roger Rulewich is principal among the latter—have done much of the hands-on designing over the years. That sort of thing is true in any business of this magnitude. But Trent Jones has been the hand at the helm.

His immediate goal is to reach the five-hundred mark, and he has enough projects on the drawing board to do that easily. He has created virtually every kind of course on every kind of land, from swamps to rocky terrain to beautiful woods. In doing so, by adhering to his belief that the design of the course rather than improvements in technology should dictate the shot values, he has changed the way the game is played and helped shape its destiny.

He also has drawn more criticism—and praise—than any other architect since men began to build golf courses deliberately.

Jones' signature has been enormous, undulating greens, hourglass fairways, extra-long tees and large water hazards strategically and scenically deployed. The famed Peachtree Golf Club in Atlanta, which Jones designed in 1948 in collaboration with Bobby Jones, was the first exemplification and is still the hallmark of this philosophy. All of these features have drawn criticism from some. An especially absurd knock is that his courses are too long for the average player. In truth, there is a specific reason for every one of the features Jones builds into his courses, and almost every one of them is aimed at making the course more playable for all levels of golfers, a concept that is considered at length in the pages that follow.

In his foreword to this book, my friend and colleague Peter Dobereiner, perhaps the best and most insightful golf writer extant, has expressed his dismay at the criticism of Jones' courses, most of that coming, of course, from the professionals who have come to feel it is fashionable to do so.

I quite agree. Some years ago, before I was aware that Trent Jones was supposed to be an ogre, I shot, if memory serves correctly, a 73 at Firestone South and won a World Series of Golf trophy. It still sits on a shelf in my den. For professional competition, Firestone measures almost 7,200 yards. It is the

Preceding pages: *Royal Country Down, #4*

24

longest and certainly one of the hardest courses on which any championship is played. Before you blink in disbelief (as my conqueror in the third flight of this year's club championship might do), let me point out that my triumph, on an admittedly exceptional day for me, came in a pre-tournament competition for writers and that sort and that we played from the *white* tees at considerably less than the maximum length. Which proves my point and Trent's. Jones builds courses that can test to the utmost the best players in the world and can, at the same time, be playable for the rest of us.

Not long ago, the Professional Golfers Association selected the 18 toughest holes in America. Interestingly, Jones, the man who supposedly designs courses that are too hard, did not have a single hole on the list.

Jones was the first golf architect who had not trained in another profession or been involved in another golf-related business. He literally created his own major, golf architecture, at Cornell University, as he will tell you about in this book.

He was a fine player as a youngster, a skill that has instilled in him an exquisite sense of shot values. He once correctly predicted the winning score in a major championship by assaying the shot values of each hole, using the decimal system, and adding them together. He probably could predict, just as accurately, the winning score in the fifth flight of the club tournament from the forward tees.

Jones also possesses a keen esthetic sense and an artistic discipline, plus an inquisitive mind that has led him on an endless quest for information. Thus his credentials were—and are—admirably balanced for the pursuit of his chosen career.

Jones has been the consummate salesman, able to find and attract financial backers for his projects, whether they be resorts, developments or private clubs. Jack Nicklaus once called him "the world's best salesman," declaring, "That man can meet a group of developers at an airport in Spain, sell them a course by sketching one out on a paper napkin and take the next plane home."

And he was the first golf architect to establish a rapport with the public, the golfers who now like to brag that their course is "a Robert Trent Jones design." As his son Rees has said, "He put the 'name' in golf architecture." This emphasis on the architect has opened the way for the large fees that many golf-course designers, Nicklaus among them, are able to command today.

Jones is the most-honored golf architect in history. He is a fellow of the American Society of Landscape Architects, an advisory member of the National Institute of Social Sciences, a member of the American Academy of Achievement and the 1972 recipient of its highest award, "The Golden Plate." In 1976 he received the American Society of Golf Course Architect's first Donald Ross Award. He was given the Distinguished Service Award by the Metropolitan Golf Writers Association that same year.

In 1980 he received Cornell University's "Distinguished Alumni" Award. The William D. Richardson Award for distinguished service and contributions to the game by the Golf Writers Association of America and the Distinguished Service Award by the New York Metropolitan Golf Association went to him in 1981, and in 1987 he was given the Old Tom Morris Award by the Golf Course Superintendents Association of America. In 1988 he was awarded a Doctorate of Humanities degree by Green Mountain College in Poultney, Vermont, and was named one of *Golf Magazine's* 100 Heroes of Golf over the last century.

The year before, Jones had been inducted into the World Golf Hall of Fame, the second architect—and the first living one—to be so honored.

To quote Charles Price, the noted golf writer and historian, Robert Trent Jones has indeed been "the game's master builder."

The second biggest hurdle in putting together a book like this is researching and compiling the facts and philosophies of a life that has spanned such time and space and has spawned such an incredible library of tales, both factual and apocryphal. He has walked with presidents and kings, the rich and famous, as well as with the commoner, and in each case there has been a story to tell.

He is the most-published and the most written-about architect ever, as well as the most-interviewed. He gives a speech, formal or informal, at the drop of a hint. There is very little of the Jones lore that has not been documented in one form or another. So what follows is a recounting of the stuff of legends. It is offered without apology, because never has so much of the man been captured within the covers of a book.

It isn't all here, of course. That would require more volumes than you might care to read and more time than I have left to write. In the world of golf, there is a Trent Jones story around every corner, at every cocktail party, on every clubhouse veranda.

Trent Jones and the Airplane could be a book by itself. Rees has remarked, "Once Dad found out he could go in the air and get there faster, he was gone." He estimates that he has flown eight million miles during his career, a total that continues to grow by some 300,000 miles annually.

He hails airplanes as if they were taxis. He does not like to wait for them, nor does he particularly care where he is going. Once he was in Heathrow Airport in London ready to board a flight to New York. A delay was announced and Jones took the next available flight out—to Los Angeles.

He was in Casablanca after the attempted palace revolution against King Hassan of Morocco, a story you will read later, and was trying to get out of the country. He booked flights to Rome and Madrid before finally flying to Malaga because "we're building a golf course there."

The point is, he has been building golf courses almost everywhere, so almost any flight will land him where there is business.

Sometimes there doesn't even have to be business. There is the story that he was in Boston's Leahy Clinic for one of his periodic checkups and tired of the stay. Unannounced, he threw his topcoat over his hospital smock, cabbed to the airport and flew to Houston to visit a friend, still in the smock when he disembarked. He denies that one, but it comes from a close, reputable source.

He says he doesn't particularly enjoy flying, but he endures it. "It's just like sitting in your chair at home," he says. What makes it more endurable for Jones than most is that he can fall asleep anywhere, anytime, and usually does. When it happened to me a couple of times during our taping sessions I thought, well, the poor fellow is getting old. Later I found out he has been doing that all his life. It makes you wonder how he ever got the perforated ulcer that has bothered him since he was a youngster. But it may explain his longevity.

Awake or asleep, I'm sure, his fertile brain keeps whirring. He is constantly considering the new and innovative, not only to design golf courses but to care for them and to improve the game in general.

For example, his large greens not only offer more pin positions but spread out wear, as do large tees, thus easing maintenance problems. The large water hazards he installs offer reservoirs for the sprinkling systems that Jones long ago envisioned would be an integral part of golf courses. He has experimented with the design and engineering of those systems. He has proved that rich topsoil is not needed to grow grass, that bogs can be turned into beautiful lakes, that rocks can be transformed into fairways, that American grasses can grow on foreign soils. Jones, you see, is an agronomist as well as an artist and designer, and so he has influenced the upkeep and costs involved in the game.

He has been a strong advocate of better education and training for course superintendents, in the areas of business and management as well as technical expertise, lecturing on the subject whenever and wherever he gets the chance. He has worked closely with the agronomy school at Michigan State, and a foundation is being established in his name at Cornell to further that cause.

Long before Deane Beman invented stadium golf courses, Jones advocated the same thing. As Herbert Warren Wind describes it in "The Story of American Golf," Jones envisioned courses on which certain tournaments would be played annually that would be designed in loop fashion, straight in and straight out, with a three-level elevated roadway surrounding the course. The lower level would be for spectators who wanted to walk, the middle level for open trucks fitted with bleachers that would follow specific matches or pairings, the top level for an observation train that would move slowly around the entire course. We haven't quite seen that yet, but perhaps we're getting there.

He is, as you shall learn, a proponent of the natural, a philosophy that stems from his love of the links, where the wind and weather created the contours at St. Andrews and all the links that follow. To that end, he is toying with the idea of using leaf-blowing machines to shape the sand on greens so the tilts and undulations will look as if nature made them.

He has a theory that would put his multiple tee positions to good use. Change the par of the course for each tee and make everybody in a group play from the tee most appropriate for the highest handicapper. "From the back tee, playing the course at 7,100 yards, the poor player has a miserable time," Jones says. "He is playing a course he has no right to play. And at resorts, especially, it ties up the course to beat hell. From the forward tees, the better player may have to shoot a 67 to equal par, and it's still a challenge."

Besides, he says, such an arrangement could cut half an hour off each round, a goal to be devoutly sought these days.

He has strong ideas on how clubhouses should be designed for the optimum traffic flow and has aided in that design on many of his projects. He has even stronger opinions on how clubs should be run—not by the members, incidentally, but by trained club managers. He and his sons own Coral Ridge Country Club in Fort Lauderdale, Florida, which gives him credibility in the matter. During one of our work sessions he suggested that when this book was finished we would write another one on those subjects.

He is a patron of the game as well. He donated the trophy for the annual Insurance Youth Classic. Beginning in 1956, he and his wife, Ione, conducted the annual Doherty Challenge Cup, one of the country's premier amateur events for women, at Coral Ridge. It is now known as the Ione D. Jones/Doherty Cup in honor of Mrs. Jones, who died in July, 1987.

I could go on, but you get the idea.

Jones has been variously described as cherubic, warmhearted, acerbic, jolly and dogmatic, among other adjectives. In truth, he is probably all of these at different times. He can be quick with criticism, yet moments later generous with his praise.

He is quick to embrace those whose values he perceives to be the same as his own, equally quick to scorn those who he feels do not measure up. Because of his playing ability when he was a young man, he is almost contemptuous— sometimes unfairly so—of architects not as skilled at the game. Nor does he have much patience with the flood of playing professionals who have turned to course design.

"There are a lot of golf architects who can't play and a lot of players who can't design," Trent grumbles. "You have to have both. You have to have good golf sense."

However one might quarrel with Trent Jones' work or his views, the one ingredient that cannot be questioned is his enthusiasm, or dedication, if you will. Golf and golf courses are seldom out of his mind. In going through Jones's files in researching this book, I found a menu from the Detroit Golf Club, which Jones was remodeling, dated August 1, 1951. On the back was a wonderful penciled sketch of the proposed second green at The County Club of Detroit in nearby Grosse Point, another of his redesign projects. By the way, for those of you who yearn for the good old days, the chef's special that evening cost $2.25 and the most expensive item on the menu was $3.90.

Bobby, the eldest Jones son, tells the story of the time he and his brother, Rees, were playing baseball in the backyard of their Montclair home when their father roared out of the house and commanded them to mow the lawn. "Our lawn is the worst on the block," he raged, "and I just lost a job because of it."

"He gave us a lesson in agronomy right there," Bobby chuckles. "It was our first architectural experience."

This ardor for the playing, the business and the building of the game has been brought together in a unique book, a volume that is *not* many things just as it *is* many others. It is not an autobiography, *per se*, of Robert Trent Jones, yet the man and his life and work flavor every chapter. It is not a history of golf courses and architects, yet Jones discusses both, especially the builders who he feels have made the most significant contributions. It is not an instructional book, yet his discussion of design and how it influences play will help golfers at every level score better by being able to "see" the hole, to understand what the architect is trying to make them do and thus be able to better plan his options and the route to the cup. It is not a manual on how to build golf courses, yet it provides an insight into that task that will make every reader an amateur architect . . . as if he isn't already.

More than that, it is a book filled with marvelous pictures from Tony Roberts and other of the world's great photographers. Thus it captures the lure and pleasure of golf both through the camera's lens and through the eyes of the man most eminently qualified to discourse on the subject.

It is, we hope, the definitive work on golf course design as it applies to and appeals to all golfers, a book of beauty and insight that will be treasured by anybody who plays the game.

I must thank many who helped me in the preparation—Rees and Robert Trent Jones Jr., the sons who provided valuable information and perception and to whom, along with their mother, this book is dedicated; Roger Rulewich, the senior associate in Jones' firm and the immediate past president of the American Society of Golf Course Architects, who was giving of his time and expertise; Jim Singerling, executive vice president of Robert Trent Jones, Florida, Inc., who was invaluable in keeping tabs on Trent and providing many other services; Arthur (Red) Hoffman, a friend of many years, a golf writer of note and a former publicist for Jones who helped gather much of the research material; Eilleen Vennell, Trent's long-time office manager; Gudren Noonan, who runs Bobby's Palo Alto office with a soft voice and an efficient hand; Richard Spray, a veteran of the Jones organizations, both senior and junior, who helped jog our memories and check our facts.

Most of all I must thank Trent Jones, for who he has been and what he has done to make golf's magnificent challenge better for all of us.

Larry Dennis
Huntington, Connecticut
October, 1988

PART
1

Chapter 1
What Is a Golf Course?

Golf . . . there is a mystery here. Why do we do it? What lures us onward to make love to, or do battle with, this inscrutable temptress?

Over the centuries golf has evolved from a pastime to a game, a competition, sometimes a profession and, for most of us, a passion that transcends mere play. But why?

There is a magnificent beauty to golf, of course. There is a constant confrontation with the elements. There is a great challenge to the physical skills and to the mind. It is at once an art and a test of strength. There is always the need to perform a stroke of uncommon precision, none ever really the same, each requiring absolute control of the muscles and the emotions, a mastery of self. Sometimes we accomplish this, but often we do not. So there is exhilaration . . . and there is frustration. There is triumph and tragedy. Usually there is all of this within a single round, often within a single hole.

Weighing all this still does not help us define the mystique, the inherent fascination and charm of the game that has never been fully understood, much less explained. Nor will I attempt to explain it here.

Certainly golf is the most difficult game to play. My good friend Sam Snead once said, "I played almost all the sports growing up, and golf is by far the hardest there is." Coming from a man who has played golf as well as anyone in history, the remark is significant.

No one ever has mastered golf. Bobby Jones, one of the greatest players ever, scored many competitive rounds in the 80s. Ben Hogan, another of the masters, has said that he might hit only eight good shots a round. There are perfect shots for everybody, but how rarely they come.

That very difficulty might—indeed, should—be enough to turn many away. Most of us encounter enough difficulty in our daily work that we need not court it during our time at play. Yet, no matter how great the anguish of a given round, we invariably return the next time, enraptured with the prospect of conquering the unconquerable. Somewhere between the joy and despair is something that brings us back.

Perhaps it is that golf is competition in a number of ways. One of the joys of golf is that we can play it with anybody, from the best player in the world to the worst, we can have a friendly wager and both of us can enjoy the round. We compete with our friends, we compete with the course, with the game itself. More than anything else, perhaps, we compete with ourselves.

Yet not everyone is competitive, and even those who are not can enjoy the game, simply for the sake of playing it. If not competition, it can be relaxation, exercise, a chance to escape, a communing with nature . . . ah, there we might have the answer, if there is one.

If you have been on a golf course in the morning, the sun glinting off the dew, the grass fresh and clean, the air sweet . . . or in the evening, as the day cools, the wind dies and the shadows lengthen . . . you may have felt at that moment that there could be no better place. You may have been right. You were at once in tune with nature and the greatest game of all.

The uniqueness of golf, and perhaps its unique appeal, lies to a great extent in its playing fields, their beauty and variety. With few exceptions, other sports have rigid boundaries. Yet not one golf course is alike. There are good courses and poor ones, great and mediocre, especially seen through the eyes of someone in my profession. Yet, to be honest, have you ever seen a golf course you didn't like?

The beauty of a golf course is as varied as nature itself. The craggy dunesland of Ireland, the flatter, undulating linksland of Scotland, the lush, heavily treed parkland of America, the open prairie, the seaside, the desert, the jungle, the mountain—each has its own attraction. Each venue, because of its

terrain, puts its particular imprint on how the game is perceived and played. We are playing the same game, with the same equipment and within the same rules, at St. Andrews, at Ballybunion, at Olympic, at Pine Valley, at Augusta, at Cypress Point, at Seminole, at Dorado Beach, at Prairie Dunes, at Desert Highlands. Yet we must play the game differently on each course, which is why golf is so frustrating, so infuriating. . .and so much fun. It is why the game is so delightfully special.

Yet there is much more to a good or great golf course than the simple accident of location. All those qualities that make golf challenging, frustrating, satisfying and enjoyable, all at the same time, must be designed into the layout of each hole and the holes altogether. Nature provides the raw material. The architect, working with that material without desecrating it, gives us the finished product.

The origins of golf are lost in time, as are the origins of the first golf course. There is evidence that St. Andrews in Scotland was the first, perhaps coming into existence in the early 1400s. Certainly it has become renowned as the home of golf, so I'll leave it at that. I happen to think the course is a masterpiece, and I have a theory on how it came about. Sailors who used to dock at the port of St. Andrews had to walk a couple of miles or so to the town. To amuse themselves on the way, they would swing a stick at a root, and the man who got there in the fewest strokes was the winner. Competition again!

Eventually they tired of the monotony and decided to break their journey into segments. They selected natural plateaus for tees and greens, dug holes in them and played from one spot to another. Perhaps they used rabbit holes for their targets. Whatever. Their sport became a succession of holes, and the first golf course had been designed.

Whether my theory is accurate makes little difference. The point is that St. Andrews, then and today, is basically as nature designed it. The rains and the wind and the ebb and flow of the tides where the River Eden runs to St. Andrews Bay and then the North Sea created the channels and ridges and furrows that eventually became the linksland dunes. There have been a few— very few—refinements over the centuries, but the natural quality of the course remains.

The Old Course does not appeal to all, especially at first sight. The uphill, downhill and sidehill lies, the bunkers in the fairways that cannot be seen from the tee and the blind shots to the green can create an initial dislike. The landscape is stark, certainly not beautiful in the same way as a lush, heavily treed parkland course.

Sam Snead, who won the British Open at St. Andrews in 1946, got his first glimpse of the course from the window of a train coming up from London. He looked out over the grey moors, then turned to a Scot sitting across the aisle. "What in the devil is that?" Sam demanded. "It looks like an old abandoned golf course."

"My God, sir," replied the dumbfounded native, "that is the Royal and Ancient Golf Club of St. Andrews, founded in 1754. And it is not now, nor ever will be, abandoned."

Perhaps only slightly embarrassed, Snead tuned to Lawson Little, his traveling companion, and said, "Down home we plant cow beets on land like that."

Others have been similarly unimpressed on their initial visits. The first time Bob Jones played there, he picked up in disgust during the third round. Yet St. Andrews eventually became his favorite course, and he a favorite of the townspeople and golf fans.

Once you have played the course a few times, you begin to appreciate its subtlety, the premium it places on making great golf shots, the risk and reward it offers and, yes, its own kind of beauty. There is a grandeur to it, a rhythmic flow that makes it still one of the world's best and most difficult courses, a true links layout after which all great courses are, or should be, modeled.

This is not to say that all courses should be laid out as links. A links course is built near the sea on a particular kind of sand and turf. More precisely, true linksland is that formed by rich soil and sediment deposited on sand dunes by a river. So a true links course is one formed by nature on an estuary, the place where a river meets the sea, as is the case with St. Andrews and the other great links of Scotland, although over the years the designation has been applied to courses that do not meet that particular qualification.

The soil is firm and drains well, the grass predominantly bent and fescue, all of which offers a hard, fast playing surface. The firmness of the turf, the rolling dunes, the wind, the lack of tree shelter all promote the unique links design. The greens are open in front, for the most part, and the greensites are natural, tucked into hollows ringed by dunes or perched on plateaus formed by the wind and sea. The terrain, with its folds and swales, is dotted by bunkers, often of the small, deep "pot" variety, most of which were originally made by nature or perhaps by sheep. Whatever theory you entertain is immaterial. To get in them is to waste a shot. The dunes are covered by the prickly whin or other rough that is unavoidable and sometimes impossible to escape from. Linksland promotes a game played on the ground, a game in which the ball can be rolled and seldom has to be lofted.

Only occasionally can a links course be emulated on inland terrain—Prairie Dunes in Kansas is one example, and that works only because the land there bears a striking resemblance to the seaside venues.

It is the natural quality of a course that counts. Fortunately, the land rarely repeats itself, so the opportunities for different and different-looking courses are endless, whether they are built on mountains, valleys, meadows or deserts. Each can have features distinctive from any other course. But no matter what the terrain—linksland, parkland, desert or mountain range—the holes should be designed to take advantage of it and blend in with it. Sometimes, if nature hasn't helped or if other considerations interfere, the architect must create features in the land. But, ideally, these features would look as if they belonged there and had always been there.

Dr. Alister MacKenzie, who had perhaps more influence on modern course design than any other architect, insisted that a course should incorporate both beauty and a natural look, even when that look was artificially created.

So the natural look of the course becomes the beauty of it. That is not inevitable, especially if there is little beauty to the land to begin with—or at least beauty that lends itself to a golf course. For example, Pete Dye is one of our foremost modern course architects who has created some marvelously natural-looking holes on land that suits itself to the purpose and some totally artificial holes on desert land that does not. Dye has become an artist in creating beauty in that latter situation. PGA West in Palm Springs is an example. It is a work of art, stunning to the eye. I suspect that most golfers in the world cannot play the course successfully, so in that respect it fails the test of a great course. But its beauty, however contrived, lures the golfer.

Given most conditions, however, I would prefer that we adhere to what nature already has done to the land. That almost always seems to be right.

At Augusta National, which he designed in collaboration with Bob Jones, MacKenzie did an especially fine job of taking advantage of the rugged terrain, routing a course that goes out and down and up and down and up again without the player really being aware of it. On the back nine, Augusta's 11th, 12th and 13th greens sit far below the clubhouse level, yet the return there is relatively easy. I call this the stepladder effect. So while the creation of individual

holes is vital, the routing of a course is the most important element of design. The good and great architects accomplish this difficult task, all the while creating the illusion that these were holes built on ground just lying there, waiting to be grassed over.

Designing a great golf course, then, is like putting together the pieces of a jigsaw puzzle. In most cases, beautiful sites, beautiful situations, hilltops, valleys and creeks are to be found. They simply must be arranged properly, all the alternatives considered, to make the holes and the course at once as challenging and as playable as possible.

A golf course can be built virtually anywhere. I have built them on sand, on lava rock, in the mountains, in the desert, in the woods and on the plains. I have built them on swamps and even on water.

In almost all cases, it is best to let the land suggest the course. Use the land and don't abuse it. Fit the holes into the terrain available, moving as little dirt as possible. And when you do have to resculpture the land, try to make it look as if it had always been that way. It has become the style among some current architects to build extra mounds and chocolate drops and bumps and install things like railroad ties. Sometimes, when you are working with a particularly featureless piece of land, some of that is necessary. But it costs an awful lot of money, and it never looks very natural or beautiful.

What makes a course great?

What is it, really, that makes a golf course great? Bob Jones had perhaps the best definition. He believed that a great course must be a source of pleasure to the greatest possible number of players and that it require strategy, the use of the mind, as well as skill, the God-given use of the muscles. If it lacked these aspects, it could not continue to hold the player's interest. He also felt that it must give the average golfer a fair chance, at the same time demanding the utmost from the more skilled player.

I could not agree more.

Beauty alone, although it certainly adds to the pleasure of playing, does not necessarily make a course great. One of the best expressions I've heard is that "there is no golf in some courses." That means the course is dull. It has no feel to it. It may be flat, the greens not built up, the bunkers all looking the same. It has no variety, no flexibility, no challenge. It simply lacks character. The basic ingredient of greatness is character, that quality of strong, individual factors that make a hole and a course stand out over others.

It boils down to playing value, which translates into shot values. They are inextricably entwined. Shot value simply means the premium placed on a particular shot, and it is dependent on the ability of an individual to perform that shot. At the same time, the parameters must be clearly defined. A perfect shot must be rewarded. A shot slightly off target should give the player some difficulty in executing his next stroke. A bad shot should carry with it a penalty, forcing the player to make a skillful shot to recover.

And the values of a hole should be clearly defined, so that the player can see at a glance what he is faced with, whether it be rough, bunkers, boundaries, trees, water or simply poor position. He should know his opportunities and his restrictions. How he reacts to these determines his worth as a player.

Considering that, we are really talking about degrees of difficulty. And we are talking about *fair* for all levels of golfers. If a professional can hit an 8-iron 140 yards but you must use a 4-iron to cover the same distance, then a particular hole location on the green might be fine for him but would be terribly unfair for you. So the architect must find a way to get you closer to the

Opposite top: *This nest of bunkers guards the corner of the 405-yard par-4 7th, a dogleg right at Oakland Hills in Birmingham, Michigan; the course is a Donald Ross design remodeled by Robert Trent Jones. Opposite bottom: The 520-yard 15th at Alister MacKenzie's Augusta National, one of the classic par-5s, offers a layup and a pitch to the green or a heroic second-shot carry over the pond that protects the front. Following pages: If you're good or lucky enough to find the island fairway on the 387-yard 2nd at Pine Valley in Clementon, New Jersey, a George Crump/H. S. Colt collaboration, you must then play a second shot over this wasteland to an elevated green and a treacherous putting surface.*

Above: *A rainbow glistens over the 16th at Tom Simpson's Ballybunion Old in Ireland, with the famed graveyard on the 1st hole in the background. Surely leprechauns guard the pot of gold at the end.*
Opposite top: *This long, narrow green with its subtle undulations awaits the player who successfully negotiates the 379-yard par-4 3rd at Muirfield in Scotland, another Tom Morris design.*
Opposite bottom: *Dunes, gorse and sea are typical of this scene, where the 6th and 11th holes converge at Royal Dornoch in the north of Scotland. The course is a design by Old Tom Morris, revised by others, including Donald Ross.*

green for your approach shot or provide a hole location on the green that you will be able to reach.

Ben Hogan, who may have played the game better than any golfer in history and certainly played it more thoughtfully than most, once said, "A good golf hole should have both character and appeal. It shouldn't ask a golfer to play shots that are beyond his ability, but it should present him with an interesting challenge and reward him when he hits the shots that are called for. Golf is a game in which you play your first shot on a hole in order to play your second from the best position, and so on. It's a thinking game, a game of controlling the ball."

In other words, a course should have the versatility to be made less punishing, but still challenging, for the average player without spoiling the character or playing value for the expert. Length is not the benchmark, but design is. No matter how far you are capable of striking the ball, each hole should force you to think out the shot you must play. Then it must make you execute it. That is the test of a great golf course.

Make the game fun for everybody. Never make a course so penal that a golfer who is not a great player will take so many strokes, be so embarrassed and so miserable that he will give up the game. The higher handicap players support the game. They *are* the game. Without them there would be no one to support the clubs and public courses, and there would be no one to appreciate the great tournament players. And how many of them would there be if they were all out there shooting 130 every day?

That philosophy may sound strange coming from a man who has a reputation, in certain circles, as a fiend when it comes to designing difficult golf course. But those circles almost always encompass the touring professionals, or those they have influenced. Yes, I design very difficult courses for that caliber of player, as well I should, for very good reasons.

Professionals complain a lot, I've found. They seem to want fairway traps from which they can reach the green, holes that are not too long, rough that is not too deep, greens that are dead-flat. That may be an exaggeration, but they do seem to object to severe tests. Perhaps if I made my living playing golf I would feel the same, but the fact is that if we turn golf into a putting contest, nobody will care and there won't be a living.

The quality of a golf course is usually in the eye of the beholder. Usually the view depends on the beholder's success that day. In the 1962 American Golf Classic in Akron, Ohio, after I had remodeled Firestone Country Club into a stern test of golf, Bob Rosburg shot 78 in the second round and damned every tree and trap on the course. The next day he shot 65 and told the press he had never played a finer competitive course.

I don't build golf courses just for the pros. I worry more about the duffer. Besides, I've never built a course on which a professional couldn't score 65 if he's playing well. Sometimes I get the idea they want me to build courses on which they can score in the 60s when they're playing badly.

I'm not a fiend. I don't hate golfers. I love golfers. That's why I build them good courses to play.

It's getting harder and harder to build those good courses for all classes of golfers, from the high handicapper to the professional. Let me give you an example that illustrates the dilemma golf course architects are facing these days.

I was called on to remodel the South Course at Oakland Hills, the fine old Donald Ross layout in Birmingham, Michigan, for the 1951 U.S. Open. I'll go into detail about that remodeling in a later chapter. It basically consisted of repositioning the fairway bunkers and tightening approaches to the greens. The purpose was to restore the playing values that had been lost because of advances in technology and the abilities of accomplished golfers. And that was

done. There were only two rounds under par in the championship, which was won with a seven-over-par total by Ben Hogan, the greatest player of that era and maybe of all time.

Perhaps the change was too abrupt, and indeed the course has since been eased with the elimination of half a dozen strategic bunkers. Nevertheless, the 1951 Open was a milestone, the coming of age of American golf course architecture.

I'm sure it was a form of culture shock, as well as the difficulty of the course, that contributed to the high scores. Subsequent championships played there bear this out. In the 1961 U.S. Open Gene Littler won with a score of 281, and eighteen players broke par. In the 1972 PGA Gary Player won with the same score, and twenty-one players were under par. In 1979 David Graham and Ben Crenshaw tied at 272, eight under, Graham winning a three-hole playoff. Graham also shot 65 in the final round despite a double-bogey on the closing hole. In the 1985 U.S. Open, plagued by rain throughout, Andy North shot a one-under-par 279 to win.

Both the United States Golf Association and the PGA feel that par is a standard and that a score around par should be the winning total in their championships. By this definition, Oakland Hills is indeed not too difficult.

The problem is that these standards need to be maintained, and that's the dilemma. Technology keeps improving. The ball travels farther. Improvement in steel and the advent of materials such as graphite and titanium have given us shafts that help the ball go farther. Metal woods and better design and construction of iron clubs have made the game easier to play. Something must be done to keep the challenge in the game.

The player is the attacker of the golf course and will use any legal means he or she can to make better scores. There is nothing wrong with that, because that's why we play golf. But the architect must defend against this attack to maintain the challenge and integrity of the game. If it becomes too easy, nobody will want to play it.

Technology must be controlled, of course, and the governing bodies of golf are attempting to do that. It's difficult to stretch the great old courses much beyond their present length, and while new courses can be built longer, there is only so far an architect can go before a course becomes unplayable for most golfers. Peter Dobereiner, the brilliant English writer who was kind enough to write the foreword to this book, once said, "As for myself, I would rather spend my last years in prison than be condemned to playing a 7,000-yard course." Most golfers would agree.

Difficult as the South Course at Oakland Hills was and is for the professionals from the back tees, it is very playable and enjoyable for the better amateur from the middle tees and for the lesser player from the forward tees. It is still a stern test, mind you, but it can be negotiated . . . with some frustration, as there always is, but usually without humiliation.

So flexibility is critical. Flexibility is created by the way the architect positions the tees, and the number of them, where he places the fairway hazards and, of course, by the way he designs the green. A more difficult shot for the better player, an easier shot for the high handicapper is the ideal. It is not always achieved, but it is the goal.

My philosophy always has been that every hole should be a difficult par and an easy bogey. Every course should be challenging, but it always should be fun to play. When Bob Jones and I designed Peachtree in Atlanta, I told him, "Bob, I know you want this to be a great championship course, but most of your members are well over sixty. They want a course on which they can have fun." Fortunately, through the use of long tees and large greens that allow great flexibility, I think we created both at Peachtree.

Every golfer gets special enjoyment from playing particular courses. He may not know why, but that doesn't matter. The fact that he does is sufficient to make those courses admirable. It means that the architect has incorporated features in the course so superior that anybody instinctively derives a joy from playing it.

So how does an architect create a course that is great for the best players in the world as well as the highest handicappers? He creates options.

In the early days of golf course design and development, most courses were *penal*, extracting penalties from the player who failed to execute the shot required. There was no other way to go than over trouble. Facing that kind of hole is disheartening to the high-handicap golfer, who sees a problem that is beyond his capabilities with no alternative available. There is no choice but to play exactly the shot required or get into trouble. Often he can't even play short because there is trouble there too. Putting such demands on most players is the mark of inept architecture—or perhaps just cruel architecture.

In many cases, the penal design of the old courses was unfair because of the degree of punishment for error. A shot that was just slightly off line might catch a deep bunker, for instance, while a *badly* missed shot would escape the trap and leave the golfer only a pitch to get close to the hole. Thus he would be the equal, or better, of a golfer who had played an almost perfect shot that missed by inches.

Pine Valley in Clementon, New Jersey, a course that many consider the best in the world and is certainly one of my favorites, is an archetypical example of the penal style of design. In this case, the course is not unfair. A badly missed shot usually is penalized more than a slightly missed shot. It is just a very difficult test. On many, if not most, of its holes, long carries over intimidating sandy wastes, chasms or water are demanded, with no alternate route available. It is a course designed for the better player, for whom it is a magnificent challenge. But many players, especially women and short-hitting men, have a great deal of trouble with it and end up in the throes of frustration when they try it. Pine Valley is a course that is exactly what it was intended to be, one of the most beautiful and demanding layouts in the world. But it is not for everybody.

The *strategic* design, on the other hand, demands that the player think his way around the course to avoid the hazards. There is no way over them. There are undulations and other subtle features that force the player to place his shots in exactly the right place or be faced with a more difficult shot into the green. So the player must plan the route to the green accordingly. The essence of strategic architecture is to encourage initiative and to reward the thinking golfer while penalizing the unthinking golfer. In strategic architecture, well-struck shots are necessary but often may be secondary to the end result. If the player has not thought through to the position he wants to be in when the shot finishes, he may find himself with an impossible next shot to the green.

Augusta National, home of the Masters Tournament, is an example. There is no rough, and no long carries over water are demanded, unless a player wants to try for the 13th and 15th, both par-5s, in two shots. But Augusta requires the player to think his way around the course, to position his ball for the shot to the green so he can get it in the right place. If he does not, he is faced with peril on the slick, undulating surfaces or an impossible recovery shot.

This undoubtedly is the better way for most golfers to play, but there still is something missing.

I decided long ago that the better way was a design I labeled *heroic*, a concept that demands a heroic carry or gamble for the better player to get into position for a birdie but one that always leaves an option for the lesser player to take the safer route. There must be a just reward for those attempting the heroic carry,

Opposite top: A *lake guarding the left side of the driving area and a majestic sweep up to a green surrounded by deep bunkers make the 384-yard 2nd at Seminole, North Palm Beach, Florida, one of Donald Ross's and golf's most striking holes.* Opposite bottom: The 4th on *Trent Jones's West Course at Broadmoor in Colorado Springs is a par-4 of only 380 yards, but a creek across the fairway and this sloping, two-tiered green pose problems.*

and there must be a way around for those unwilling to take the risk. Without the alternate route, heroic carries are unfair. Without the reward, heroic carries are meaningless.

If you can play a difficult 200-yard shot over a lake, you will have a chance for that birdie and certainly can make par. If you do not successfully make the shot, you will pay the penalty, and you know it before you start. If you are not capable of that shot, there must be a way for you to go around the lake. It can cost you an extra stroke, and it certainly will diminish your chance for a birdie or a par. But it won't cost you two strokes, and it will always give you the opportunity, through skillful play, to still make your par or birdie. In any event, it will be an easy bogey.

At the same time, that route, less risky and demanding, must not be boring or condescendingly easy. There still must be the excitement of meeting your own challenge. It may be a lesser challenge than that faced by the scratch player or the tournament player, but it is a challenge to you that can be met with skillful play within the limits of your particular ability level.

Two heroic holes come quickly to mind. One is the 16th at Cypress Point, one of the most heralded par-3s in the world. It demands a tee shot of at least 220 yards across an inlet of the ocean far below. To fail is death, at least to your score. But there is a strategic route, dry land to the left to which the conservative golfer can play with an iron. Then he can make a pitch to the green for a possible par or a bogey. Obviously, one's abilities must be carefully assessed before the first shot is made.

Another is the 13th hole on the East Course I designed at Dorado Beach in Puerto Rico, a 540-yard par-5 that is one of my favorites. The hole is sharply S-shaped, bending to the left from the landing area and back to the right into the green. There is a large pond in the left corner of the first dogleg and an even larger one guarding the right side of the fairway and green.

The cautious route is straight down the fairway off the tee, avoiding the pond to the left, then straight again on the second shot, steering away from the water right. This gives the player no chance to reach the green in two, but if the first two shots are properly played, a relatively easy pitch is left to the

Opposite: The shot to the green on the par-4 10th at Oak Hill in Rochester, New York, a stern 432-yarder, must carry this creek that wanders across this fairway and the 11th. Trent Jones caught the architectural bug while watching Donald Ross design this course. Below: At 399 yards from an elevated tee, the 15th at Shinnecock Hills on Long Island is not long for the good player, but bunkers at the corner of the dogleg and around the green await the errant shot. The hole is a typical William Flynn design. Following pages: The tee shot on the par-3 9th at Merion, Hugh Wilson's gem in Ardmore, Pennsylvania, must carry up to 195 yards and circumvent water in front and bunkers all around to find the putting surface.

elevated green. If a player cannot hit the ball far enough to reach the corner of the second dogleg in two shots, he or she can play a medium-length shot across water to the green in the hope of getting home in three. Or the third shot can be struck down the fairway, again leaving an easy pitch home, a putt for a par and, at worst, a comfortable bogey.

The bold and capable player, on the other hand, can hit the tee shot across the water on the left, considerably shortening the hole. If that shot is successful, the player is faced with another long carry across water to reach the green in two. And the Atlantic Ocean, by the way, lies just thirty yards beyond. If he chooses to take this route and makes it, a birdie or even an eagle awaits. If he fails, the water and a high score lurk.

The hole is demanding, but it is fair to all, and it clearly demonstrates the rewards and penalties that should be built into all great holes.

When you look at a golf hole, the problems should be immediately visible—the lakes, creeks, bunkers, trees, the fairway with its tilts and contours and varying widths, all should be right there for you to see. And you should carefully—if quickly—consider all this. You should be able to develop your strategy, based on your ability and the situation in the round at the moment. The more intriguing the challenge, the better the hole and the course is and the more fun you will have in coping with it.

The point is that every player should recognize his or her abilities, the potential and the limitations. If the occasion is right, try always to take advantage of your potential. But never exceed your limitations. It invariably brings you to grief.

Herbert Warren Wind, perhaps the world's foremost golf historian, once wrote an analysis of Merion in Philadelphia, Seminole in Florida and Cypress Point on the Monterey Peninsula. All are relatively short courses, and all are among the world's best.

Said Wind, "They are a treat for golfers of various levels of ability because the strategic concept of their holes makes proper positioning of the ball and not the ability to hit it a mile the cardinal requirement. In their individual ways they encourage initiative but, intrinsically, they are courses that reward golf sense and ball control. Conversely, a golfer must recognize his limitations because, if he overreaches himself, sooner or later he will be severely punished. Each of them has some great and exciting holes, but even on the plainer holes the shot values are sound. Each has a wide variety of holes. And each has a stretch of memorable closing holes."

Seldom if ever has there been a better description of a great golf course.

The best way to get better at golf, of course, is to find a good instructor and learn. If you were just starting at skiing, you probably wouldn't go out without a lesson. But too many players do just that when they take up golf. They don't learn how to hold the club, how to stand to the ball, how to swing properly, the mechanics and strategies of the game. As I said before, you can enjoy the game without playing it well, but it's a lot more fun if you do.

After you have become as mechanically proficient as your time and talent will allow, you can further improve your scores by becoming aware of what the architects had in mind when they designed the golf courses you play and the strategy you should adopt in overcoming the obstacles they have built in.

The good architect, of course, creates the strategy that you should follow, that you must follow, if you are to make a good score. By properly contouring the greens to allow for a variety of hole locations, by contouring the fairways to force you to play in a certain direction and by proper placement of bunkers and tees he can dictate the way the hole should be played according to the placement of the cup and the tee blocks. Given this quality, this flexibility in design, a hole and course can be made to play a number of different ways.

Then it is simply up to you, the player, to find the best way.

Above: *The 18th at Riviera in Los Angeles, designed by George Moore, is one of the most challenging finishing holes in golf, a 454-yard par-4 that requires an uphill tee shot over a precipice, then an accurate long iron or wood, also uphill, into a green that drops off sharply on the right. Opposite top: The 6th hole on the Five Farms East course at Baltimore Country Club, an A. W. Tillinghast classic, is a 574-yard par-5, a sharp dogleg left that requires the second shot to clear these bunkers to set up a pitch into the green. Opposite bottom: A. W. Tillinghast considered the 10th green at Winged Foot West in Mamaroneck, New York, the finest he ever designed. The 190-yard par-3 requires a long iron or wood shot over a valley to a sloping, two-tiered green protected by deep bunkers on the right, a bunker at the front left and woods beyond.*

Architects

The first golf course architect, of course, was the Lord, and he was the best there has ever been. All we have been able to do since is emulate nature. Sometimes that has been done badly, but often it has been done very well.

St. Andrews is the premier example of God's work. It is certainly the greatest course in the world today not created by an architect, although it has been refined by the likes of Allan Robertson, Old Tom Morris and Alister MacKenzie.

The course began to assume the form it has today sometime during the 1700s when putting surfaces were introduced and attention was paid to keeping them smooth and puttable. In those early stages, St. Andrews consisted of twenty-two holes, running out and back in the shape of a shepherd's crook, twenty of the holes sharing ten common greens (with but one cup on each). The Society of St. Andrews Golfers decided, in 1764, to consolidate the four starting holes into two long ones, which eliminated a total of two holes in each direction and resulted in the 18-hole course that has become the standard today.

There may or may not be any truth to the legend that the Scots consumed a jigger of whisky per hole, and since a bottle of Scotch contained eighteen jiggers, counted the round over when the bottle was empty.

In 1832 the St. Andrews golfers began cutting two cups in each green, creating (at the time) eight double greens. Several years later, with play and congestion increasing, the course was widened, the double greens were expanded into huge surfaces as wide as 100 yards and a new 17th green was built. St. Andrews now had four single greens—the first, ninth, 17th and 18th—and fourteen double putting surfaces. It remains that way today.

Golf, meanwhile, was spreading around the globe, wherever the Scots and other disciples happened to land—to England on a seven-hole course at Blackheath in 1608, to the United States as early as 1779, to India in the early 1800s, to France, Hong Kong, South Africa, Australia, New Zealand and Canada by later in the century. Almost all the early courses incorporated only a few holes, were laid out informally and were generally not very good, at least by the standards of the Scottish links. The need for course architects was desperate indeed.

Robertson, the professional and clubmaker at St. Andrews, became the first recognized designer when he performed the revamping of that course in the mid-1800s. He also designed a ten-hole course at Barry, Angus, Scotland, in 1842 that was the basis for Carnoustie, one of the fine championship courses.

Soon others followed, most of them golf professionals and greenkeepers who were solicited to design new courses. Our profession, a noble one in most cases in the century or so that has ensued, had been founded, however casually.

It is not the intention here to launch into a history of course architecture. That has been done, most notably by Ron Whitten and Geoff Cornish, whose book, *The Golf Course*, is the preeminent work on the subject and will be a resource for historians from now on.

There have been thousands of individuals, architects or not, who have built great, good, bad and indifferent golf courses over the centuries. I will leave the compilation of their achievements, notable or not, to Whitten, Cornish and whoever else might attempt it. Instead, I will deal briefly with some of my favorite architects, describing their influence on course design and the way golf is played. Recognizing what they have done, why they may have done it and where they have done it might help you play better. In any event, it should help you better enjoy this delightful game and its magnificent venues, which is really the purpose of this book.

It is perhaps heretical to say it, but the early great courses might indeed have been more accidents of location than genius of design. Certainly we know that of St. Andrews, and a critical look at the early courses in Scotland and

England bears out that contention. Old Tom Morris, renowned for his ability to take advantage of the natural land, produced such jewels as Muirfield, Royal Dornoch and Prestwick in Scotland, Royal County Down in Newcastle, Northern Ireland, and Lahinch on the west coast of Ireland. Despite a few quirks and oddities on each course, they are still among the best in the world. County Down's outgoing side may be the best nine holes of golf in the world, except for the relatively featureless greens, and certainly the entire venue is one of golf's most beautiful. Incidentally, Old Tom was commissioned to do County Down for "not more than 4." I have no idea if he brought the job in under that, but we might not take on the task today for that amount. On the other hand, given a chance at that land, maybe we would.

It was at County Down and at Muirfield, both of which he did at about the same time, that Morris introduced perhaps his greatest contribution to architecture when he created the "double-loop" routing. Instead of the traditional nine holes out and nine back, both of Muirfield's nines start and end at the clubhouse. The front nine runs clockwise, the back nine counterclockwise. This takes full advantage of all wind conditions and forces the player to deal with the breezes from all angles. It was a significant development in golf course design.

Yet Morris also produced many courses that, at least by modern standards, are disappointing. Back then there was no way to move the earth around, which goes back to my premise that what you were given to work with determined what you produced. Old Tom, a great player, obviously knew playing values, and given the opportunity he could build great holes and great courses. But if the land wasn't right, usually the courses weren't either.

That is still true to a great extent today. Now we can move as much dirt as we want anywhere we want it, but it takes considerable skill to make as great a course as one built on naturally exciting terrain.

The great architects at the turn of the century and beyond—Willie Park, Jr., J. F. Abercromby, Herbert Fowler, H. S. Colt and Tom Simpson—turned inland from the links and began designing courses on the heathlands near London. On this rolling terrain, where the sandy soil that is much like linksland is covered with trees and undergrowth, a new phase of golf course design began. These architects were not afraid to move dirt where it was required, although the task was difficult with the implements available at the time. But always, when they altered the land, they attempted to create a natural look that emulated the links as much as possible. Trees, an unknown quantity on the links, had to be dealt with and the holes routed around and through them. In this respect, then, these men were the forerunners of modern course architecture. Their contributions to the design concept of courses that we see all over the world today were immense.

Abercromby plied his trade primarily in the heathlands—Worplesdon Golf Club, Coombe Hill Golf Club and the Old Course at Addington Golf Club, all in Surrey, were his hallmark works. The other architects were more peripatetic. Park, considered by some to have set the standards for those who followed, is best known for Sunningdale and Huntercombe near London. He also built some seventy courses in the United States, including the championship North Course at Olympia Fields in Chicago and Woodway Country Club and New Haven Country Club in Connecticut.

Fowler created the fine Walton Heath course in Surrey and completely redesigned the links of the Royal North Devon Golf Club at Westward Ho! He also kept busy in the United States, where perhaps his best-known creation was Eastward Ho! on Cape Cod.

Simpson, who did much of his work on the Continent, probably performed his greatest feat when he remodeled the Old Course at Ballybunion on

Opposite: *The 5th at Old Marsh in West Palm Beach, Florida, with its rumpled fairway, bunkers and threatening water, exemplifies the sculptured beauty and difficulty of a Pete Dye course.*
Above: Old Tom Morris was one of the earliest golf course architects, and has greatly influenced the profession, both in terms of his philosophy and the courses he left: Royal County Down in Northern Ireland, Lahinch in Ireland, Royal Dornoch and Prestwick in Scotland among them.

57

Top: *The 1st on the Lower Course at Baltusrol in Springfield, New Jersey, designed by A. W. Tillinghast and remodeled by Robert Trent Jones, is a relatively easy par-5 opener for the members at 479 yards. But for USGA competitions, which are regularly conducted at the club, it becomes a 469-yard par-4 that stretches a player to the limits right off the bat. Above: The challenging 8th at A. W. Tillinghast's San Francisco Golf, a shortish par-4 at 388 yards, offers a subtle elegance. The fairway twists downhill to the landing area, then up to an elevated green surrounded by bunkers.*

the west coast of Ireland. It remains today one of the world's most marvelous layouts.

The original course at Sunningdale was considerably altered by Colt while he served as the club's secretary, mainly to accommodate the greater length of the rubber-cored Haskell ball introduced at the turn of the century. He also designed a second eighteen at Sunningdale, did two courses at Wentworth and laid out the course at Swinley Forest Golf Club on the heathlands, which he considered his best work. Others might disagree. He was equally adept on the links as inland, as he proved with his remodeling of the two courses at Royal Portrush in Northern Ireland. The Dunluce course there, site of the only British Open ever played on Irish soil, has been acclaimed by some as the world's best layout. Certainly it is one of the most spectacular.

Colt also designed the Eden Course at St. Andrews and the marvelous County Sligo Golf Club at Ross's Point on the northwest coast of Ireland. The latter was done with the help of C. H. Alison and Alister MacKenzie, who apprenticed under him. MacKenzie also aided in the Eden design. Alison became Colt's partner for twenty years and designed most of the courses that bear their name in America. These included such fine layouts as Briarwood, Knollwood and North Shore in the Chicago area, Burning Tree in Maryland, Canoe Brook in New Jersey, Century, Old Oaks and Fresh Meadow in New York and Milwaukee Country Club in Wisconsin.

MacKenzie also was a partner for a short time, so it is clear that Colt put a definite stamp on twentieth-century course architecture. Perhaps his greatest contribution, at least in the United States, was made at Pine Valley. George Crump is generally credited as the architect of the course often ranked number one in the world, but evidence exists that Colt actually was responsible for much of the design.

Colt, Alison and MacKenzie, all English-born, along with Park and Donald Ross, the Scots, are the foreigners who had perhaps the most influence on American golf courses and architecture. Their use of the land in creating beautiful, natural-looking courses and testing shot values was masterful and has been widely copied, by me and virtually every other architect who considers these factors sacrosanct in the building of a golf course. Some designers don't pay much attention to these values, but all the good ones do.

MacKenzie was a physician who served as a surgeon with the Somerset Light Infantry during the Boer War, during which he became infatuated with the Boers' use of camouflage. It was an interest that was to stand him in good stead when he later abandoned medicine for the practice of golf course architecture. That decision was made after he met Colt, who was hired in 1907 to build a course for the Alwoodley Golf Club in Leeds, of which MacKenzie was an honorary secretary.

His new career was interrupted by World War I, during which he served not as a physician but as a camouflage expert for the British Army. After the war he took up architecture in earnest and from the mid-1920s on became one of the giants of the business. His most noted works outside the United States are the West Course at Royal Melbourne, another of the world's great designs, and the remodeling of Titirangi in New Zealand.

MacKenzie's reputation was made in the United States when he was selected to design Cypress Point. He took a marvelous piece of land on the Monterey Peninsula and made absolutely the best use of it, combining inland terrain with seaside holes to create a layout that embodies all that is desirable in a golf course— beauty, excitement, memorability and great shot values. Cypress Point, completed in 1928, has since been consistently ranked among the best in the United States and the world.

Cypress Point led to another opportunity for MacKenzie that resulted in a course even better known. Bob Jones, defending his U.S. Amateur championship in 1929 at nearby Pebble Beach, had heard of Cypress Point and played it before the tournament began. Jones was so impressed that, when he retired from competitive golf after completing the Grand Slam in 1930, he hired MacKenzie to build his dream course in Augusta, Georgia. The Augusta National Golf Club, annual site of the Masters Tournament, remains today a premier example of beauty, strategic design and playability, an enjoyable challenge for the amateur of any skill level and a demanding test for the tournament player.

MacKenzie came along in the age of penal architecture, but he recognized the need to accommodate the less proficient player and became the first to practice strategic design on a grand scale. His contribution to the advancement of architecture, and it was a great one, lay to a great extent in the list of 13 essential features published in 1920 in his marvelous little book, *Golf Architecture*. The list is worth reproducing here:

1. The course, where possible, should be arranged in two loops of nine holes.

2. There should be a large proportion of good two-shot holes, two or three drive-and-pitch holes, and at least four one-shot holes.

3. There should be little walking between the greens and tees, and the course should be arranged so that in the first instance there is always a slight walk forwards from the green to the next tee; then the holes are sufficiently elastic to be lengthened in the future if necessary.

4. The greens and fairways should be sufficiently undulating, but there should be no hill climbing.

5. Every hole should have a different character.

6. There should be a minimum of blindness for the approach shots.

7. The course should have beautiful surroundings, and all the artificial features should have so natural an appearance that a stranger is unable to distinguish them from nature itself.

8. There should be a sufficient number of heroic carries from the tee, but the course should be arranged so that the weaker player with the loss of a stroke or portion of a stroke shall always have an alternative route open to him.

9. There should be infinite variety in the strokes required to play the various holes—viz., interesting brassy shots, iron shots, pitch and run-up shots.

10. There should be a complete absence of the annoyance and irritation caused by the necessity of searching for lost balls.

11. The course should be so interesting that even the plus man is constantly stimulated to improve his game in attempting shots he has hitherto been unable to play.

12. The course should be so arranged that the long handicap player, or even the absolute beginner, should be able to enjoy his round in spite of the fact that he is piling up a big score.

13. The course should be equally good during winter and summer, the texture of the greens and fairways should be perfect, and the approaches should have the same consistency as the greens.

Simple enough. The best things usually are. But that foresight provided us with the basis of modern design that we all follow today. We don't always make it in every respect, but the guidelines are as meaningful today as they were when MacKenzie put them on paper.

In addition to that insightful, common-sense approach, MacKenzie was blessed with a finely tuned artistic sense. He sometimes was guilty of exaggeration, especially with his greens. The sixth at Augusta with its mound at the top right is an example. MacKenzie would do this occasionally on every one of

The 4th at the Country Club in Brookline, Massachusetts, a 338-yard par-4 remodeled by Rees Jones for the 1988 U.S. Open, offers the longer hitter a chance to drive the green, but bunkers protect the putting surface and severe trouble awaits a shot hit slightly left or short.

his courses, and this is my only objection to his approach. But always the artistry is apparent. There is a dramatic boldness to his work, with flowing lines and undulations set off by massive bunkers. But it all blends with the surroundings to look as though it belongs.

MacKenzie was more than just a designer of great courses. He was attentive to the details of course construction and the maintenance of a course and its grasses. He was, then, the consummate architect.

MacKenzie was unique among the great architects, especially the earlier ones, in that he was not a good player. I always have believed that a good architect must be able to play the game well. In this way he can best determine the shot values that go into the design of a course. All of the earliest architects were golf professionals. Colt was the first noted architect who was not, but he was a fine amateur player. And most of today's successful designers, if not professionals, are proficient amateurs.

I was a good player in my younger days, and I'm proud of the fact that Bob Jones once said, "When Trent designs a hole, he is able to test every yard of it himself for true shot value."

MacKenzie could not, but he was able to overcome this deficiency with keen observation and a sense of playing values that went far beyond his limited physical ability. And, in the case of Augusta National, the presence of Bob Jones undoubtedly helped a great deal.

I have learned much from MacKenzie, whom I met late in his career and early in mine. I also have been influenced by Ross, who grew up on the links of Dornoch and trained under Old Tom Morris at St. Andrews. At the age of twenty he returned to Dornoch, where he spent the next seven years as professional and greenkeeper. There he learned more about course maintenance and

architecture from John Sutherland, the club secretary and a student of those arts. In 1898 he migrated to the United States, and in the next half century he became this country's best-known and most active designer of golf courses. Although he did the bulk of his work in North Carolina, Florida and the Northeast, he constructed courses in every area of the country. There is no need to recount all the marvelous layouts for which he is responsible. The best are Seminole in Florida, Pinehurst No. 2 in North Carolina, Oakland Hills South in Michigan, Oak Hill in Rochester, New York, Scioto and Inverness in Ohio, the Broadmoor in Colorado, Salem in Massachusetts, Wannamoisett in Rhode Island, Plainfield in New Jersey, Aronimink in Philadelphia, Bob O'Link in the Chicago area.

Ross certainly was of the strategic school. He believed that golf should be a pleasure, not a penance, and that a beautiful, natural course would be far better received by the majority of players than an artificial layout that demanded too much of most.

He was a master at designing courses that would test all the shots, particularly the long irons and the approach to the green. He did not believe in penal driving areas. He believed that the tee shot, the longest shot, should be allowed the most room for error, and often his fairways seem inordinately wide. But almost always the drive has to be played into a specific area of the fairway to afford the ideal shot into the hole.

And he was a genius at designing greens and the bunkering and mounding around them, blending everything into the surrounding landscape. His favorite pattern was the crowned green that ran off at the edges, effectively reducing the landing area on the green and rewarding the player who could make a high, soft shot into the target. Ross's greens also place a high premium on the ability to chip and hit precise little pitches.

Opposite top: *Royal Melbourne, Cypress Point and Augusta National are the best-known monuments to the architectural genius of Alister MacKenzie.* Opposite bottom: *The 12th at Southern Hills in Tulsa, Oklahoma, a Perry Maxwell jewel, was once described by Ben Hogan as "the greatest par-4 12th hole in the United States." It stretches 456 yards, doglegging left downhill to a green guarded by water and bunkers.* Above: *The 18th at Bay Hill outside Orlando, Florida, has been remodeled by owner Arnold Palmer from Dick Wilson's original design. A 456-yard par-4, the hole now features a boomerang-shaped green sweeping around a lake that must be carried if the pin is tucked on the right. Bunkers surround the back and left, and present an explosion to a putting surface that slopes sharply to the water. It is justifiably considered one of the hardest finishing holes in golf.*

61

Donald Ross, the Scot from Dornoch, popularized golf course architecture in the United States.

"Contours and slopes," he said, "have been used to break up greens which are so designed as to always give the player near the cup an opportunity for one putt but have minimized the opportunity to get down in less than the regulation number for the golfer whose play to the green has been less accurate."

He means that if you don't hit it awfully close, you're not going to make a birdie. And if you miss the green, don't plan on getting it up and down.

Ross felt the green area was so important that, when laying out a course, he first looked for greensites and usually built the hole backward from there. His holes began with the target. That is not the way most architects worked, nor is it the way I have worked in most cases. But for Ross it was effective.

Unfortunately, Ross and his company got so big (more than 3,000 employees were building his courses by 1925) that, by his own admission, he never saw many of the courses that bear his name. And many were handled by local construction companies who often changed his intended design. That was too bad for those who paid for his name, but for the purist there is no mistaking a Ross course.

Ross also was a fine player who won the North and South Open three times and consistently finished well in the U.S. Open, as high as fifth in 1903, before he gave up his playing career to concentrate on building courses.

Charles Blair Macdonald, who grew up in Chicago, was the first American golf architect and deservedly is known as "The Father of American Golf Course Architecture." After studying for two years at St. Andrews University, where he fell in love with the game, Macdonald returned home and eventually built two courses for the members of the Chicago Club, one at Belmont in 1893 and another in Wheaton in 1895. These were the first two 18-hole courses in the United States. The latter became the Chicago Golf Club that today ranks as one of the finest in the country after having been extensively revised by Seth Raynor, a Macdonald protégé, in 1923.

In the early 1900s Macdonald began to consider building a course that would be patterned after the best holes in Great Britain. Eventually, on a rolling seaside stretch of land on Long Island, near Southampton and abutting Shinnecock Hills, he built The National Golf Links of America. There he recreated, among other great holes of Britain, the Alps of Prestwick, the famed Road Hole at St. Andrews and, most successfully, North Berwick's Redan, a one-shot hole with the green angling away from the player and protected by a bunker on the left front. Many consider Macdonald's Redan better than the original.

Macdonald also used the rippling land to its best advantage, as he usually did, to create his own holes that may be better than the imitations. The result was a course that caught America's imagination and catapulted Macdonald into prominence and demand. The National was the best links ever built in this country at that time. It may not be today, but it still stands as a monument to a man who, like all great architects, believed that golf holes should be arranged on the natural terrain, that artificiality was totally out of place on a course. Macdonald, a believer in variety and bold bunkering, sometimes created mounds and blind holes that would be anathemas on modern courses, but most of these were in his attempts to imitate the older British configurations.

Macdonald was one of the great characters in American golf. A fine player, he lost the first two unofficial national amateur championships at Newport Golf Club and St. Andrew's Golf Club, then, out of cantankerousness or pomposity, insisted that an official championship had to be conducted by an official association of golf clubs rather than a single club. This led to the formation, in December of 1894, of the Amateur Golf Association of the United States, which later became the United States Golf Association.

Macdonald was elected second vice president of the new association and the next year won the first official United States Amateur Championship, also conducted at Newport. But his greatest contributions lay ahead.

After he completed the National, Macdonald designed many other fine courses, among them the Mid-Ocean Club in Bermuda. The Yale University Golf Course in New Haven, Connecticut, is the most memorable, built over incredibly rugged land and reflecting the boldness and dimension of his architectural philosophy. But Yale or any of the others cannot quite approach the stature of the National Golf Links, which forever will remain his monument.

Macdonald's success undoubtedly encouraged other Americans to follow, and thereafter golf architecture was no longer the exclusive realm of the Scots. Some of those who passed for course designers were really only stake planters —"Eighteen stakes on a Sunday afternoon" became a popular method of laying out courses. Eventually, however, there began to emerge a new breed of architects with the skill and knowledge to produce good and great designs.

One of these was Perry Maxwell, a retired Oklahoma banker of Scottish descent who served for three years in the early 1930s as Alister MacKenzie's assistant. After MacKenzie's death in 1934, Maxwell supervised the completion of some of his courses, including the wonderful Ohio State University Scarlet course in Columbus.

On his own, Maxwell was known for his severely undulating greens, with contours so significant that they came to have a name of their own, the "Maxwell Rolls." He was hired to redesign greens at Augusta National (the first, 10th and 14th are examples of his work), Pine Valley and the National Golf Links, among other courses.

Maxwell built the first nine holes at Prairie Dunes (the second nine was finished twenty years later by his son, Press, using his father's basic plan). He built three new holes (the third, fourth and fifth) at Colonial in Fort Worth for the 1941 U.S. Open, and they may be the three best holes on the course. Among the many fine courses he designed, the most notable may be the magnificent Southern Hills Country Club layout in Tulsa, consistently ranked among the best in the country and the world.

Albert Warren Tillinghast, another great character in American golf architecture, emerged during the first quarter of the century as a giant of the business. Tillie, who came from a wealthy Philadelphia background, was a hard-drinking bon vivant with immeasurable talent in many areas—a good golfer, a writer, editor and historian, an artist, a fine golf photographer and collector, a sportsman and a raconteur. He was one of the founders of the PGA of America and a staunch believer in turfgrass research and the USGA Green Section.

Above all, Tillinghast was a superb golf course architect with a flair for beauty and an uncanny eye for shot values. His courses are marked by variety and imagination. He hated blind shots and hidden hazards, and he felt that overly large putting surfaces placed too much premium on putting and discouraged good iron play. It is a philosophy that I, in particular, might argue with, but Tillie believed in it. Therefore his greens are characteristically small, tightly bunkered, usually dished in and sloping, sometimes to the extreme. But almost always he allows an opening, no matter how small, through which a shot can be run onto the putting surface.

He was not as prolific as Ross, for example, but the list of Tillinghast's greatest courses is startling in its depth and variety—Winged Foot East and West in New York, with Quaker Ridge right next door and Bethpage Black, one of the country's finest municipal courses, just a short drive away; Baltusrol Upper and Lower, Somerset Hills, Ridgewood and Shackamaxon in New Jersey; the East Course at Baltimore Country Club's Five Farms; San Francisco Golf Club; the Oklahoma City Golf and Country Club and Tulsa Country Club; Pittsburgh Field Club, Philadelphia Cricket Club and Sunnehanna in Penn-

Charles Blair Macdonald stands as the first American gold course architect, counting National Golf Links, Chicago Golf and Yale as his principal achievements.

sylvania; Newport in Rhode Island; Brooklawn in Connecticut; Westmoreland in Chicago; Rochester Golf and Country Club and Golden Valley in Minnesota; Swope Park in Kansas City; Brook Hollow and Cedar Crest in Dallas. And those are but a few of his fine designs.

Like all talented architects, Tillinghast was a master at taking the land available and shaping it to his uses in the most natural manner. For example, at Winged Foot the ground was rocky, so he took advantage of the rock ledges by building his greens on them, which is why so many of the greens there are elevated. Then he washed sand against the sides to make the deep bunkers for which the place is noted.

At San Francisco Golf, on the other hand, the soil is sandy, so many of his greens there are nestled down in hollows. If you want to understand why the good architect does what he does, examine the land and the surroundings he had to work with.

There must have been something in the Philadelphia air in the early 1900s. Tillinghast's friends included George Thomas, who moved to California and became an "amateur" but brilliant designer, with courses like Riviera and Los Angeles Country Club North to his credit; Hugh Wilson, who designed the wonderful East course at Merion in 1912 and helped finish Pine Valley; and George Crump, who built Pine Valley with the help of H. S. Colt.

William S. Flynn, who apprenticed under Wilson on the Merion job and served for a time as the club's greenkeeper, settled in Philadelphia and became, in collaboration with Howard Toomey, one of the country's premier architects after World War I. Flynn handled the design, Toomey the construction and business matters. Notable among Flynn's many fine courses are Shinnecock Hills in Southampton, Upper Cascades at the Homestead in Virginia, the Spring Mill Course at the Philadelphia Country Club, Cherry Hills in Denver and the James River course at the Country Club of Virginia in Richmond. He also built the Primrose nine at The Country Club in Brookline, Massachusetts, several holes of which are incorporated when championships are played there.

Flynn's finest, of course, was Shinnecock, finished in 1931. It more closely resembles a links than any course not really built on seaside ground, although it is close enough to get the ocean winds off two surrounding bays and Long Island Sound. There is a sweep and a majesty to Shinnecock that, along with its natural quality, puts it high among the world's best courses.

Flynn, a disciple of Hugh Wilson, in turn spawned apprentices like William Gordon, Robert (Red) Lawrence and Dick Wilson, all of whom became prominent in the field.

Dick Wilson, a counterpart and, you might say, a rival of mine during the 1950s and 1960s, created many wonderful courses, including Bay Hill in Orlando, the Doral Blue course in Miami, Meadow Brook and Deepdale on Long Island, Cog Hill No. 4 outside of Chicago (one of the best public courses in the world), La Costa outside of San Diego and the JDM Country Club courses in Palm Beach Gardens, Florida. His *pièce de résistance*, of course, is Pine Tree in Boynton Beach, Florida. It has been called the greatest flat course in the world, and while it may or may not be that, considering all the wonderful links courses on flat land, it is a marvelous example of Wilson's work. His greens are almost always plateaued, often set on a diagonal to the approach shot and offering a variety of hole locations, and he used the land to its best advantage. The holes he built seemed to have been there forever. There is no greater accolade.

Wilson was assisted in much of his work by Joe Lee and Robert Von Hagge, both of whom have gone on to successful careers of their own. Lee took over Wilson's business when Dick died in 1965 and has since, on his own, built some of the country's most enjoyable courses.

Stanley Thompson, the Canadian who was my first boss and mentor and

Opposite top: *The picturesque 14th hole at Harbour Town on Hilton Head Island, South Carolina, one of Pete Dye's best designs, is a relatively short par-3 at just 155 yards, but the shot is over water all the way. Water right and bunkers at the back left corner will catch shots that go astray. Opposite bottom: At 193 yards, the 8th at Butler National in Oak Brook, Illinois, is tough enough. Water in front and to the right, and woods that loom on the left and behind, make it one of golf's scariest par-3s on a George Fazio design that is one of golf's hardest. Above: A. W. Tillinghast was not as prolific as some architects, but virtually every one of his courses is a distinctive gem.*

later my partner, was another who filled the roles of character and genius. I will discuss his contributions at greater length in the next chapter.

Those were and are the giants. More are looming, but it takes maturity and the perspective of time to establish any individual and his work in the firmament.

Pete Dye is in the forefront of the so-called modern architects. Dye is sixty-three as this is written, but he did not begin designing courses until the mid-1960s, so he has made his mark in a relative hurry. He, too, draws from the Scottish courses with their smallish greens, undulating fairways, pot bunkers and bulkheading with railroad ties, and his style has had a great influence on architecture in the last two decades.

As I suggested earlier, Dye has done marvelously natural work where the land has allowed it. Crooked Stick outside of Indianapolis, his first major work, is an example. It was finished in 1966. The Golf Club in New Albany, Ohio, near Columbus, was completed shortly thereafter, and Dye did a beautiful job of weaving the holes through forest, linkslike open spaces and water. It is a relatively unknown course, because no tournaments of note ever are played on it, but it is a gem.

So is Harbour Town Golf Links on Hilton Head Island in South Carolina, It is a shortish course, with very small greens, carved out of the pines and cypress, but despite this still has a linksland flavor.

Oak Tree in Edmond, Oklahoma, site of the 1988 PGA Championship and the first Dye course to host a major championship, is another of his artistic creations. He has not made a links on the plains, but there is a strong resemblance. There is a certain artificiality to the course, which perhaps is unavoidable, but the Scottish characteristics—the deep bunkers, rolling fairways and severely contoured greens—are there.

Dye is an artist, a sculptor. In a sense, he does some of his best work with bad land. PGA West, as I indicated, may not be a great course because it is too hard for the majority of players. But it is a magnificent example of making something out of nothing.

He is a hands-on designer. He does not draw, does not make detailed plans. Instead, he goes on site and directs the work. He puts a bump here and a bump there, and the result usually is spectacular. Dye often overuses the railroad ties, bulkheading bunkers, lakes and everything in sight, which contributes to the sometimes artificial look of his courses. But they always are striking and beautiful.

More important, Dye is a good player and has a well-defined sense of shot values. So, with few exceptions, his courses are great and fair tests as well as appealing to the eye.

Tom Fazio is one of the best of the younger designers. He looks at the work of others and emulates what he likes, ignoring what he doesn't like, and he has excellent feel and judgment for what is good. It is no crime to emulate. We have all done it over the centuries. It is how you learn, by taking the best characteristics of what has gone before and using your imagination to try to make them better. That's what Tom Fazio and other fine architects can do.

Tom began working with his uncle, George Fazio, in the early 1960s and eventually became a full partner. George, who died in 1986, designed such great courses as Butler National in Chicago and Jupiter Hills in Florida. He and Tom also did remodeling work on Winged Foot West and Inverness in Toledo, in both cases to prepare them for U.S. Open Championships, and Oak Hill in Rochester to spruce it up for the 1980 PGA Championship.

Tom now has surpassed George as an architect. He has the ability to do the utmost with good land, creating beautiful and natural-looking holes that have variety and challenge to them. In addition to the first three courses at PGA National in Palm Beach Gardens, Florida, where the Champions course has been the site of a Ryder Cup Match and the 1987 PGA Championship, the younger Fazio has to his credit such wonderful courses as Wild Dunes in South Carolina, The Vintage Club in Palm Springs, the Golf Club of Oklahoma in Tulsa, Wade Hampton in North Carolina and Barton.Creek in Texas.

Jack Nicklaus, who has been balancing his careers as a great player and a golf course designer for about fifteen years at this writing, has built great golf courses—Muirfield Village in Ohio, Shoal Creek in Alabama, Desert Highlands in Arizona, Grand Cypress and Loxahatchee in Florida and others. There is no question Nicklaus understands shot values, not only for a player of his caliber but for the amateur as well. Nicklaus's problem has been that too often he fails to visualize his holes on the first attempt and must rebuild them to make them right. He winds up with good holes, but it's expensive. He also has shown a tendency toward artificiality, as in the cones or mounds on his courses that are supposed to resemble dunes but don't. They also are expensive to maintain. All this is not uncommon with any architect, and Nicklaus will learn as he spends more years in the business. For some of us, fifteen years is no time at all.

Without sounding too much like a proud father, which I am, I'd say the

Opposite: *Also similar to Augusta National's famed 12th hole is the par-3 12th at Muirfield Village, Jack Nicklaus's course in Dublin, Ohio. Shown here from the lower tee, the hole usually plays from an elevated tee and requires a 156-yard carry over water to a green set into a lovely hillside.* Above: *George Fazio, another fine player turned architect, created many outstanding courses, including Edgewood Tahoe in Nevada, Moselem Springs in Pennsylvania, Butler National in Illinois and Jupiter Hills in Florida.*

best two architects today are my sons, Robert Trent, Jr., and Rees. Both started with my firm, and some of our best courses were built under their direction. Since going out on their own they have created a great many wonderful courses. I will tell more about them and the work they have done in the following chapters.

There are many talented and technically competent architects working today, some of whom perhaps don't get the recognition they deserve because they don't have their own firms and are tied in with the so-called bigger names. Roger Rulewich, my chief designer, is one of these. A former president of the American Society of Golf Course Architects, he is one of the best in the business and has a wonderful feel for routing a golf course.

Don Knott, who works for my son Bobby, is another whose talents remain largely unrecognized. He is a good player with an architectural background as well, so he has a feel for the playability of the course as well as the technical aspects that go into building it.

The quality and depth of talent in the business of golf course architecture today reflects, I feel, the demand for that talent and the dedication to the profession that the practitioners bring.

Golf course architecture has come a long way since the days when designers basically followed the dictates of nature. Today it is a combination of professions—engineering, agronomy, horticulture and landscape design, plus knowledge of the game itself.

What follows in this book is a look at what I and others have contributed to the development of the profession and what it means to you, the individual who plays and supports this wonderful game.

Chapter 2
Robert Trent Jones, Man and Builder

Below: *Robert Trent Jones tees off at the ceremonies opening his course at Green Lakes State Park in Fayetteville, New York, in 1935.* Bottom: *The young Bob Jones ready to play in Rochester, New York, in 1926.* Opposite: *The 8th at Banff Springs in Alberta, Canada, fronted by water and set against a band of the Rockies, is a 205-yard par-3 known as The Cauldron, for obvious reasons. It is another beauty by Stanley Thompson.*

I was twelve years old, living in East Rochester, New York, and I had heard you could make money as a caddie at the Country Club of Rochester. So I took the trolley car from East Rochester and had to walk about a mile and a half to the club. As I was walking down the road, a white Packard roadster came toward me, and in it was a handsome, black-haired man. As the car swept past, carrying Walter Hagen in his usual grand style, I knew right then I had to somehow get involved with golf. Never in my wildest dreams could I have imagined how great that involvement would be.

Hagen was to leave soon for a new job as the professional at Oakland Hills in Detroit, but he would return to Rochester periodically for exhibitions or just to visit, and I would get a chance to caddie for him or somebody in his foursome. The next year, in fact, he played an exhibition at the club with Harry Vardon and Ted Ray. I was very much taken with Vardon's smooth swing and, when I started playing, tried to imitate him. Nobody could imitate Hagen and that sway he had.

Of course, like most kids who knew anything about golf in those days, I was a Bobby Jones fan. I had been since he won his first two matches in the U.S. Amateur at the age of fourteen two years before. Overwhelmed by the fact that we had the same name, I began to follow his career closely. How could I have known that our lives would some day become entwined?

I learned to play golf at a course called Genundawah, a nine-hole layout in East Rochester, using a mid-iron I had bought for fifty cents from a rack of old clubs in the pro shop. For a while that was the only club I had. The course was built on a residue of Lake Ontario, on what we called a "blow sand" area, and it was just like undulating linksland. I was fourteen years old. The green-keeper was a German gardener who told me and a friend of mine that we could play on the course if we would cut the greens every day after school. So we did. One of us would steer the mower and the other would pull with a rope, because it was too heavy for one kid to push. We would go fast, and when we finished, we played golf. I was shooting par on the course within a year or so. I also was learning some things about golf courses . . . like how to grow grass on sand. There was no fairway irrigation on the course. They tied the sand down by planting wheat. When it grew to a certain height they would cut it and throw down the grass seed, which would be held by the single stalks of the wheat.

One incident at Genundawah comes to mind, and it's particularly interesting some sixty-eight years later. A doctor at the club said he would give a mashie-niblick to the winner of the caddie tournament. I won it with a 39, and he gave me his old mashie-niblick. I was upset, because a new design with wide grooves that put a lot of backspin on the ball had just appeared on the market. So I went to the doctor and said, "You know, you gave me a club and I'm very appreciative, but I really wanted one of those new mashie-niblicks with the wide grooves." So he got it for me, and when you hit the ball it would take the paint off, and the ball would really back up on the greens.

Later that year the United States Golf Association declared the wide grooves illegal, just as it did in 1988. Which only goes to show there really isn't much new in golf equipment.

Incidentally, I was plenty upset at the ruling.

By the time I was sixteen I was being called the most promising young golfer in the Rochester area. That year I entered a 36-hole Open tournament sponsored by the Rochester *Journal-American* at Genesee Valley Park. I had passed up a junior tournament the week before, thinking I couldn't enter both. In the morning round I carried my own bag and shot 76. In the afternoon, with a caddie, I shot 69, a course record, and finished as low amateur, one stroke behind the winning professional.

Right then I began to consider broader horizons as a player, but I had a

stomach ailment that flared up. It turned out to be a duodenal ulcer, and I played no competitive golf for the next two years. During that period I decided the life of a tournament golfer was not for me.

I was born in 1906 in Ince, England, and my parents emigrated to East Rochester when I was three years old. My father, William Reese Jones, worked in the railroad car shops there, and college was not in the financial picture. At that point, in fact, I had dropped out of high school and was working as a draftsman for Merchants Despatch Transportation, Inc., a subsidiary of the New York Central that maintains and operates railroad refrigerator cars.

The job was frustrating, and I began looking for something else to do. I had spent some time watching Donald Ross build Oak Hill in Rochester, and I was still in love with golf. I thought that maybe building courses might be the answer for me, but I didn't know how to go about learning the business. There were no technical schools for it, and you couldn't go to a university and major in golf course architecture.

I discussed this with Ray Humburg, who was the head of the engineering department at Merchants Despatch. He was a graduate of the Cornell College of Engineering and felt that would be the best school for me. It had schools in the various disciplines, and golf course architecture really is a combination of professions.

In the meantime my reputation as a player in the Rochester area got me a job at Sodus Country Club, a small club with a nine-hole course in Sodus Bay, New York, overlooking Lake Ontario. I was the professional, the green-keeper and the manager. The club had a small white clubhouse with only a snack bar and only about fifty members. One of these members, however, was

a wealthy gentleman named James Bashford, and he ended up giving my career its start.

I told Bashford of my dream, and he was sympathetic. He drove me to Cornell in his limousine and introduced me to the dean of the College of Agriculture. And he gave me $1,000 a year for a couple of years to help me out.

I had to get permission from the university authorities to enter as a special student, and I went through tutoring in the summer of 1926 in mathematics, chemistry and drawing. That fall I entered Cornell and virtually designed my own curriculum.

I studied landscape architecture in the College of Architecture, hydraulics and surveying in the College of Engineering, agronomy and horticulture in the College of Agriculture. I also studied economics, chemistry, public speaking, journalism and business law. After I had finished at Cornell I also took a course in art at Rochester Technical Institute, which developed the ability to sketch that was to help me so much throughout my career.

It wasn't all work. I was elected president of the university chapter of Delta Kappa Epsilon. And during my second year I met Ione Tefft Davis, a beauty from Montclair, New Jersey, who was a Phi Beta Kappa student at Wells College in nearby Aurora, New York. That was the most important thing that happened to me at Cornell . . . or ever.

I returned during the summers to Sodus, and the money I made there, along with Bashford's help, got me through. One summer he also got me a job teaching at Hollywood Golf and Country Club, his club in Hollywood, Florida. It was there I suffered a traumatic, but eventually helpful, experience.

I had resumed playing some competitive golf and had entered the first La Gorce Open at Miami Beach. Among the top professionals playing were Johnny Farrell, Gene Sarazen, Macdonald Smith, Bobby Cruickshank, Al Watrous and Tommy Armour. One of the few stars missing was Bobby Jones himself. As it turned out, I was to fill in for him, in a way.

I was nervous enough, and when they called "Robert Jones" to the first tee, the crowd pressed around, wondering if this was THE Bobby Jones. It was not, as my sudden attack of stage fright proved. Playing the first nine in a cold sweat, I was out in 43, and it didn't get much better coming home. But I did finish the tournament, improving each round, and the experience stood me in good stead. In my next tournament, the 1927 Canadian Open, I shot 303 and finished tenth. The tournament was won, by the way, by Tommy Armour. But competitive golf was to become mostly a thing of the past for me. And eventually any further Bobby Jones mix-ups would be straightened away.

Because I was a special student, of course, I did not receive a degree from Cornell. But I got what I went for—the education, the knowledge to design and build golf courses.

I was twenty-four years old when I finished. The year was 1930, not the best of all possible times to be starting in business.

After a couple of remodeling jobs, my first major assignment was to design a course for the Midvale Golf and Country Club near Rochester. Midvale also called in Stanley Thompson, a Canadian architect with considerable credentials. I'm certain they wanted somebody to look over my shoulder, to make sure the young kid didn't mess things up. As it turned out, that was a great stroke of good fortune for me.

Although he died in 1952 at the age of fifty-eight, Stanley Thompson remains Canada's greatest architect, as well as one of golf's greatest characters. A charming, fun-loving guy, he could talk almost anybody out of almost anything . . . and usually did. But not every time. When he built Jasper Park for the Canadian National Railway, he ran out of money on his $500,000 budget, but he conjured more cash out of the company and continued on. However, when he decided to contour the ninth fairway so the golfer looking at it would see the voluptuous figure of Cleopatra, he ran afoul of Sir Harry Thornton, then the head of the railway. Sir Harry was appalled and Thompson modified the curves. But the hole is still called "Cleopatra."

Thompson's modus operandi was in keeping with his personality. He would walk a property to get the feel of it, never taking a note, then sit back with a bottle of scotch and a good cigar and design the course. And they were always good. Jasper Park and Banff Springs in Alberta, Capilano in Vancouver, Cape Breton Highlands in Nova Scotia—all wonderful, beautiful layouts.

Beauty and naturalness were Thompson's hallmarks. He once wrote: "Nature must always be the architect's model. The lines of bunkers and greens must not be sharp or harsh, but easy and rolling. The development of the natural features and planning the artificial work to conform to them requires a great deal of care and forethought. In clearing fairways, it is good to have an eye to the beautiful. Often it is possible, by clearing away undesirable and unnecessary trees on the margin of fairways, to open up a view of some attractive picture and frame it with foliage . . . oftentimes the natural beauty of many a golf course, which the average player assumes was always present, has been created by the skill of the engineer who can see opportunities for beauty in the rough woods, swamps or fields that mean nothing to the unskilled eye. The absence or presence of the above features, among others, will decide whether continuous play on a course becomes monotonous or otherwise."

It was this philosophy, so like mine, that drew us together once we met at the Midvale project. He asked me to come to work for him, which I did, and we soon became partners.

Midvale was an interesting project. We formed the greens with slip-scrapers and teams of horses. It was virtually a hand operation, and it took seven days with four or five teams to shape a green. So I had a lot of time to think about what I wanted to do with them. I would make sketches, then watch while the work was done. It was very valuable experience.

Opposite: Kananaskis, a Trent Jones and Roger Rulewich creation in Alberta, Canada, is a spectacular example of mountain design. Following pages: The 2nd, a 527-yard par-5 guarded by water, is typical of the beauty at Peachtree in Atlanta, perhaps the course that solidified the Trent Jones reputation.

Scenes from Peachtree (clockwise from top left): *the 14th, a 180-yard par-3 with water left; the 12th, a par-4 of 440 yards set into the woods with typical Trent Jones bunkering; the 13th, another long and well-bunkered par-4; the 6th, a lovely and demanding par-3 at 216 yards.*

We didn't make a lot of friends during the construction. The entire area was very sandy with little water, so we would get sludge from the city disposal plant eighteen miles away and haul it in by the truckload. And did it smell awful! But when we worked it into the soil it helped hold the moisture, so the grass grew very quickly and well.

But the club went broke just before we finished, and we didn't collect our $9,000 fee. That was to happen with our next three jobs during those hard times, but my partnership with Thompson remained strong until 1938, and our friendship lasted until Stanley's death.

We soon turned north to Canada, where there was still some money with which to build courses. I routed the holes for Thompson at Capilano, worked on some short courses in Ontario and Quebec and helped him with the course at Banff, where they were having trouble with winterkill on the greens. Every winter the greens would die. I discovered that they were putting the fungicide down too early, so it would wash away and not be effective. I simply suggested they put a dose on early and another later to protect the greens all winter, and that seemed to solve the problem.

Some fifty years later, while we were building the courses at Kananaskis, the course superintendent from Banff came over one day and said to me, "You know, I'm just finding out that if I put fungicide down twice, I can keep the greens over the winter." I just smiled and told him I was glad to know that.

The Depression worsened and golf course construction became almost nonexistent. We started a two-course project for General Electric on Carleton Island, on the U.S. side of the St. Lawrence River, but GE sold the island in 1932 when we had completed only fourteen holes. Thompson then went to Rio de Janiero, where his brother-in-law had lined up some jobs. I stayed home and drew up detailed plans for the courses from the topographical maps Stanley sent me.

I had another course that didn't work out, at least at the time, but it may have indirectly started another career. I was to build a course for Colgate University in Hamilton, New York, in 1932, just after Gene Sarazen had won the British and U.S. Opens. I went to him and asked if he would like to help design his ideal golf course, just as Bobby Jones was doing in Augusta. He agreed, and on the five-hour train ride he kept me entertained with fascinating stories about his career. Gene was also to deliver a speech at Colgate, but on the ride to the campus the next day I could see he was getting very nervous.

When we got to the hall, about six hundred students were waiting for us. Bill Reid, the director of athletics, introduced Sarazen, the audience gave him a big hand, and Gene stood up and said, "Fellows, I'm happy to be here." And he sat down.

I quickly stood up and said, "Now, Gene, why don't you tell the audience about your match with Walter Hagen?" So he started telling the story, and soon he was at ease, strutting around like Hagen, mimicking him. Then I asked him another question, and another, and he had the students sitting on the edge of their chairs for about an hour.

When we got ready to leave, Sarazen whispered to me, "Listen, I'm going to do this at all the colleges." And he ended up speaking to about twenty of them.

The golf course, which was to be built with WPA labor, was shot down because one of the professors complained to Washington, and there was no other money. The first nine finally got built in 1955, the second in 1964. But I guess it was worth the wait. In 1977 the national collegiate championship was conducted on the course.

With little else happening in the United States, it seemed time for desperate measures. In 1934 I returned to Rochester, where a greenkeeper had built an awful course in Durand-Eastman Park. I went to Patrick Slavin, the director of parks, and said, "You know, your golf course is not very good." And he threw me out of his office.

Well, Fay Blanchard, the managing editor of the *Journal-American*, was a good friend and golfing buddy of mine, so I told him the story. He wanted me to give him some material for the sports editor, and soon the newspaper came out with a shot at Slavin for building such a bad golf course. Two weeks later it printed another blast.

Slavin then called me into the office and said, "You little son of a bitch, how do I get the newspapers off my back?"

Quite innocently I replied, "Well, let's do it right this time."

He agreed, but he told me the city council would only allow $1,500 for my fee, and I couldn't live on that for a year. But the Works Progress Administration was going strong then, and I asked him if he could buy grass under the WPA program. He said he could, and I said, "You just bought $8,000 worth of grass." I owned a nursery at Midvale that wasn't doing anything because there was nobody to sell the grass to, and that worked out just fine.

Top: *The 11th at Augusta National, remodeled by Robert Trent Jones into a 455-yard par-4, presents this perilous second shot into a green threatened by water on the left.* Above: *Augusta's par-3 16th, another Trent Jones creation, demands a tee shot of 170 yards or more over water that also guards the left of the two-tiered, sloping green.*

Above: *The fourth at Baltusrol is one of the world's best-known par-3s, demanding a 194-yard carry over water. Trent Jones remodeled it before the 1954 U.S. Open and promptly proved its playability by making a hole in one. Below: An aerial view of the Dunes in Myrtle Beach, South Carolina, shows the 575-yard par-5 doglegging around a lake in the left center of the picture. Regarded as Robert Trent Jones's classic heroic shot, it offers the player a chance to bite off as much as he chooses on the second shot.*

The area in which I was to build the course was pretty bad, virtually a swamp. At one point Slavin called me in and said, "This project is your doing, and they're calling it 'Slavin's Folly.' The city engineers say there is no way on God's earth you can build a golf course on that property. It's quicksand."

So I called on one of my professors at Cornell who had taught me drainage, and he came in and inspected what I was doing. He told Slavin, "Let the kid alone. He's doing all right."

In more than half a century of building golf courses, that was one of the hardest jobs I've had, at least until I encountered Mauna Kea thirty years later. But I built it, and the course drew raves from the local players and press. That gave me the experience, as well as the confidence, to build some pretty good golf courses on some pretty ugly pieces of land throughout my career.

Slavin was impressed enough, I guess, to offer me a job as assistant director of parks. "You'll never make any money as a golf course architect," he said. But I turned him down. I wanted to build golf courses.

In the next four years I built five more public courses that the federal government basically paid for. I saw nothing wrong with that at the time, nor do I now. If the WPA could pay the unemployed to rake leaves, I didn't see why a golf course wasn't a legitimate project. It is self-liquidating, and it provides something permanent and beautiful for the community.

All the courses I built with WPA funds—two in Illinois and four in New York, including Durand-Eastman—have been profitable. I also like to think they have been models for other public courses, which must handle heavy traffic and punishment.

One of those courses was Green Lakes State Park Golf Club not far from Syracuse, which I built in 1935. There were some beautiful geological formations, including a glacier lake, and it was a marvelous area for a golf course.

One already existed on the property. It had been built by Laurie Cox, a professor of landscape architecture at Syracuse University. I think he also was the lacrosse coach, but he knew nothing about golf, and the course was pretty bad. He had built all the holes on a hill, and every time you hit a shot the ball would run all the way to the bottom. I explained to Jim Evans, who was the director of state parks in the New York central region, what I wanted to do with the new one. I figured I could route the holes around the back of the hill and end up with eighteen holes on the flat without using the hill at all. He agreed. But he was afraid the first thing the state legislature would do was cut out my fee, so he offered to lease the course to me for a dollar a year. I agreed on one condition—there was a Civilian Conservation Corps camp nearby, and I wanted to use CCC labor on the golf course until we could break even.

He said, "Okay, I'll do it, but we'll both probably go to jail." So I did, and we came out with a lovely course. At the time, Spalding was sending a team of professionals—Jimmy Thomson, Horton Smith, Lawson Little and Craig Wood—around the country to sell golf. I asked if they would put on an exhibition to open the course. They agreed, I promoted it on area radio stations for a month and a half beforehand, and we got 10,000 people out there to watch.

The course became successful immediately. We were charging green fees of a dollar on weekdays, two dollars on the weekends. Before long I was making about $10,000 to $12,000 a year out of it, which was a lot of money then, and it got us through the Depression.

The following year I decided we needed another exhibition to open the season, so I signed up Sam Snead and Gene Sarazen to come up for $100 apiece and play against a couple of the local professionals. They drove up in their own car, paid their own hotel bills, everything, so they didn't have much left at the end of it.

Top: *The 9th at Trent Jones's Point O'Woods in Benton Harbor, Michigan, is a par-3 of 192 yards that requires a precise shot to avoid water on the left and bunkers that surround the green.*
Above: *The 13th on the West Course at Broadmoor is a downhill par-4 of only 353 yards, but these bunkers and a greenside pond must be avoided.*

I asked Sam if he wanted to do it again next year, and he said, "Okay, but not for what you paid us this time." I asked him what he wanted and he said, "The gate." So they came up the next year, and I gave them each $98. Snead said, "Hey, there were a lot of people out there." I replied, "I know, Sam, but we have no fences around the course and most of them were sneaking in without paying."

I told the story in 1987 when I was inducted into the World Golf Hall of Fame at Pinehurst, and a fellow came up to me and said, "I loved that Snead story. You're the only guy who ever put anything over on Sam."

When the war started, gasoline became so scarce that you couldn't drive anywhere, and golf was a low-priority item. So our play dropped at Green Lakes and I decided to give it back to the state. But it will always be one of my favorite places. Just recently the clubhouse there was named after me.

Early on I discovered that being involved with golf, especially as a golf course architect, could get you associated with the rich and famous. I became acquainted with Lowell Thomas, the commentator, and we grew to be great friends. He asked me to do a nine-hole course for him on his estate in Pawling, New York, which I completed in 1935. During the preliminary stages I took Gene Sarazen up there, and as we were looking over the site, a man on horseback approached. It turned out to be Tom Dewey, who was to become the governor of New York and almost president of the United States. In his gruff, deep voice he asked, "How are you going to lay out the course?" I explained my plan, and he said, "Well, I guess that looks all right." And he rode away. I was so happy he approved. "What a nice guy," I said. Sarazen, as was his wont, expressed a different opinion . . . after Dewey was out of earshot, of course.

About that time I got a call from Lester Norris, who wanted me to build a nine-hole course on an estate near St. Charles, Illinois. I didn't know who he was, but I took the Twentieth Century Limited to Chicago, and he met me at the LaSalle Station with a big Buick and drove me fifty miles to St. Charles. He told me he was chairman of the park board and wanted to build a course on this land adjacent to the Fox River. I thought he just had some kind of a secretarial job. It wasn't until I had agreed to do the job that I found out he was the president of Texaco and was married to the niece of John "Bet-A-Million" Gates, who happened to be the largest stockholder in Texaco and a multimillionaire in her own right.

I had married Ione in 1934. She became my rock, the foundation of my career. She ran the office in the early years, which gave me time to dream and to travel all over the world. She was a great personality, a lovely and gracious person, and everybody loved her. Herb Graffis, one of the world's great and beloved golf writers and aficionados, once called her "the best public relations man in America."

Robert Trent, Jr., was born in 1939, Rees in 1941. As it turns out, that was the beginning of perhaps a dynasty and certainly, I hope, a legacy.

The second Great War put the world on hold, and with it golf. Stanley Thompson and I had amicably dissolved our partnership three years before. Now I was on my own, with an office in New York and a home in Montclair, New Jersey. Only a few remodeling jobs were available during the early 1940s, and I spent a little time working as a turf consultant for the government, which was trying to figure out why airport runways were breaking down.

New courses were catch-as-catch-can. I did start working on a course for the United States Military Academy at West Point, using prisoners of war to do the labor and blasting the holes out of solid rock. But the war ended and we ran out of money, and the course had only twelve holes until it was finally finished in 1950.

Opposite top: *Another heroic hole by Trent Jones is the 13th at Dorado East in Puerto Rico, a double-dogleg par-5 that wanders 540 yards through and around water, offering options both off the tee and on the second or third shots to the green.*
Opposite bottom: *The par-4 8th at Firestone South is a 450-yarder that sweeps downhill to this bunker-guarded green.*

I took Gene Sarazen up there one day and asked him if he wanted to go down and watch the prisoners at work cutting up trees with a chain saw. He said, "Mussolini and the Italians surrendered yesterday, and there's no way I'm going to get close to a bunch of German POWs."

I also did a course for the IBM corporation at its headquarters in Poughkeepsie, New York, a project that started in 1942 and, at one point, provided a severe test of my diplomacy.

Thomas J. Watson, the head of IBM at the time, was walking the property with me, along with several of his minions, and he pointed to a large hill and suggested that we put a tee up there to take advantage of the beautiful view. I replied that it was a pretty steep climb to the top, and he said, "Well, they're out here for the exercise, aren't they?" I said, "Well, yes. Why don't we all climb up there." I think he was in better shape than I, but we both arrived at the top totally winded, and the rest of his troops in their shirts and ties straggled along minutes later.

Watson said, "Well, I guess we can forget about this hill. Go ahead and build the course the way you want."

When we finished in 1945 I was urged to take my fee—it was $13,000, as I recall—in stock. But I had a family to feed and refused. I've occasionally wondered what that stock would be worth now.

Better times were soon to come. Bob Jones wanted to build a golf course.

Often it is difficult to pinpoint the event, the circumstance, that launches a career, or at least accelerates it. For me the moment is relatively easy to determine. Peachtree did it.

Frankly, I was a very well-known golf course architect by 1945, which probably is why I was selected to design Peachtree. Ed Dudley, the professional at Augusta National at the time, recommended me to Jones, who liked what I had done. And the two Joneses got along famously, although he caused me to change my name.

On our first meeting, he suggested we play nine holes at East Lake, his club in Atlanta. Bob Jones the architect played with borrowed clubs and shot 36 for the nine holes. Bob Jones the player shot 29, as I recall, knocking down the flag with every shot. He had just returned from the army, was in his early forties and had not yet come down with the debilitating illness that eventually was to take his life.

At one point in the round, on a 210-yard par-3 hole, I struck my tee shot three feet from the hole. Jones turned to a group of members who had caught up with us and said, "This is Bobby Jones." Later, on our return to town, he said to me, "What are we going to call you?" I said, "There can be only one Bobby Jones in Atlanta, and that's you. From now on, I'll be Trent Jones." It's a family name that comes from the River Trent in England, and I've been Trent ever since, both north and south of the Mason-Dixon line.

Bob Jones and I became good friends, and I came to admire the man greatly. We know what a great player he was, but he was much more than that—a lawyer, of course, a marvelous writer and student of words, a sportsman and, most of all, a gracious gentleman. His temper as a youngster is legendary, but he controlled it quite nicely throughout his adult life. Only occasionally would it peek through.

One night we were having dinner at a restaurant and some oaf came up to Bob and said, "Bob, don't you think Ben Hogan is the greatest player there's ever been?" Jones' neck reddened perceptibly but, ever courteous, he replied, "You know, the only thing you can hope to be is the best in your time."

He was that, and he was one of the best of all time in many ways.

Jones gives credit to Dick Garlington for the idea of building another golf course in Atlanta. Garlington was on the USGA Green Section Committee,

Opposite: *Two of Robert Trent Jones's western projects in the 1960s were the Wigwam in Litchfield, Arizona, (above) whose Gold Course is still ranked among the top 100 in the country by Golf Digest and Pauma Valley (below), north of San Diego, one of Jones's unheralded masterpieces.*

was a long-time chairman of the Green Committee at the Atlanta Athletic Club and was, at the time, the club's president. He certainly contributed to the success of the course and the club, but Bob Jones, despite his modesty, was the driving force.

The planning began in May of 1945. We chose a tract of 240 acres at the intersection of Peachtree and Dunwoody Roads in DeKalb County north of Atlanta. It was part of the Ashford estate and site of the historic Cobb Caldwell mansion, which was meant to be only a temporary clubhouse but is so charming that it remains today as the club's home.

Shortly after that I learned the meaning of clout. I was at a luncheon with Bob Jones and about a dozen of his friends and influential Atlantans. He said, "Fellows, it's taking me five or six hours to play a round at East Lake, and if I have to do that I'm going to give up golf. Some of us think there should be a new course in town. We have picked out the land, Trent here has made a layout, and we want to buy it. I would like your support, so I'll need a check for $100,000 apiece from you by next Monday morning."

And he got the money. That taught me that when I got into big ventures, I wanted a partner with muscle.

The site was gently rolling and gorgeous. The course, which we designed to play up and down the valleys rather than over the hills, expresses the philosophy of both Joneses and reflects the qualities of Augusta National that Bob wanted to echo. It is a broad, expansive layout with no parallel or adjoining fairways and long tees that allow it to be played from under 6,000 yards to more than 7,000—7,400 yards, in fact, if anybody wanted to stretch it to the extreme. The greens were extraordinarily large for the time, averaging some 8,000 square feet. The 10th green, at more than 10,000 square feet, was one of the largest in the country then. All were boldly contoured. This was in keeping with the emphasis both of us placed on the value of a number of excellent hole locations, with a great range of difficulty, on each green.

The flexibility in tee placements and hole locations, plus the variety of bunkering and other hazards, allows the course to be played an infinite number of ways. I believed at the time, and still believe, that the course would set a standard for modern golf course architecture. Certainly its features have been incorporated into countless courses, mine and others.

Peachtree and my association with Bob Jones led to my doing a great deal of work on Augusta National, starting with the remodeling of the 18th green in 1946, subsequent work on other greens and the reconstruction of the 16th hole in 1947 and the 11th hole in 1950. I will discuss this further in later chapters.

During that period I designed the Dunes at Myrtle Beach on a lovely piece of land studded with live oaks where the Singleton Swash empties into the Atlantic Ocean. If it was not a true seaside course, it was as close as I had come to one at that point. I was able to work the water in on several holes, including the 13th that became one of the world's famous par-5s and perhaps the best example of my philosophy of heroic architecture. Certainly it was, and still is, one of my landmark courses.

In 1949 I was hired to remodel Oakland Hills for the 1951 U.S. Open. The details of that task are given elsewhere in this book. It's enough to say here that the job made me famous or notorious, depending on whose opinion you want to entertain.

For sure, the Oakland Hills remodeling and the publicity it generated gave further impetus to my career. Herb Wind wrote a complimentary—and widely read—article in *The New Yorker* that appeared shortly after the '51 Open. As it turned out, the timing was perfect. Money was becoming more available after a brief recession before 1950. Clubs around the country were in the mood to remodel their courses, and new construction was beginning to boom. Archi-

*Scenes from Spyglass (top to bottom):
the 14th, a 555-yard par-5 with water in
front of a shallow green; the 7th, an elegant 515-yard par-5 with a pond to the
left of a tiny green; the 4th, a 365-yard
dogleg par-4 to a long green surrounded
by mounds; the 2nd, an uphill par-4 of
350 yards to a monstrous green.*

Hazeltine in Chaska, Minnesota, one of Trent Jones's most controversial courses, is also one of his best. The course was the site of the 1970 U.S. Open, which is scheduled there in 1991. This is the 16th hole.

tects suddenly were in demand, and I had become perhaps the best-known in the world.

Even President Dwight D. Eisenhower was after me. As our first real golfing president, he perhaps contributed more to the golf boom in the 1940s and 1950s than any other man, with the possible exception of Arnold Palmer, and he wanted me to build a hole at Camp David that he could play during his respites there. Actually, we built one green with three tees so he could play it different distances, ranging, as I recall from about 90 to 130 yards.

My work at Oakland Hills spawned requests to remodel or touch up other sites for major championships—Baltusrol in New Jersey for the 1954 U.S. Open, The Olympic Club in San Francisco for the 1955 Open, Oak Hill in my home town of Rochester for the 1956 Open and again for the 1968 Championship, Southern Hills in Tulsa, Oklahoma, for the 1958 Open and Congressional in Bethesda, Maryland, for the 1964 Open. I became known as the "Open Doctor."

It was at Baltusrol, of course, that I struck one of history's famous golf shots, perhaps the best-known shot ever hit outside of tournament competition.

Certainly it was the ultimate squelch. Shortly after the remodeling of the Lower Course was finished, I was challenged by a critic who contended I had made the fourth hole too difficult. Suggesting that the hole, which I had lengthened to play at 194 yards over water, be tested to determine what needed to be done, I led my critic, along with tournament chairman C. P. Burgess and professional Johnny Farrell, to the tee. Each of the three put his tee shot on the green. Then I struck a mashie shot that landed six feet in front of the hole and went into the cup on the first hop.

"Gentlemen," I said, "I think the hole is eminently fair."

I had almost done the same thing a few years before at Rockrimmon Country Club near Stamford, Connecticut. I had built the ninth hole as a par-3 that played from an elevated tee across a lake to a green on a plateau. I figured the hole at 170 yards, which would require only a good 4-iron to reach it, but the club's committee members thought it looked much longer and would demand some kind of wood shot. They didn't want a hole like that. I sent Frank Duane, my assistant on the project, back to the car to get my 4-iron and a couple of balls. I needed just one, striking a shot that landed three feet short of the pin and stayed there. That ended the argument.

Skill is necessary in building a golf course that satisfies the client, but sometimes you need a little luck too.

During the 1950s I built a bunch of big, strong courses that still rank among my best works—the Dunes; Bellerive and Old Warson in St. Louis; Point O'Woods in Benton Harbor, Michigan; Shady Oaks in Fort Worth and the Houston Country Club in Texas; along with the first step in remodeling the Broadmoor in Colorado Springs. Bellerive was the site of the 1965 U.S. Open. The 1971 Ryder Cup Match was played at Old Warson. Point O'Woods is the perennial site of the Western Amateur. The Broadmoor has been host to many big tournaments, including two U.S. Amateur Championships.

In 1956 I completed Coral Ridge in Fort Lauderdale, Florida, a club that I and my sons still own and a course with which I still tinker. It is a fine flat course that has been the site of our annual Ione Jones/Doherty Cup tournament, one of the nation's highlight events for women amateurs. And it does have a considerable degree of difficulty. Sam Snead and Ben Hogan both have played it a lot, and Snead still holds the course record of 69. When Jack Nicklaus turned professional and won the U.S. Open, he moved to Fort Lauderdale and we made him an honorary member. To my knowledge, he never broke par at Coral Ridge.

At the end of the decade Firestone became another benchmark in my career. The South Course had been built in 1929 by Bert Way, and I was asked to remodel it for the 1960 PGA Championship. For economic reasons I followed his fairway routings in doing the redesign, which resulted in a lot of parallel fairways. But when I finished, that was about all that was left of Way's original course. I added fifty bunkers and two ponds, built two new greens and enlarged the remaining sixteen to two and three times their original size, building in the contours that provide adequate pin positions for tournament play.

The course came out at 7,180 yards officially, playing to a par of 70. It was, and perhaps still is, the longest par-70 course in America on which tournaments are regularly played. And the critics immediately swung into action. It was a "typical Jones course," they said, "long, hard and boring." Well, it is certainly long and difficult, but it is hardly boring. Despite the parallel fairways—and there I had no choice—there is a diversity of water, sand, fairway and green designs that provide a different challenge on almost every hole.

Firestone South has stood the test over the years. It has been the site of three PGA Championships, and the winning scores have been one over par, even par and four under par. The old American Golf Classic was played there thirteen times, the winning scores ranging from twelve under par to one over. (The 1976, and last, AGC was played over Firestone North, which I built in 1969.) And the South Course has been the site of the World Series of Golf since its inception in 1962. Since the switch to seventy-two holes in 1976, the

Trent Jones has spent a career dividing his time between airplanes and golf carts.

Opposite: *Scenes from Mauna Kea (clockwise from top left): the 17th, a strong par-5 fronted by a bunker; the 6th, a short but demanding par-4; the 13th, a par-4 to an elevated green; the downhill 11th, a long and exacting par-3; the 18th, another marvelous downhill par-4 of 428 yards to a difficult putting surface; the 9th, a gorgeous par-4 that can play anywhere from 340 to 427 yards, sweeping downhill to a well-protected green.*

winning scores have ranged from thirteen under to two under.

Is this, then, a course that is too long and hard? I prefer to think of it as a course on which par is the standard, although that standard usually is beaten by today's great players. But when they do, they have played extremely well. Nor have the longer hitters dominated the course, with the exception of Jack Nicklaus, who has made a fortune at Firestone over the years. In 1988, in fact, the World Series was won by Mike Reid, one of the Tour's shorter hitters, at five under par.

Actually, as the years have passed, the criticism has turned into praise, and I really believe Firestone has earned the respect and admiration of most Tour pros. And from the member tees, by the way, it is an exceedingly pleasant, although still challenging, course to play.

I gave the anti-Jones forces more ammunition with Bellerive, which went on public display for the 1965 U.S. Open. At 7,190 yards with a par of 70, it remains, at this writing, the longest course over which an Open has been played. The experts were predicting that only Arnold Palmer and Jack Nicklaus could play it, but they were never factors in a championship won by Gary Player in a playoff over Kel Nagle. Both were considered shorter hitters then. Each shot 282, two over par, for the 72-hole route, and Player won the next day with 71. Again, par was the standard that the United States Golf Association and I, along with a lot of other purists, feel it should be.

In the 1950s I also began to branch out beyond the continental borders, creating the Cotton Bay Club in the Bahamas, the Brasilia Golf Club for the new capitol of Brazil and the original Dorado Beach course in Puerto Rico for Laurance Rockefeller. The Canada Cup, later to become the World Cup, was played there in 1961. It was the beginning of an "overseas" career that would take me around the world building courses.

It has been said that I ushered in a new era in golf architecture during this period. I'll leave that for others to decide. Certainly many of the design factors that went into my layouts had appeared in courses over the centuries. But I do feel that the introduction of the heroic concept, skillfully mixed with the strategic and, occasionally, the penal, set new standards for the modern golf course.

I followed the same strategy in my many remodeling jobs. I did not want stretches of rough from the tee to the fairway or hazards in spots that would penalize and paralyze the higher handicappers. I spent a lot of time taking out cross-bunkering and other penal attributes of the older courses and putting in options that would help those players. In effect, I was cleaning up architecture.

I was not alone. Dick Wilson, in particular, was building long, tough courses that adhered to the heroic concept. I'm sure we copied some features from each other, and I suppose in a way we were rivals. But there was plenty of work for everybody.

These were rich years, about to become better. I was ably assisted during the decade by Frank Duane in design work and by Bill Baldwin and John Schmeisser, who headed our construction teams, and I was soon to get more help from my sons. Bobby joined the firm in 1962 and established a west coast office in Palo Alto, California. Rees came aboard in 1965, soon taking over supervision of the east coast office in Montclair. That helped not only in the design of courses but also in the business end of the operation. I was spending more and more time in the air, and poor Ione was struggling with the details at home. When Bobby and Rees arrived, it took a lot of pressure off her.

Roger Rulewich, a Yale graduate like Bobby and Rees, joined us in 1961. I kept waiting to hear "The Whiffenpoof Song" echoing through the office halls. Several years later we opened an office in Spain under the direction of Cabell Robinson, a college friend of Rees.

And business boomed. During the 1960s the Jones firm produced courses

like the Wigwam in Arizona; Pauma Valley and Silverado in California; the Eisenhower Golf Course for the Air Force Academy in Colorado Springs; Black Hall and Fairview in Connecticut; Royal Kaanapali, a future World Cup site, on Maui, Hawaii; Boyne Highlands in Michigan; Incline Village in Tahoe, Nevada; Palmetto Dunes on Hilton Head in South Carolina; Sugarbush and Woodstock in Vermont; Golden Horseshoe and Lower Cascades in Virginia; and Half Moon-Rose Hall at Montego Bay in Jamaica. Rees and I also designed Ferncrost Village Golf Club in Danvers, Massachussetts, and The Rail Golf Club in Springfield, Illinois. Both courses now are annual venues for LPGA tournaments.

By 1970 Rees and I had finished Inverrary in Lauderhill, Florida, site of the Inverrary Classic for several years and the 1976 Tournament Players Championship. At the same time we built Turnberry Isle in North Miami.

Rees and Rulewich were instrumental in building Panther Valley Country Club in Allamuchy, New Jersey. It was a difficult job that had to be cut out of rock and gravel. We also had to cope with a swamp. Finished in 1969, the club is part of an upscale real estate development.

Rees and I also designed Montauk Downs in Montauk, New York, now listed among the top public courses in America by *Golf Digest*. In 1967 we finished twenty-seven holes for the Atlanta Athletic Club, eighteen of which were to be combined for the 1976 U.S. Open and the 1981 PGA Championship. We also added nine holes at Tanglewood Golf Club, a public course outside Clemmons, North Carolina, that we had built in 1954. In 1972 we were to add another nine, and two nines of the complex were combined for the 1974 PGA Championship.

We also built two more nines for Rockefeller at Dorado Beach. The other significant courses of the decade were Hazeltine National in Chaska, Minne-

sota, Spyglass Hill Golf Links on the Monterey Peninsula, Sotogrande in Spain and Mauna Kea on the land of Hawaii.

Spyglass was completed in 1966 and was put into the Bing Crosby Pro-Am rotation the next year, joining Pebble Beach and Cypress Point. Spyglass contains an unusual mixture of seaside, links-type holes and parkland atmosphere. The first five holes, starting from deep in the woods and heading immediately to the sea, demand target golf through sandy wastes, deliberately reminiscent of Pine Valley but with the water in the background and buffeted by the ocean winds. The rest of the course winds through towering Monterey pines and cypress in the Del Monte Forest. Hundreds of trees had to be felled during the construction process, and some sophisticated engineering procedures were utilized in dealing with a deep ravine that cut across the property. But the course turned out to be one of our finest and has been consistently on everybody's list of best courses.

And the screams came again. The pros didn't like the length (which is only a little more than 6,800 yards) or the greens. In fairness to them, and to the Joneses, the course was not ready to be put into tournament play. One full season is not enough to grow grass, especially on the greens. There was frost that first year and the greens were hard, not to mention that some pins were placed where they never belonged, given the conditions. We had tilted the aprons on several greens to give the players a better look for the approach, and the holes in some cases were cut so close to the aprons that a putt might not stop rolling until it was off the green. That, of course, has been corrected. Also, because the subsurface of the soil is clay, the course becomes very wet during periods of heavy rainfall. The budget did not provide for enough money to guarantee extensive drainage, and unfortunately the Crosby, now the AT&T, is played during a rainy period, so it always plays very long during the tournament.

We did some remodeling on some of the greens. The course has matured and the complaints have mostly gone away. I know of no course in the world that isn't better five years after it is opened. Like fine wine, a golf course gets better with age.

Hazeltine was finished in 1963, and when the pros finally got around to playing it in the 1970 U.S. Open, there was the usual reaction. Jack Nicklaus started it with an article in *Sports Illustrated* stating that most, if not all, of the holes were blind. The criticism was particularly unfair, because to my knowledge Nicklaus had not seen the course when he dictated the story. When I arrived at the site before the Open, I conducted a press conference and went over every hole, pointing out that the fact the green cannot be seen from the tee does not make it a blind hole. "Maybe Jack Nicklaus is blind," I remarked.

Dave Hill, who was to finish second in the Open, said, "They ruined a good cow pasture," or words to that effect, a comment that understandably did not sit well with either the USGA or the good folks at Hazeltine.

Tony Jacklin, who won the Open, loved the course.

There *were* some problems with Hazeltine. Totten P. Heffelfinger, a former USGA president and a driving force behind the founding of Hazeltine, had insisted that a children's course be built alongside the championship layout. This required land we would have preferred to use for the regular course, adversely affecting four holes on the front nine.

Since 1970 we have changed those holes and done further remodeling, and even Dave Hill now says he likes the course. At this writing, my son Rees is doing more work on the course for the next U.S. Open there, scheduled for 1991. As I say, it usually takes time and refinement to make a great golf course.

In 1963 I built Sotogrande at Cadiz on the Costa del Sol for Joseph McMicking, an entrepreneur who walked into my New York office one day. He said he wanted to build a golf course in Spain and had heard I was the man to

do it. Joe and I became great friends, and the project turned out to be quite an experience. On my first trip to Cadiz I asked Joe about a series of stone towers along the shoreline. He said they were used to watch for the coming of the Phoenicians. When they were spotted, fires would be lighted along the coast to warn the populace. That was more than 2,000 years ago, he pointed out, and I thought, "We've been in existence 200 years and we think *we're* old!"

Sotogrande was significant in that here I brought American golf, and American grasses, to Europe for the first time. I built long tees and big greens with subtle contours that allowed a variety of hole locations. Although the sea provides only a visual backdrop, water was brought into play on seven holes, five of them on the incoming nine. There is a selection of short and long holes, along with a variety of shotmaking requirements. The course from the championship tees measures a stern 6,910 yard.

The fairways are of Bermuda grass (it took only two sacks of sprigs from Tifton, Georgia, to provide a nursery from which all the fairways were planted). We originally tried Bermuda on the greens but found that Penncross bent worked better. Good local sand was not to be found for the bunkers, so we used crushed marble from Andalusian quarries. It works admirably, not only as a substance to play from but also for the white, gleaming accent points to the holes it provides. And we installed a fully automatic irrigation system, mandatory in the hot climate of southern Spain.

With the rugged Sierra Blanca mountains looming over the lush green turf, the course is one of the most beautiful anywhere, and it quickly gained a reputation as one of Europe's best tests.

We built a short course at Sotogrande at the same time and in 1975 we finished a second full eighteen, the New Course to go with the Old.

In 1985 the new Course at Sotogrande was purchased by Jaime-Ortiz Patino and a group of investors, who formed the Valderrama Golf Club, an exclusive private club designed to attract members, friends and business associates from around the world.

I was called in to remodel the course. The changes I made did not alter the intrinsic character but did enhance the shotmaking values, transforming Valderrama into a challenging championship course. In my opinion, it is better than the Old Course at Sotogrande.

The course, with bentgrass tees, fairways and greens and 328 Bermuda in the rough, measures just more than 7,000 yards and is spectacular for both its beauty and difficulty. The 4th hole, I believe, is one of the best par-5s in the world.

In 1988 the first Volvo Masters, the culmination of the European Tour, was played at Valderrama, and four of the best players in the world finished at the top, Nick Faldo of England won with a total of 284, four under par. Seve Ballesteros of Spain was second at two under, Sandy Lyle of England was even par and Ian Woosnam of Wales was fourth at one over. As at all great courses, the cream rises to the top.

There was criticism, as there always is, of the rough and the overall difficulty of the course. But Ballesteros called it the best course in Europe and one of the best in the world.

At this writing, the plans are to make the course the permanent home of the tournament, which I think is a fitting tribute to the course and to Patino, who engineered the original event and who has helped make the course what it is.

William F. Quinn, Hawaii's first state governor, asked Laurance Rockefeller in 1960 if he could build a major resort that would attract tourists to the islands. Rockefeller, the chairman of Rockresorts, Inc., was willing, but not without feasibility studies and a personal inspection of possible sites.

Since I had done the original course at Dorado Beach (and was to do more for him there and at neighboring Cerromar), he invited me to Hawaii. As we were flying over the Big Island he suddenly said, "That's the kind of beach I'm looking for." He was looking at Kaunaoa Bay, a half-mile crescent-shaped cove protected by rock outcroppings, ringed by sand and scrub. It was part of the Parker Ranch, a 246,000-acre tract along the Kawaihae Coast on the northwest shoulder of the island. The land folded into the foothills of the Kohola Mountains, with Mauna Kea Mountain standing in snowcapped splendor some twenty-eight miles to the southeast. Mauna Loa, still an active volcano, towered over the island forty miles to the south.

On the ground it did not look as good. Located on the leeward side of the island with scant annual rainfall, the land was hostile, almost like a moonscape. It was the most challenging terrain I had ever faced. But the potential certainly was there. As I will detail in later chapters, we were able to build one of the world's most beautiful and spectacular courses, arising lush and green out of this rugged terrain, landscaped with flowering shrubs and trees, palms lining the broad fairways and white sand glistening in its 106 bunkers.

Rockefeller built a hotel and environs to go with the course. Today the Mauna Kea Beach Hotel is still one of the best half-dozen resorts in the world and is the standard for all the other magnificent venues that have sprung up to accommodate Hawaii's now-burgeoning tourist trade.

I built the course to fit the land. If you have the land, you can add the beauty.

From the championship tees Mauna Kea is a big course, stretching to 7,144 yards. From there it can be an extremely difficult course, especially if the wind blows, which it usually does. It can be played at 6,593 yards from the regular tees, and the women can play it at 5,644.

Dar Es Salaam in Morocco, which Trent Jones built for King Hassan II, lies peacefully here, but the project once put Jones's life in danger.

Strangely enough, neither Mauna Kea nor Sotogrande has ever been characterized as "long, hard and boring," nor as a "typical Trent Jones course." Perhaps that is because neither is a stop on the American Tour and therefore is not subject to the scrutiny of the professionals who look at a course with an eye toward how many birdies they can make in the easiest fashion.

Almost as big a challenge as Mauna Kea was the job we did at Eugene Country Club in Oregon. It began as a remodeling and finished as one of the most startling reversals, literally, that I have ever heard of. It was a nice course that wound through beautiful trees 100 feet or more high. But somehow it seemed all wrong. We tramped the property and studied it. I wanted to reroute some holes, but that would have meant removing some of those magnificent trees. Bobby, who had played in the national collegiate championship there ten years earlier, kept saying, "Dad, you can't do that."

Finally I figured out what was wrong. Wherever the water came into play it was in front of the tee instead of the green. So we discussed reversing a few of the holes. Then I suggested we reverse the entire course. I took the idea to the board of directors, and it was so shocking that they bought it. Not without a fight, of course. The membership had to vote on it, and it was a year before we got approval, by one vote. A lot of folks don't want to give up their favorite holes, you understand.

So we reversed the course, building championship greens in place of the tiny ones there and adding a few other embellishments. When it was finished, most of the members who had been against it came to us and told us how glad they were we had done it.

Eugene today is one of the great unknown courses in the country. It requested the U.S. Open and would have been an excellent venue, but its parking facilities are too limited. It was the site of the 1978 national collegiate championship, won by Scott Simpson, and was in the fifth ten of the latest *Golf Digest* ranking of the 100 greatest courses.

Sometimes the unusual must be done to build a golf course. That was the case with Birnam Wood, an elegant private club for seniors—fifty years and older—in Santa Barbara, California, that I designed for Robert McLean, publisher of the Philadelphia *Bulletin*. Actually, I bought into the project, because I believed in the idea. To get around the zoning laws, which called for lots that were a minimum of one acre, which would not have left enough land for a golf course, I suggested that we ask each of the landowners to lend us half his lot, in perpetuity, for the golf course. They agreed, and with a little arguing in front of the zoning commission, we got the job done.

We have used that ploy on other occasions to get around some zoning regulations. In the end, everybody was happy with it. The property owners had a golf course that they wouldn't otherwise have had, and they didn't have to maintain half their lawns.

Two of our most exciting projects in the late sixties and early seventies never got done. The first was the proposed $15 million Beverly Hills Country Club, located in a canyon five minutes from the heart of Beverly Hills, right next to Mary Pickford's house. Dean Martin was associated with the project, which was to be financed with the sale of 600 equity memberships. Actually, the course was located in a virtual crater, a steep-walled canyon that posed severe design problems. We cut off the tops of ridges to raise the valley floor 400 feet so we could put the course there. We moved 10 million cubic yards of dirt and must have spent $4 or $5 million on earthmoving alone. Bobby and I had spent two years working on the design, and it was going to be a magnificent course. But there were money problems and some other trouble that cropped up. Martin got out of the project, and we never could finish it.

Our proposed golf course in Moscow, the first in Russia, ended on an equally disappointing note. Dr. Armand Hammer, the head of Occidental Petroleum, was trying to build a hotel, conference center and office complex in Moscow and apparently had convinced Leonid Brezhnev that he needed a golf course for all the foreign visitors as well as the ambassadors from the various countries. In 1974 Dr. Hammer invited Bobby and me to do the course, and after inspecting several sites we finally settled on a tract of land just outside the city. A Russian project engineer had been appointed and we were ready to go, but for some reason we never got final approval from the government. Whether it was the Afghanistan crisis that was looming or that golf was considered a capitalistic endeavor, I'll never know.

I had suggested to the mayor of Moscow that such a course would be an ideal site for the World Cup. He wanted instead to introduce golf into the Olympics, scheduled for Moscow in 1980. I think you need thirty-two countries participating to get approval for a demonstration sport. We could have done that, but I have an idea the Russians decided they didn't want to bring in all those countries and finish last in the competition.

At any rate, the course didn't happen at the time. But now, some fourteen years later, Bobby is building one. *Glasnost* will make birdies fly in the Soviet Union . . . or at least a few pars.

As I indicated earlier, one of the bonuses that accrues to a golf architect is the chance to get an inside look at the fascinating world of big business and the men who control it. In the early sixties I was approached by Henry Mercer, the shipping magnate who lived in Rumson, New Jersey. He was trying to get more business from the Japanese and felt that wooing them with golf was the best way. But they were not allowed to play at the club he belonged to, so Henry decided to build his own course on his cattle farm near Colts Neck.

I finished Hominy Hill Golf Club for him in 1965, and not long after that I was there on a Sunday afternoon. Mercer had some Japanese gentlemen as his guests, playing the golf course. He drew me aside and said, "I've been trying to get their business for ten years, and I got it today. Their business will pay for this golf course five times over."

The course was and is an excellent layout. It has since been sold to the county, and in 1983 the U.S. Public Links was played there.

Rockefeller, for whom I designed or worked on ten courses, was my major client and my entre into the realm of high finance. I also become friends with Yoshiaki Tsutsumi, one of Japan's high-powered business leaders for whom Bobby and I built the Karuizawa complex.

My work at Sotogrande led to design opportunities for the Aga Kahn, for whom I built the Pevero Golf Club at Costa Smeralda on Sardinia in 1970, and for King Hassan II of Morocco. From 1970 to 1974 we did forty-five holes at Royal Golf Dar Es Salaam in Rabat. It was a pleasant association, although at one point it almost cost me my life.

The king, to put it kindly, is a golf nut. He decided he wanted to build a first-class golf course, and Fred Corcoran, the late golf entrepreneur who founded the PGA Tour and was a friend of the king's, put us in touch with him. When Bobby and I first met him, we found him inside the palace walls playing golf on a little course he had constructed there, pausing every once in a while to sign some papers.

We made the deal to do the course, which turned out to be two 18-hole layouts and an additional nine before we were finished. That was fine, but the extracurricular activities were not always so comfortable.

At one point the king invited me to a birthday party, his fortieth, I believe, to be held at his palace on the ocean between Rabat and Casablanca. The festivities were to include a round of golf, although not on a course I had designed.

Just before attending, I was in Paris, where I ran into John Laupheimer,

Robert Trent Jones and Eamon Allen, the course superintendent at Ballybunion Golf Club, survey the progress on Ballybunion's New Course.

then a Philadelphia businessman who was later to become a USGA executive and then commissioner of the Ladies Professional Golf Association. I told John where I was going and he asked to come along.

When we drove into the palace grounds in my rental car, there were soldiers who wouldn't let me park where I normally did. I explained to them that I was a friend of the king and his chief of staff, and they finally let me by. But when I got to the area, I saw only one car parked there and figured something was wrong. So I drove back to the lot where everybody else was parked and put the car there.

John and I wandered over to the first tee, where the prizes for the golf event were about to be awarded. About that time, a group of cadets in battle fatigues showed up and started firing at the palace. I asked somebody what was going on, and he said, "It must be part of the entertainment." I said, "This is not entertainment, because chunks of the palace are coming off."

This, of course, was an attempted coup. We beat a retreat into an old railroad car parked by the first tee and used as a shelter, and just as we did a bomb exploded on the putting green. The cadets came after our group, which included the king's military staff. It was probably fortunate for them that they were all in golf clothes.

We were forced out of the railroad car and made to walk to a nearby corner of the golf course, where they lined us up. Anytime someone would try to sit down, they would nudge him with a bayonet. I had on a Dorado Beach cap, and one of the soldiers grabbed it, threw it on the ground and stomped on it. I don't know if he didn't like me or Dorado Beach.

Eventually a soldier came up to me and said, "*Diplomatique?*" I thought, "This is it. I'm a diplomat." So I pulled out my passport and showed it to him. Laupheimer did the same. We were pulled away from the others and told we didn't have to stand up anymore, that we could go sit down. "But don't sit too close to the bushes," we were warned, "because somebody might come through and shoot you."

At that point Laupheimer said, "I wonder if I have double indemnity."

After about an hour and a half, with dusk falling, a man came out of the palace and said, "The king is alive. Long live the king. You may go."

As we were walking back to our car, we passed the place where I had first intended to park. The lone car there had been blown to bits. I was thankful I didn't have to explain that one to the rental car company.

The Joneses turned out a lot of good courses in the early seventies—the Karuizawa courses, the courses for King Hassan, the two Cerromar courses for Rockefeller at Dorado Beach, the two new nines at the Dorado Beach Golf and Tennis Club, Pevero Golf Club on Sardinia for the Aga Kahn, Port Royal in Bermuda, the first of three courses at Horseshoe Bay in Texas, which Bobby handled, the Chanticleer Course for Greenville Country Club in South Carolina. Rees was primarily responsible for Arcadian Shores, a fine course in Myrtle Beach, South Carolina.

Rees and I designed the Craig Burn Club in Elma, New York, for our good friend Bobby Goodyear, a student of golf course architecture. This is an example of how a knowledgeable client can contribute to the making of a great course. Craig Burn, opened in 1971, was a forerunner of the return to natural golf courses that we have seen in the 1980s. It is one of our most innovative designs and is perhaps our best unknown gem.

Rees and I also did The Springs Golf Club in Spring Green, Wisconsin, another on the *Golf Digest* list of best public courses. Which goes back to the point I made much earlier in this book, that we build golf courses for people, not just for the U.S. Opens.

The architects Jones at Spyglass in 1967—from left: Bob Jr., Trent and Rees.

The 13th hole at Ballybunion New, a 387-yard par-4, has what Robert Trent Jones calls one of the most spectacular natural greensites in the world. With a larger dune walling off the left side of the green, a bunker in front and a steep drop-off to the right, a precise second shot is required to get safely onto the putting surface.

Bobby did twenty-seven magnificent holes for us at Princeville on Kauai, and Pacific Harbour in Fiji. Those were, respectively, the sites of the 1978 World Cup and World Amateur Championships. It was the first time the two events have been played in the same year on courses designed by the same architect.

The rest of the decade was not the best, for golf course architects in general and Robert Trent Jones in particular. The real estate market collapsed in 1974 and a lot of developers, not well-financed to begin with, ran out of money. Lots of people, including course architects, were not getting paid. And both Bobby and Rees left my firm about that time and started their own design businesses.

Disputes over how to run the business was one reason for the split. Rees always contended I was too much of an optimist, but I'd been through hard times before, a lot harder than this. They both had growing young families, and I think they both felt they simply had to get out on their own. Bobby had been working in the burgeoning Pacific Basin, while I spent a great deal of time in Europe. In retrospect, it was good that they left. Otherwise they would have had to wait until I died to establish their reputations. That would have been too bad, because the reputations of both are growing bigger and bigger in the world of golf.

Life and work do go on. Business was slower for awhile, but we did turn out some fine courses in the later years of the decade—Troia in Portugal and Nueva Andalucia in Spain with the help of Cabell Robinson are a couple of examples. In 1978 we also remodeled Glyfada in Athens, Greece, for the 1979 World Cup.

As we moved into the eighties, we built the two Kananaskis courses in Alberta, Canada, Castelgondolfo in Italy, Rivershore in Kamloops, British Columbia, two more wonderful courses at Horseshoe Bay and one at Metedeconk National in New Jersey.

In the making are two great sister courses, Vidauban near St. Tropez in France and The Robert Trent Jones International in Prince William County, Virginia, outside Washington, D.C. Both are on large, scenic tracts of land that will house both corporate-oriented courses and complexes as well as private clubs. When finished, they will rank high among my finest works, from the standpoint of marvelous golf courses as well as unparalleled facilities for the combination of golf and business.

Then there is Ballybunion. When I was hired to build a new course to complement one of the world's finest layouts on the west coast of Ireland, I was given both a once-in-a-lifetime opportunity and a terrifying challenge. Perched high on the dunes near the Mouth of the Shannon, where the Cashen River empties into the Atlantic Ocean, the property I had to work with is perhaps the finest piece of linksland in the world, certainly the finest I have ever seen.

Natural sites for greens, bunkers and passage through the dunes were everywhere, and our job was to seek them out. I think we took good advantage of them. The course winds through craggy, grass-covered dunes, skirting the seashore and turning back into the higher land, offering a spectacular combination of long and short holes that demand power, precision and imagination.

Finished in 1984, Ballybunion New has been castigated, of course, as too long and difficult, too hard to walk, and so forth and so forth.

Well, it *is* difficult, but it measures just under 6,500 yards from the championship tees, hardly a backbreaker by modern standards. And it *is* hard to walk, but so is Ballybunion Old, as well as most other links courses in Ireland. I am biased, of course, but I would ignore the critics and instead embrace the words of those whom I consider to be knowledgeable observers who have called it the finest links course in the world. Only the test of time will determine if it is that.

It would be difficult for me to pick a favorite course. But as one who has modeled his design philosophy on linksland courses, I might lean heavily, after fifty-two years in this business, toward the best true links course I've had the opportunity to design.

My firm has designed and remodeled some four hundred and fifty golf courses in forty-three of the United States and thirty-four countries. National and international championships have been played on thirty-six of those courses. We have enough courses on the drawing board or in stages of construction that I should achieve my personal goal of five hundred or more. But if I am to be remembered, I hope it is not just for the golf courses I have built but for other contributions as well to the game I love, to the game that has been my life.

I introduced roping to American tournament golf, at the 1954 U.S. Open at Baltusrol. It had been done before at St. Andrews for the British Open and on the 13th hole at Augusta National, but never in other tournaments or national championship play. There were only three or four groups at the time for which the spectators needed to be kept from crowding close to the players, but I felt it needed to be done, not only for the protection of the players but also, from an architect's point of view, to keep the rough that was in play from being trampled down. There wasn't much sense in letting the rough grow to penalize the errant shot, then having the gallery trample it down to the point where the ball would sit nicely on top of it. The USGA agreed, after heated discussion, and the idea caught on. Now no tournament could be conducted without it.

To my knowledge, I was the first to really measure how far the tournament professionals drove the ball. With the permission of the USGA, I set up a system to do this at the U.S. Open at Oak Hill in 1956. My motives again were selfish, of course. I wanted to see how far they really hit the ball so I could design my courses accordingly. As I recall, Roberto de Vicenzo was the longest driver on the hole I was measuring with a belt of 280 yards.

I am proud of the work I have done in fostering the education and training of golf course superintendents. The golf course superintendent now must be a professional, knowledgeable not only in the science of his profession but also about business and personnel management. And he must be regarded as such by the people who govern the clubs and courses around the world. Without a qualified caretaker, the best course in the world will fall into disrepair and cease to become a proper arena for golfers.

Now we are ensuring that this will be an ongoing thing. The Robert Trent Jones Foundation is being established to introduce courses of study at Cornell University in the fields of architecture, maintenance and club management. The courses, which will be incorporated into the existing school structures, will involve the technical, business, management and public relations aspects of these professions. Scholarships also will be made available through the foundation. In addition, a museum, library and archives will be established.

I was one of the charter members of the American Society of Golf Course Architects, founded in 1947 in New York City. Donald Ross was there, along with eleven others. He was named Honorary President. Robert Bruce Harris was named president, my pal Stanley Thompson was the vice president and I was chosen to be the secretary-treasurer. Today I am the only living founder of the organization, whose stated purpose was and is "to protect and upgrade the profession and to advance concepts and techniques of design consistent with the spirit of the game by collective thought."

It is still a rather select group, with stringent qualifications for membership. At this writing there are just eighty-one regular members and thirteen associate members, but the influence of the association in advancing the design, construction and maintenance of golf courses, with all the attendant ramifi-

Following pages: Golden Valley in Japan, in its spectacular mountain setting, is a Robert Trent Jones Jr., creation.

cations, has become significant around the world.

I was elected president of the ASGCA in 1951, and in 1976 I was the recipient of its first Donald Ross Award, now given annually to a member of the golf industry who has made a significant contribution to golf in general and golf course architecture specifically.

I have received many other honors, including the Old Tom Morris Award given by the Golf Course Superintendents Association of America. I have been elected to the World Golf Hall of Fame.

I appreciate all those kindnesses. But I am most grateful for simply having had the chance to contribute. If I have helped golfers—from the duffer to the professional—enjoy this game just a little more, it has all been worthwhile.

I think I have done that. And I am most proud of the legacy that I am leaving. I have trained many men who have gone out on their own to do what I have tried to do—build better golf courses for more people. These include my two sons, and of them I am proudest of all.

Although neither Bobby nor Rees decided to become golf course architects until they were adults, I suppose it was inevitable that they did. They literally grew up in the business. I used to take them on my business trips, to look at property or supervise courses we were doing. Even our family vacations were in places where I was building courses. Both boys were running bulldozers before they were old enough to drive.

Both played golf, although Bobby was the better of the two. He became a fine amateur who has played a lot of competitive golf. He was on the Eastern Intercollegiate championship team at Yale, from where he graduated in 1961. He played first man on the team his senior year, and has won several tournaments over the years. Rees, who also played at Yale, was always a good tournament player as a youngster. Bobby had a lot of lessons from the likes of Tommy Armour and Claude Harmon, but I was the only teacher Rees ever had. He could have been as good as Bobby, but he was into baseball for awhile and never worked as hard at golf as he might have. He was proud of the fact that he was as good as he was without having taken lessons from anybody but me, but even he admits now he should have gone to some experts. Still, he's a six-handicap today and could be better if he had time to improve his short game.

Bobby graduated from Yale in 1961 and went to Stanford Law School for a year, but the law was not for him. That turned out to be a break for the golfers of the world. Rees graduated from Yale in 1963 and, having decided to become a golf architect, studied landscape architecture at the Harvard School of Design.

Each designed some magnificent courses with my firm, and each has continued to get better since he left. They learned from me, but they have continued growing on their own. I like to think their design principles are much like mine, but their expressions are different. I also have learned from them, and some of our later courses reflect, their ingenuity and innovative approaches.

Bobby is the quintessential naturalist, letting the land dictate the design of his holes and courses. His creations are sometimes more flamboyant than mine, but he always does a wonderful job of blending his work with the surroundings. His holes and courses are in harmony with the environment. He considers golf an outdoor chess game and so puts great emphasis on the mental aspects of the game. His courses tend to be more strategic, with some mixture of penal and heroic holes. He believes that all elements of the game—strength, accuracy, club selection and finesse—should be tested, that a Ben Crenshaw should not be allowed to win just because he's the best putter.

Bobby describes his style as "eclectic." His courses cannot be stereotyped. Each is different from the other. And he has built a string of great ones around the world—Joondalup and the National in Australia; Pondak Indah in Indo-

Robert Trent Jones, Jr., designs in Japan include Onuma (left) and Pine Lake (top). Joondalup in Australia (above) is one of his newest and best creations.

nesia; Pine Lake, Golden Valley and Onuma in Japan; Spanish Bay and Poppy
Hills on the Monterey Peninsula; Princeville on Kauai, Hawaii; Sugarloaf in
Maine; SentryWorld in Wisconsin, which was named by *Golf Digest* in 1984
as the best new course of the year and was the site of the 1986 U.S. Women's
Public Links Championship. And that's just a start.

Rees's courses could fit the same description, although perhaps in a more
subtle manner. Rees does not believe so much in length as I do but in smaller,
well-fortified targets surrounded by varied features. He leaves a lot of his greens
open in front, believing that hazards to the sides penalize the good player more
than the higher handicapper. He uses grassy hollows and swales around the
green, trying to penalize the shot to the degree it is missed, retaining the ball
closer to the putting surface if it is only slightly off-line.

Many of the greens Rees builds sweep up in the front, like those at St.
Andrews, a style I have always preferred. His greens are marked by more gentle
transitions as opposed to abrupt terraces. Long putts will break, but putts from
close around the hole will be relatively easy.

Rees considers himself a multi-themed architect, which means that he is
constantly seeking variety, trying to give the player a new experience on every
hole, not just on every course. As a result, his later courses have become more
visually exciting. He also classifies himself as an "architect of definition" rather
than one of deception. He wants the golfer to know what he has to contend
with, and Rees works very hard at showing him the intended target, both off
the tee and into the green.

Rees has concentrated on building in the east and south, mostly real estate
development and resort courses. In addition to those he designed while with
my firm, he has turned out gems like Pinehurst No. 7 and the new eighteen
for Bryan Park in North Carolina, Stoney Creek in Virginia, Jones Creek in
Georgia, Charleston National, Woodside Plantation and Haig Point in South
Carolina. Ron Whitten in *Golf Digest* called Haig Point, a private course located
on Daufuskie Island, better than neighboring Harbour Town, long one of
America's 100 best.

Rees's courses can be demanding, but he strives always to make them
playable for all. Like his father and brother, he offers options to accommodate
all skill levels. "We design our courses generally for people who play golf, not
only for golfers," he has said. "Why take this great form of recreation and turn
it into a torture? The battle should be fun and fair."

Both Rees and Bobby have served prominently in the American Society
of Golf Course Architects. In 1978, Rees became, at the age of 36, the young-
est president ever to serve the society. Bobby rose to the presidency in 1989.

At times my sons and I have been disputants, sometimes combatants. I
suppose that's true in all father-son relationships, and it becomes especially
intense when all work in the same profession. I don't know how good a father
I have been, nor do I know how good they consider me to have been. As much
as I was gone, a great deal of their upbringing was left to their mother, and
thank God she was so good and strong.

I do know that I love them, and I am proud of them, as individuals and
masters of their profession. If this is indeed the legacy Ione and I have left, it
is the greatest contribution we could have made.

I've had a wonderful life. I had a wonderful wife, my kids have turned out
well, I have four wonderful grandchildren and I've met wonderful people. I've
also been able to spend my life doing what I wanted to do, making a living at
this marvelous game while working in the best of all possible atmospheres.

I've been very lucky. I guess sometimes you make your own luck, but you
have to have some help, too. I just thank God for his blessings.

Chapter 3
The Building of a Golf Course

erbert Warren Wind, the noted author and golf historian, once said: "I think it's the easiest thing in the world to criticize a finished course . . . But it's helpful if one occasionally sees a golf course before it is finished. When you see it in its rough, rude form, the landscape that the golf course architect takes over tells you something. I've been frightened a great deal when I've walked out and seen the land that certain friends had to work with—part of it swamp, no natural features in sight and the worst sort of trees. On top of it, the man has a low budget to work with . . . you wonder how he is going to get it so that the featureless land really plays, and when you return to this land and see what he's done with it, then you can appreciate the work that the professional architect is able to do."

As a matter of fact, it's often frightening to an architect to think of any piece of land being made into a course, mainly because of what that transformation entails. The design of a course is difficult enough. What goes before and after the designing is enough to drive a man mad, especially these days. Building a golf course is a lot more complicated and difficult than the layman could imagine. Most of the millions of golfers around the world who enjoy themselves at the game have no idea what goes into the making of their playgrounds.

Nature doesn't make golf courses any more. Man does . . . and at the same time man puts up a lot of roadblocks to the accomplishment of that task.

In the next chapter I will discuss the designing of a golf course and the theories and philosophies that go into that design. In this chapter I will examine the problems that surround the implementation of that design, the exigencies of planning and construction that transform the raw piece of land into something of beauty and playability.

With the proliferation of real estate developments in the 1970s and 1980s, golf course construction has boomed. The growth in the popularity of the game and the expansion in the number of players has fueled that explosion. Much of the development is in the south, southwest and west regions, the warmer climates, for obvious reasons, but the northern part of the United States is keeping pace. Whether his project is in Florida, California, Arizona, Illinois, Ohio or Maine, the developer eventually asks himself if he needs a golf course. The answer usually is yes. Nor is that mindset limited to the U.S. All kinds of housing, business and industrial developments are being spawned around the world, and a golf course is almost always an integral part of each.

This means architects are busy. We used to have to drum up business. Now it comes to us. And much as I hate to say it, we get calls and letters in our office from people who don't even know who Robert Trent Jones is. All they know is that we are golf course architects, and since they are going to build a golf course, they figure they need one.

Many of these come from towns and counties that have come up with a list of architects and have sent out a mass mailing to find out who is interested in doing the project. Which brings up the first problem an architect faces before he ever begins to think about designing the course. Every job requires a proposal, of course, but dealing with governmental bodies complicates the process. Working in the public domain means you have to bid for everything, you have to accept contractors you may not want to work with and you have to prepare a lot of specifications, contract documents and information, including material with which a golf course architect usually doesn't concern himself. The project may have a smaller budget, so the fee may be less and you can't do all the things you want with the golf course. It's the old business of working with bureaucracy. So the architect might spend days putting together this complicated proposal and then not get the job anyway. So he has nothing to show for the time and money he has spent.

This is part of the cost of doing business. But, given a choice, an architect would much rather work with a club or private developer than a body in the public domain. And today most of the better architects have that choice, which is unfortunate for a municipality that wants to build a fine public course.

Once the architect signs a contract to build a course, whether public or private, the real problems begin.

The major hurdle to be leaped before anything can begin is consideration for the environment. It has become a primary issue in building almost anything, particularly a golf course. With everything that man is doing these days to *really* rape the land, environmental protection has become a cause celebre and the environmentalists have become, in some circles, national heroes. This is all well and good, because the environment must be protected. But it does create a great deal of difficulty for people trying to build golf courses.

Flood plains and wetland areas, for example, dictate which parts of a property you can and cannot use. These are not just marshes and swamps but also freshwater wetlands—in Florida, along the coasts, in the middle of Michigan, almost everywhere. Basically they are not to be disturbed, although sometimes certain alterations are permitted and can be worked into the design. But this requires a lengthy process that the architect must go through to show the authorities that there will be no detrimental impact on the environment in these areas. Engineering drawings and other material must be submitted. All that certainly affects where and how we lay out a golf course and what kind of construction work we propose to do.

Wetlands seem to be our biggest single issue right now, and it's interesting how wetlands often are determined. States set up different sets of regulations. In Connecticut, for example, soil types are the primary consideration in designating wetlands, whether the land is wet or not. In New Jersey the type of vegetation usually is the determinant. In other states there may be different criteria. That's why on almost every job we do we work with a local engineer who knows the area, the people, the regulations and how the system works better than we do. He can submit the proper detailed information to the agencies so we can get permission to do the work. We would not hire an environmental engineer from Massachusetts to do a job in Arizona. The whole process is getting so big and complicated that nowadays engineering companies have departments that handle nothing but environmental issues.

Wetlands can be a serious problem for a developer because few, if any, are designated until somebody wants to build on them. So the developer who buys a piece of land doesn't know what he's getting. Wetland areas usually are indicated on small-scale mapping, but the critical areas on specific sites have to be investigated once a proposal is made by the developer. Then the authorities come out and set the boundaries, and suddenly the developer has some pieces of land he can't use. It would certainly be better for the developer if wetland areas could be designated before he buys the property so he knows exactly what he's getting and what he can and can't do with the land. Perhaps some day that will happen.

At Metedeconk, a development in New Jersey on which we built a course, the authorities took 220 acres along a river out of the parcel, designating them as wetlands that could not be used. Not only that, they designated a buffer area between the wetlands and any development, something that is often done. So the owners had to buy additional land for housing, because the financial pro forma was based on a selling a certain amount of lots and houses to make the project viable.

In this case we were allowed to use the golf course as the buffer, although that doesn't always happen, and we were able to work around the edges, going into the wet areas to dig out ponds and lakes. We were happy about that, and

Opposite: The blind spider, the world's smallest daddy-longlegs, delayed construction at Kiahuna on Kauai, Hawaii, for a year, but he couldn't stop Robert Trent Jones Jr. from making the long par-4 17th a strong test. Following pages: Whether they satisfy the environmental commission's demand for native vegetation, red poppies color the 3rd at Spanish Bay, the smashing Robert Trent Jones Jr. links course on the Monterey Peninsula in California.

it's a very nice side of the golf course. Wetlands really make good neighbors for an architect. They prevent the developer from building houses all around the course, and they add to the aesthetic value if properly incorporated into the design. But they do cost the developer land and money.

Sensitivity to wildlife has become a strong concern of the naturalists and therefore to the golf course builder. My son Bobby has had his Edgewood Park course in San Mateo County, California, delayed for ten years by a group seeking to protect the bay checkerspot butterfly, only one and a half inches long but obviously powerful in its influence. At Kiahuna on Kauai, Hawaii, the blind spider, which happens to be the smallest daddy-longlegs in the world, delayed construction for a year.

When Bobby built Spanish Bay, the last course to be allowed on the Monterey Peninsula, he was forced to revegetate all the dunes on the property, tearing out plants such as ice plant and pampas grass that had been growing there but which the coastal commission said were not native to the area, then replanting with native growth, whatever that means.

In Arizona, when a course is built in the desert, environmental authorities insist that all vegetation that is cleared must be saved and transplanted in appropriate locations. Often a particular kind of plant, such as a cactus, must be replanted in exactly the same direction as it originally grew so the sun will strike it the same way. So the cactus or tree or plant must be dug up, placed in a box while construction is going on, then replanted someplace else. It's a process that can cost up to $1,000 apiece for the larger plants, adding shocking amounts to the cost of building the course.

Environmental problems after the course is completed must be considered. Those basically are in the area of maintenance and the use of pesticides

Below: The 15th at Troon Village, the Jay Morrish/Tom Weiskopf course outside Scottsdale, Arizona, is a dainty par-3 at 139 yards set in a beautiful desert environment that had to be protected, which undoubtedly is why peril lurks between tee and green. Opposite: Whether it be a Skyland (top), Robert Trent Jones Jr.'s fine mountain course at Crested Butte, Colorado, or a Bel-Air in the posh environs of Los Angeles (bottom), a golf course has a positive impact on the environment.

Stages of construction (clockwise from top left): Crushing lava at Mauna Kea; building the 6th tee at Mauna Kea; routing the fairway on the 6th at Dorado East; grading a fairway at Kananaskis; building a fairway approach at Dorado East; grassing the 1st green at Mauna Kea. Opposite: Sprinkler heads jut above an unfinished fairway at Kananaskis.

Controls and wires and pipes are part of golf course construction—at Gordon Lakes, Fort Gordon, Georgia (above) and Firestone North in Akron, Ohio.

and fertilizers and their impact on ground water that runs off into other bodies of water. Soil erosion also is carefully monitored.

The International, our new complex in Prince William County outside Washington, D.C., is an excellent example. The courses are being built on the Manassas Reservoir, which supplies drinking water to the surrounding area. Naturally, officials have been concerned about the impact of our work. We were directed to build dikes, retention ponds and basins all over the property. It was quite an elaborate system. If they could be placed in the rough or woods and out of the way, there was no problem. But a lot of them cut into fairways with their rigid grades. Sometimes trees had to be cleared to build them, trees that we would have left on the golf course, which is sad. We could soften those harsh lines, blending them into the contours of the course, as long as we didn't destroy their intent. That's where creative design can overcome problems and restore the natural, flowing look of a golf course.

Erosion control is a major factor. If you have ever seen a golf course under construction, you often see bales of hay piled in certain places. This is to prevent soil movement when it rains, keeping it from being carried into a water course, clogging up drains or whatever. At The International, where the need is to keep soil out of the reservoir, we used "soak fences"—fiberglass or some other fabric staked around the perimeter and buried in the ground to prevent the soil from getting through. When the golf course is grassed in, the soak fences can be yanked out.

All this must be done before we are given permission to start disturbing the soil. Also necessary is a lot of discussion on the chemicals that will be used on the course and what happens to them. This really involves the superintendent and the people who will be running the course after it is completed and the architect leaves. Environmental officials are terribly concerned about such things, as is the public.

In the case of a golf course, some of these fears usually are unjustified, and we have to convince them that golf courses are not harmful to the environment. For example, the chemicals we put on a golf course don't travel the way people think they do. They just assume that the first rain that comes along will wash all the chemicals into the river or the reservoir or their wells. But the wise superintendent uses the materials very carefully, putting them down in controlled quantities, not only for environmental reasons but to save money and to do the job effectively. They take much more care than the average homeowner, who throws the stuff on his lawn in relatively much greater quantities.

Actually, farmers have been the guiltiest parties in creating environmental problems and the attendant concerns. They continually open up the ground by plowing, creating soil movement and erosion, and they don't fertilize and use pesticides nearly as carefully as golf course superintendents. Yet farmers are exempted from a lot of the controls that are imposed on golf course owners.

In truth, golf courses are beneficial to the environment and the community in many ways. First is their aesthetic value. They are, in effect, beautiful oases that break up a concrete world and provide recreational activity for millions of individuals. Second, and perhaps most important, a golf course acts as an air conditioner and cleaner, a natural drainage area, a space for water reclamation . . . a balance to nature, as it were.

All plants give off moisture, and this is especially true with areas of thick turf like those found on golf courses. When this moisture evaporates, it has a cooling effect on the atmosphere. The 100 or so acres of turf on an 18-hole course have the cooling effect of a 7,000-ton air conditioner.

The leafy surfaces of the vegetation on a golf course also attract the millions of tons of particle matter that is dispersed into the atmosphere by industry

Following pages: *The building of a hole, the 185-yard downhill 6th at Treetops in Gaylord, Michigan—from rough grading to finish grading to grassing to completion.*

and by automobiles, thus serving as a natural air cleaner. And through the process of photosynthesis, plant matter converts carbon dioxide into oxygen and helps restore the quality of the air.

A golf course also has a tremendous social and economic impact on a community, in a passive but positive sort of way. If all golf course areas were converted into housing developments or shopping malls, the strain on water supplies, sewer systems and the other structures of modern civilization, not to mention school systems and other facilities, would be considerable.

That's why states and municipalities have passed "greenbelt" legislation giving golf courses and land used for similar natural purposes some tax advantages. Still, the struggle goes on when a new course is proposed, and it becomes necessary for the architect, the superintendent, the owner or developer—all people in golf—to effectively present their case to the citizens, whether it be at public hearing or through literature or whatever vehicle is available to them. There is a great need to assemble information that will give the public the hard facts on the advantages of a golf course.

In many cases opposition to a golf course stems not from an objection to the course itself but to what usually goes with the course—housing, office parks and so forth. Sometimes, in view of what some developers do, the opposition is justified. I suspect most people would love to have a golf course nearby, but they don't want all the other things. But in their broad-brush attack on the project, the golf course is included. The citizens go to a governmental body, so now it becomes a political situation. There is almost always a public hearing, the press takes notice and the people get involved, especially the ones who are against it.

It all results in constraints and, usually, delays that end up costing the

developer a lot of money. In the long run, of course, it costs the customer and the golf course user.

How much does it cost to build a golf course? For a good one, between $3.5 and $5 million. This does not include the cost of the land, the clubhouse or the bar stock. The golf course business is no place for the weak and timid . . . or the shoestring operator.

Once the red tape is cut through and all the necessary permits obtained, the architect can proceed with the design, routing the course and staking the holes and the key features of each. Treelines and individual trees to be preserved will be flagged. Then the heavy work begins.

We have our own construction force, for the simple reason that we might lose control of the project if we did not. In the long run, it also saves the client money, because he doesn't have to put out bids. The architect can incorporate the cost into his budget at a more realistic and reasonable level. A few other architects—my sons Bobby and Rees among them—also have their own companies, but most designers hire outside contractors.

The construction of a golf course can be roughly divided into eight basic areas, all related in one way or the other—clearing and grubbing the land; doing the earthwork; grading, contouring and establishing the drainage; shaping the greens, tees and fairway bunkers; finishing the construction of the greens, tees and fairway bunkers; developing the fairways and rough; installing the irrigation system; and setting up the pumping station for that system.

This is not intended to be a manual on how to build a golf course, so I will pass lightly over many of the technical aspects. But there is much more to the transformation from raw land to finished course than the layman realizes. Knowing what goes into the making of it may help you better appreciate your playground.

Opposite and above: *After the land is graded, the trenches are dug and the pipes are laid, the finished hole emerges. . . . here the 5th at Treetops. Following pages: From forest and swampland, architect Pete Dye created a sculpture at the Players Club in Ponte Vedra, Florida. This is the par-5 11th hole.*

133

Above: *Flowers add to the beauty and pleasure of a golf course. From the top: Flame-of-the-Woods, often found in Florida; the rose, in this case the Alexander rose cultivated in Scotland; the water lily, another favorite in Florida and elsewhere. Opposite: Ice plant (top), generic to the Monterey Peninsula, is beautiful, but don't try to hit out of it. Former U.S. Open champion Jerry Pate once did and ruined his shoulder. Even more beautiful—and much less dangerous—are the azaleas (bottom) that bloom each spring at Augusta National, here behind the 12th green.*

The first task is to clear, and that basically means everything that would ruin a good fairway or interfere with a golf shot. All the trees, stumps, roots, limbs, brush and other debris must be removed from the specified areas. This is done with heavy earthmoving equipment, tractors, chippers, chain saws, whatever is necessary.

This operation usually is done in three phases, giving the designer a chance to make adjustments after each.

All the material that is cleared must be removed or, usually, burned. This must be done carefully, of course, and in compliance with local ordinances and Environmental Protection Agency regulations.

Burning is not without its hazards. When we were first clearing the land at Spyglass on the Monterey Peninsula, we were burning material in the 13th fairway. The fire got temporarily out of control, and for a while I thought we were going to burn down the whole Del Monte Forest.

Once the initial clearing is done, grubbing must be performed, and grubbing is just that—roots, rocks and other unwanted material must be dug out of the ground. If you have ever tried to dig up a fresh garden plot, perhaps you can understand the magnitude of doing the same thing on up to 100 acres. It's done by machine, of course, but it has to be done thoroughly. Nobody wants to smash into a root or a rock on a 5-iron shot to the green.

Large boulders and ledge rock must be dealt with almost on an individual basis. If the designer determines they cannot be left, often the only option is blasting. This is done *very* carefully.

The final stage of the process involves raking to a depth of twelve to fifteen inches, filling holes and pockets and grading, smoothing and leveling, creating flowing contours acceptable to the designer.

Any existing roadways on the property, if they are not to be used as roads, also must be broken up and filled in to blend with the rest of the area.

Damage to trees and foliage that are to remain as part of the course must be avoided. And the topsoil must be taken care of.

The topsoil that exists in all work areas must be conserved for earthwork. None of it should be buried or wasted in grading operations. Basically, the topsoil covering in cleared areas should be six inches. The rest should be stripped and stockpiled at green, tee and fairway bunker sites to be used in grading and shaping there. The construction crew also must excavate for ponds and embankments, stripping the topsoil for use in other areas.

Next, grading and contouring must be done on all areas other than greens, tees and fairway bunkers. This includes fairways, all rough areas and all disturbed areas. Areas overgrown with grass, weeds or other plant material must be turned over by plowing or disking or other methods and incorporated into the seedbed if possible. If the growth is not suitable for that, it must be stripped and disposed of. Then swales must be excavated and mounds, crowns and ridges must be established, all planned for optimum drainage, all graded to specific degrees of sloping and all developed to blend with surrounding contours, including the greens, tees and bunkers that are yet to be formed. Once the grading is done, topsoil is spread over all the areas to a minimum depth of six inches.

Shaping and molding the subgrade of the greens and greenside bunkers is done with smaller machines, following the design of the architect to insure that the contours blend with the surroundings. The same is true with fairway bunkers, also done with smooth, flowing lines, and tees, which are done flat, sloping no more than one degree from front to back and smooth on the sides for easy mowing. The subgrades of all must be compacted to prevent future settling or water-holding depressions.

Some 80,000 flowers surround the par-3 7th at Sentry World, the showcase hole on the Robert Trent Jones Jr. design.

After fertilization the greens are seeded with a type of bentgrass, spread by hand and raked lightly into the seedbed, or sprigged with a Bermuda grass in the hotter climes.

Underdrains of perforated pipe at least four inches in diameter then are installed in the subgrade of the green, set into trenches over crushed stone or gravel and sloping uniformly to allow for proper drainage into adjacent rough areas or other appropriate locations. The trenches then are filled with gravel or stone, after which a four-inch layer of the same is spread over the entire green, following the contours of the subgrade.

Similar drainage is needed in the traps, which are graded to drain to one or more low points, depending on the design. Dry wells filled with gravel or crushed stone are dug at these low points. Pipe also is installed from the outside edge of each trap, draining into swales, ditches, ponds or other out-of-play areas.

When the gravel is uniformly spread over the green, a seedbed mixture of 80 percent sand and 20 percent peat or other organic material is carefully applied to an uncompacted depth of twelve inches. Then it is compacted, firmed and smoothed by mechanical means, always maintaining the established contours. That same seedbed mixture often is spread over tees to a depth of four to six inches and is spilled over onto the top of all side slopes.

The amount of skill and care that goes into this entire process determines how acceptable, or unacceptable, the contours of the putting surface will be. Careful work also prevents settling and later rebuilding, an expensive proposition.

The type and amount of sand placed in a bunker is critical. Sand should be spread at a depth of four to six inches above the subgrade. The consistency should be reasonably firm or the ball will bury, creating a near-impossible shot even for the better players and certainly an impossible one for the higher handicappers. For example, at the 1977 U.S. Open at Southern Hills in Tulsa, which traditionally has used a powdery sand anyway, too much sand was dumped into the bunkers at too late a date. There was too much of it to begin with, and it never had time to settle and pack. The result was that in some bunkers the ball would bury out of sight. I believe that sand traps should be hazards, but that was carrying things too far.

We prefer a coarser, white sand for bunkers because it provides a firmer surface and drains better. This kind of sand can be found on seaside beaches. Inland sand that provides a good playing surface can be found, but it usually requires a careful search.

The development of fairway and rough areas basically has to do with the preparation of a suitable turf bed, smooth and properly contoured. This involves scarifying and loosening the soil (remember, it already has been cleared and

Above: *The home of the Royal and Ancient, one of the world's oldest and stateliest clubhouses, overlooks the 1st tee and 18th green of the Old Course at St. Andrews. Following pages: The clubhouse at Royal Lytham & St. Annes in Lancashire is typical of many in England and Scotland.*

The Stanford White-designed clubhouse at Shinnecock Hills, seen here from the 16th hole, sits on the property's highest hill and majestically overlooks the course.

grubbed) with a disk or harrow, then fine-grading it by machine or even by hand in certain difficult places. All stones, roots and other objectionable material still remaining must be cleared away. All areas must be graded to provide proper surface drainage. Undulations and variations in grade that will not permit the use of normal mowing equipment must be eliminated.

Seedbed preparation, of course, includes the edges and slopes of ponds, which must be planted as near to the water's edge as possible. Sometimes the water level must be lowered for this purpose.

Fertilization and seeding follow. Fairways can be seeded with a mixture of bentgrasses or bluegrasses in the temperate climates or sprigged with one of the Bermuda varieties in warmer areas. Roughs can be planted with a mixture of bluegrasses, ryegrasses and fescue, or Bermuda or centipede grass where it's hot.

Again, this is not a treatise on the technical qualities of grasses. All have different qualities, some good and some bad, as far as durability and playability are concerned. Bermuda is wiry, bent is fine. The various strains of ryes, bluegrass and fescue fall somewhere in between. All, depending on how they are cultivated and mowed, can provide playing surfaces that range from good to excellent, as can grasses like zoysia and *poa annua*, a strain of bluegrass. But all are susceptible to climatic conditions, thriving or dying in certain locales and temperatures. Suffice it to say that the architect and the superintendent had better know which grasses to plant for the particular location, and how to take care of them, or there can be major problems with the fairways and the greens down the road.

Before the final grading and seeding, of course, the irrigation system for fairways, greens and tees must be installed. This is an extremely complicated project that must be well planned and carefully executed if it is to do the job in the years to come. We have always preferred to plan that job ourselves, even when almost every other architectural firm was hiring an outside firm to do it.

The first step is to find a water source. That's one of the first questions we ask when we investigate a property: Where is the water going to come from? People who want a course built usually don't consider the quantity of water needed. They'll say, "Yes, we have a good stream over here or a creek over there. We have enough water." But they don't know what enough water is. Up to a million gallons a day might be needed, depending on the coverage you want and the typical weather conditions, and numbers like that always surprise people. They might have been thinking in terms of a million gallons a week or a month.

A little stream isn't going to do the job, especially if it only flows during seasonal wet periods. So the irrigation designer must figure out climatic conditions and how much water really will be needed in a particular area. Then he must go about finding a water source, whether it means tapping into a municipal water supply (which is rarely done), drilling wells, pumping it in from a lake or river or creating lakes and filling them for the purpose. Properly constructed lakes or catch basins are valuable for reclaiming and recycling water used on a golf course, which is an environmental plus not usually appreciated.

The most important task is to lay out the system itself to properly distribute the water where you want it. That involves pipe and wire, control valves,

The three-story, Spanish-style clubhouse at Riviera in Los Angeles contains 82,000 square feet of space perched on the rim of Santa Monica Canyon, through which the golf course winds.

valves that actuate the sprinkler heads and so forth. Most modern systems are controlled by computer, so that must be properly programmed. All these elements must be pulled together into the design of the system.

There are a multitude of options, different manufacturers, different types of equipment. These must be discussed with the owner and the superintendent, who might have some strong preferences. Certainly the budget is a consideration.

Hiring or having a good irrigation designer and a reliable contractor is vital. Then the actual staking of the head locations must be supervised. An irrigation designer can take the plan for a golf course and spot his pipes and his sprinkler heads, but when he gets into the field he often finds they don't fit. The hole may have been changed, widened here or narrowed there, so now he must adjust his locations to get the proper coverage.

Then the contractor takes over, and he must know what he's doing. Like a surgeon, an irrigation contractor buries his mistakes. Since you can't stand over his shoulder while he's doing the entire job, you must trust that he's doing it correctly. Digging and replacing, not to mention finding a problem in the first place, are expensive propositions.

Once the seeding is done and the job is accepted by the club or owner, all maintenance—watering, fertilizing and control of disease, weeds and pests—becomes his responsibility. That's why it is vital that the architect and course superintendent work closely together through all stages of the planning and construction. It is critical to the architect and his reputation that the superintendent be knowledgeable and skilled, because the nature and value of the course in years to come rests in his hands. And that's why I've been so involved in improving the educational opportunities, the research capabilities and the overall quality of that profession.

The knowledgeable architect's job doesn't always end with the golf course itself. We get involved with decorative flower plantings and the like around the course and the clubhouse. Often we advise on the construction of the clubhouse itself. I've probably been involved with 150 or so clubhouses, because most building architects are not that familiar with golf and don't know how to make a clubhouse functional. They are not aware of things like golf car storage and traffic flow between the clubhouse, the locker room and the golf course. A golf course architect, who has worked with this sort of thing throughout his career, can be a great help in coming up with the right design.

The preceding is a capsule version of a time-consuming project. On average, given normal weather conditions, it takes twelve to eighteen months to construct a golf course. In Florida, on flat terrain with no particular problems, we might do it in a year, but in the North or elsewhere in the world it usually takes longer, perhaps up to two years if the terrain is rugged and/or the land is rocky, or if the weather doesn't cooperate. Then the course must be planted and the grass must grow. Grass grows pretty quickly in warm climates, but elsewhere it can take another year after planting before the course is playable.

That growing time can be cut by as much as six months, of course, by sodding the course. Expensive as that may be, it might be worth it to a developer to get the course in play and begin pulling in revenue that much sooner.

The construction scenario you have just read is a textbook version. It can vary to a greater or lesser extent depending on the land and location of the course.

In planning and building a course, you must consider what we call the "liabilities of the property." Excessive rock is a liability. So is clay, which will create growing and drainage problems. Perhaps the biggest liability is a swamp, because you have to drain it and usually fill in the area provided you are allowed to today.

A property that is totally treed is a liability in one respect, but it is definitely an asset in other ways. It will cost the builder money to clear the fairways, but when you are finished you have all those remaining trees framing the course. It would take you twenty or more years to achieve the same result if you had to plant them . . . and that would cost a lot of money too.

Sand is definitely *not* a liability. It's an asset. You can grow great grass on sand, although nobody thought so until I built Dorado Beach in Puerto Rico for Laurance Rockefeller in 1958.

The property was basically all sand. At the time, the United States Golf Association's Green Section was recommending a mixture of 60 percent soil, 30 percent sand and 10 percent other ingredients, especially for greens. I said, "Hell, I'm not going to put topsoil on the sand. They grow grass on sand all over the British Isles, and I don't see any reason we can't do it here." Which led to another interesting experience.

Near the Dorado Beach site was the Berwind Country Club course. It was built on clay and they had terrible problems. The course would flood every time it rained. So Rockefeller, basically out of the goodness of his heart, invited the members to come in with him on the Dorado Beach project. A committee from the club, headed by an army colonel, came to see us. The colonel said, "Mr. Rockefeller, we're not interested in doing anything with you. I've been the chairman of the greens at eleven army posts, and I don't think you can grow grass on sand."

Rockefeller turned to me and asked, "Trent, what about that?" I said, "You *can* grow grass on sand. All you need is water and fertilizer. We have the water here and you have the money to buy the fertilizer."

What I had figured out was that if you planted grass in sand, the roots would grow deeper. If you put drainage underneath, you eliminate excessive moisture, and moisture is what causes the "brown patch," the dead patches we see so often on golf courses. Create a pond into which you run the drainage system. As soon as the water begins running into the pond, you know there is enough moisture in the soil.

I had a hard time selling the concept to the USGA. They told me I would use too much water. I said that if you stopped watering when the moisture level was adequate, that wouldn't happen. And the grass also would not be susceptible to brown patch.

So we went ahead and built the course at Dorado Beach basically on sand. When we opened, it was like a carpet. I played with Rockefeller on opening day, and when we got to the 18th green he said, "Trent, this is the most gorgeous turf I've ever seen."

For a while, at least, the USGA Green Section was angry as hell with me. But they have since seen the light. Now we build greens that are a mixture of sand and some humus to provide a cushion, so the sand doesn't compact and the ball will bite when it lands rather than bounce and roll over the green.

On rare occasions we are forced to tell a developer or a club-builder that the land he has chosen is not suitable for a golf course. But I've really found very few places in my career where a golf course can't be put.

Before I built Mauna Kea on Hawaii for Rockefeller in 1963, we took a walking tour of the property, and I was excited. The terrain was undulating, almost like linksland. There were elevations for the tees, nice pockets for the greens, everything you would want for a great course. But the land was desolate, covered with brown volcanic rock, cinder, large boulders and scrublike vegetation in the higher areas, impenetrable jungle in the valleys that was fed by moisture from the ocean. The average annual rainfall was only eight inches, and Rockefeller doubted that we could build a course on it.

I said, "It depends on whether I can work with the lava rock, if it can be

Opposite: *At Sugarloaf, the white birches through which the holes were routed stand like sentinels lined up along the fairways.* Following pages: Pages 148-149: *Old Trail, a Tom Fazio creation in Jupiter, Florida, near the Everglades, shows that beauty and playability can be created from marshland. Pages 150-151: Another gorgeous and testing mountain design from Robert Trent Jones Jr. is Beaver Creek near Vail. Here is the spectacular 191-yard par-3 2nd hole, showing the steep drop from the elevated tee to the green below*

Below: *The 15th at Valderrama is a par-3 beauty, 226 yards from the back tee but with a number of other tees available to the player with less strength. It is an example of the care that a good architect takes to insure that a hole and a course is playable for every golfer.*

crushed and used as a soil base to grow grass. If it can, and if there is enough water, I can build a golf course."

We determined that, with enough water, the lava rock could support plant life. Using a bulldozer fitted with a specially ribbed roller, we crushed the lava into a red dust the consistency of talcum powder and spread almost a foot of it over the course. The wind would blow the dust around, and it was awful. The construction crew had to wear face masks, and we ruined lots of pairs of pants, because the stuff wouldn't come out. But we improvised a watering system to stabilize the crushed lava, mixed it with coral sand from nearby Kawaihea Harbor and put the seed down. When it sprouted, we got the cleanest grass you've ever seen. There were no weeds, because nothing had ever grown in the material before.

We also had to deal with basal rock, a cinder residue of the lava flow that had covered the area eons before. It was totally unworkable, and the larger portions had to be blasted, buried or bulldozed. But those portions that we could handle we used as coarse foundation for tees and greens and to fill in fissures and crevices.

We drilled two wells 400 feet deep that produce a million gallons of water a day, installed one of the first fully-automatic underground irrigation systems and produced "an oasis in the desert."

That was the first one. Now there are five or six courses along the island coast that might never have been built without using those procedures.

While we were building the Pevero Golf Club for the Aga Kahn at Costa Smeralda in Sardinia in the early 1970s, he called a meeting to discuss grassing the golf course. He had called in four Italian agronomists who told him that, because there was very little topsoil on the island, he had to bring in enough topsoil to spread a foot of it over the entire course, and it was going to cost millions.

In the meantime, I had discovered that there was a lot of disintegrated granite on the property that could be crushed into dust and, with proper nutrients added, be used as soil. I said, "Your highness, it's your money, but if you want to take a chance on spending $35,000 for seed, I don't think you'll have to

spend millions for topsoil." Two years later they played the Italian Open there on lush grass growing in granite. It saved the Aga Kahn $2.5 million, and his staff is still upset with me. One said to me afterward, "We hate you. Every time it comes to spending money, he relates your story to us."

Sometimes you don't even need land, per se, for a course. We built Marine Park in Brooklyn for the New York City Department of Parks on swampland, filling it in with both garbage and inorganic refuse, spreading a heavy layer of sand over each layer of organic fill. It took a long time, some eighteen years between inception and completion in 1963, but it was a fine course when it was finished. And as this is being written, we're building a course called Stockley Park, near Heathrow Airport outside of London, on an old garbage dump, using a similar technique. There, incidentally, we found newspapers one hundred years old that you could still read.

Sometimes, when you build a course, things are not as they seem. My son Bobby built Spanish Bay, the marvelous linksland course on the Monterey Peninsula in California, on land on which a company had been mining sand. Most of it had been taken out, right down to the rock. So Bobby had to bring sand back in and reshape it into undulating linksland. He did a wonderful job, and the terrain looks like it had been there forever, formed by nature.

Mountain courses have a lot going for them—spectacular scenery, clean air and cooler summer temperatures. But they present construction problems not found on flatter land. I have built more than twenty-five of them, and the grades and rock always provide plenty of headaches. For that reason, I always try to build them in a valley, if possible.

Stanley Thompson built the Banff Springs Hotel course in Canada in the 1920s. It is the granddaddy of mountain courses and still one of the best, located in a valley where the Bow and Spray rivers converge and surrounded by mountains 10,000 feet high on all sides. Building the course in those days was a monumental achievement, and it could be done only because the Canadian Pacific Railroad, the developer of the resort, was willing to spend $250,000 on a monstrous earthmoving project. The company transported hundreds of gondola cars filled with tons of soil 1,000 miles over the Rockies, providing the fill that covered the entire golf course.

Today sophisticated earthmoving equipment lets us build courses on sites we never would have considered forty years ago. And the new strains of grasses and irrigation systems make it possible to have courses at elevations that previously could support only sparse underbrush, evergreens and wild animals.

Animals, by the way, sometimes can make building a course more exciting than you want. When we were working on the Broadmoor course in Colorado, for example, Bill Baldwin and I were out looking at a green early one morning when out of the woods about 100 feet away came a mountain lion. I didn't think he was interested in joining us for a round, and I said, "Bill, let's get the hell out of here." We started back to the jeep and Bill, who was a big, tall fellow, started running and got way ahead of me. I said, "Bill, don't run. They chase you if you run."

Bill said, "Okay, I won't run, but I'm going to walk damned fast."

At Kananaskis, a way had to be found to tranquilize bears and remove them from the property while the course was under construction. Vegetation also had to be spread around the perimeter of the course to head off migrating elk. We also had to buy plastic swans to scare off Canadian geese that were littering the greens and lakes.

Building you a lovely place to play is, as I hope you now can see, a gargantuan task. Perhaps the next time you are out there among the beautiful trees, hitting off the lush turf and putting on the smooth greens, you might be conscious of how this oasis came into being, and perhaps you will enjoy it that much more.

Following pages: *The Balsams is an old Donald Ross course set in the pastoral beauty of Dixville Notch, New Hampshire.*

153

Chapter 4
The Designing of a Course

Roger Rulewich, the chief designer in my firm and one of the finest architects in the country, once admitted to what may be a recurring nightmare for the men who build golf courses.

"You just hope," he grinned wryly, "that when you go to the opening ceremony you don't discover that you only have seventeen holes on the course."

That hasn't happened yet, at least with my firm, but it illustrates the pressure the architect is under to design a good mix of holes and then route them properly.

Putting eighteen holes on a piece of property is like putting together a jigsaw puzzle. The architect will walk the land, probably several times, and carefully study the topographical maps. Then he gets an almost instinctive feel for how the course should be routed—at least I know I do, although it is instinct supplemented by a lot of that hard work before the ground can be broken. After I had designed a lot of courses, I got to the point where, after I examined the topo map and walked the land, I could visualize where the clubhouse should be and how the course should be routed according to the terrain. Then it becomes a matter of adjustment in designing the individual holes to fit the basic route plan.

The primary criterion is to use the terrain to build holes that will require good golf shots. When designing options into a hole, the architect must take into account the length, the shape of the fairway, the positioning of the hazards and the placement and contour of the green, combining all that with a keen knowledge of shot values. And of course there must be a balance of holes, the right mix of par-3s, par-4s and par-5s, and the right mix of length and variety among them—straight holes, doglegs, semi-doglegs, with a variety of contouring, slopes and undulations on each. Establishing a change of pace as the player goes through the round is essential to making a course challenging and intriguing. Four par-5 holes in a row, or four par-3s, or ten par-4s, would not be aesthetically pleasing. It also would be boring. It's not always easy, but I've never found a piece of land yet on which that change of pace couldn't be accomplished.

First you settle on the basic routing of the course. You might have to make two or three routings, especially on rugged land with a lot of change of pace. You do have to get from point A to point B on each hole, you must have eighteen holes per course, and you have to start at the first tee and wind up at the 18th green, both somewhere in the vicinity of the clubhouse. Usually the ninth green and the tenth tee have to be close by as well. It doesn't always fit together the first time you do a routing, so you do it again, always checking by walking or riding the land while you're doing it. At this stage you're doing it all on paper instead of with a bulldozer, so all it's costing is time. Trial-and-error architecture, building and then knocking down and building again, is very expensive.

Ideally, the land *would* dictate all your holes, but it doesn't always work out that way. You work the course and the individual holes through the land as best you can, but there may be a few hard spots along the way. To make the pattern of holes work, you may have to cross from one point to another and build a hole there, and you may have to work a little harder on that hole.

When you look at your layout of the course you can usually tell that you have a whole bunch of holes that are really nice, but there may be one or two stinkers in there. So if you are going to keep the other holes as good as they can be, you are going to have to work extra hard on a few. You may have to spend more money for grading, or whatever it might be, to make these holes match the others.

Sometimes it's amusing to walk a site with the client, who is familiar with his own property. He's been over the land innumerable times, and he has the holes fixed in his mind. He'll say, "Isn't that a great hole?" And as you walk he'll point out another good hole, and another. And you have to agree that they're all nice holes. But you have to remind him that the goal is to build an 18-hole loop and get back to the clubhouse, and some of those great holes may not fit into the overall pattern of the golf course.

That's what owners usually overlook. They may see eighteen great holes out there, but if you built all eighteen of them, anything might happen. The course might end up in a different county. Or you could never play them from one to the other . . . or the golfer might have to walk half a mile between holes to do it.

So in laying out a course you often are forced into doing things with the property that are less than ideal. Golf is a continuous game. You finish one hole and go on to the next one. You just can't go out and play one hole at a time, no matter how wonderful that hole may be. It has to fit the total plan.

You really can't have any preconceived ideas about the kind of golf course you're going to build. If someone tells you he wants a tournament course, or if it's going to be a public course with heavy play, or some other specific type of

Golf course design starts with a schematic of the route plan, this one of the Robert Trent Jones project at Vidauban in France.

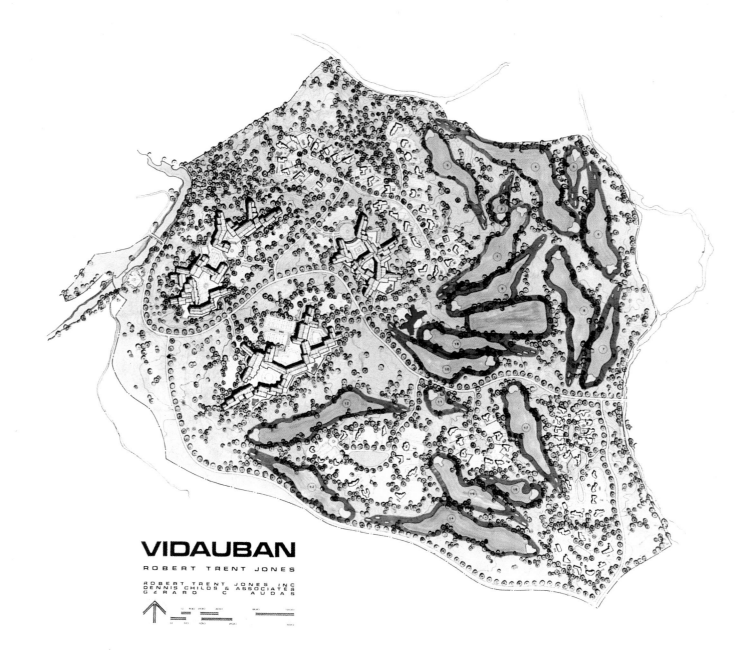

VIDAUBAN

ROBERT TRENT JONES

ROBERT TRENT JONES INC
DENNIS CHILDS & ASSOCIATES
GÉRARD C AUDAS

EIGHTH HOLE
345 YDS.

Designed + Sketched   Robert Trent Jones. 1936

Artistic talent and training have always been valuable tools for Trent Jones. Shown here and on the next page are his renderings of greens for the Norris estate at St. Charles, Illinois.

course, you might have some notions about what you're going to build. But you can't develop any concrete ideas until you actually see the land. We get a lot of clients who call us up and start describing the property, but it's best that we just go to the site and look it over. We're trained to see an awful lot very quickly when we look at a property. A person who is not experienced in that regard can't get the visual impressions that a good architect can register immediately.

When an architect starts working with a client on a new piece of land, he usually has to have a lot of sensitivity, as well as a great deal of diplomacy. Everyone who shows us property has prejudices—they bought it or took an option on it, and they like it. They think it's a great piece of land on which to build a great golf course. The members of any country club—no matter what kind of course they have or where it ranks in the scheme of things, think they have a great course. They have memories and stories to tell, and the place has value to them. It's the same with a builder or developer. He now has become emotionally involved.

That's why we've been called in, to build a golf course. Now we must offer a separate and objective opinion, and sometimes we've got to be pretty straightforward. The property may not be be as good as the owner thinks it is. Or it may be good property for a development but not that good for a golf course.

FOX
RIVER.

FOURTH HOLE
175 YDS.

Designed & sketched Robert Trent Jones.

Our first priority is the quality of the course. We'll build a good one, no matter what kind of land, but sometimes you have to tell the owner or developer that it's going to take a little more work or more money than normal because of the nature of the property.

Sometimes you're fortunate enough to have a client who says, "Here's the land. Build me the best golf course you can." Nowadays, when most courses are part of real estate developments, that is rare. We would rather not have to work with housing. I don't know of any architect who likes to do it. But it's a fact of life, one of the realities that is contributing to the boom in golf course construction in the 1980s.

Originally a golf course was just that and nothing more, except perhaps apple trees. Now there are a lot more golf courses associated with real estate developments than there are private clubs or municipal courses. So, in this regard, the golf course and its ancillary activities has become a way of life. The kids can walk or ride their bikes to the club, where they can play golf or tennis or swim. Mother doesn't have to be a chauffeur. And she and dad can get to the course quickly, too. It's an appeal that makes a golf course and a country club an indispensable part of any development.

So now you become a land-planner as well as a golf course architect. You

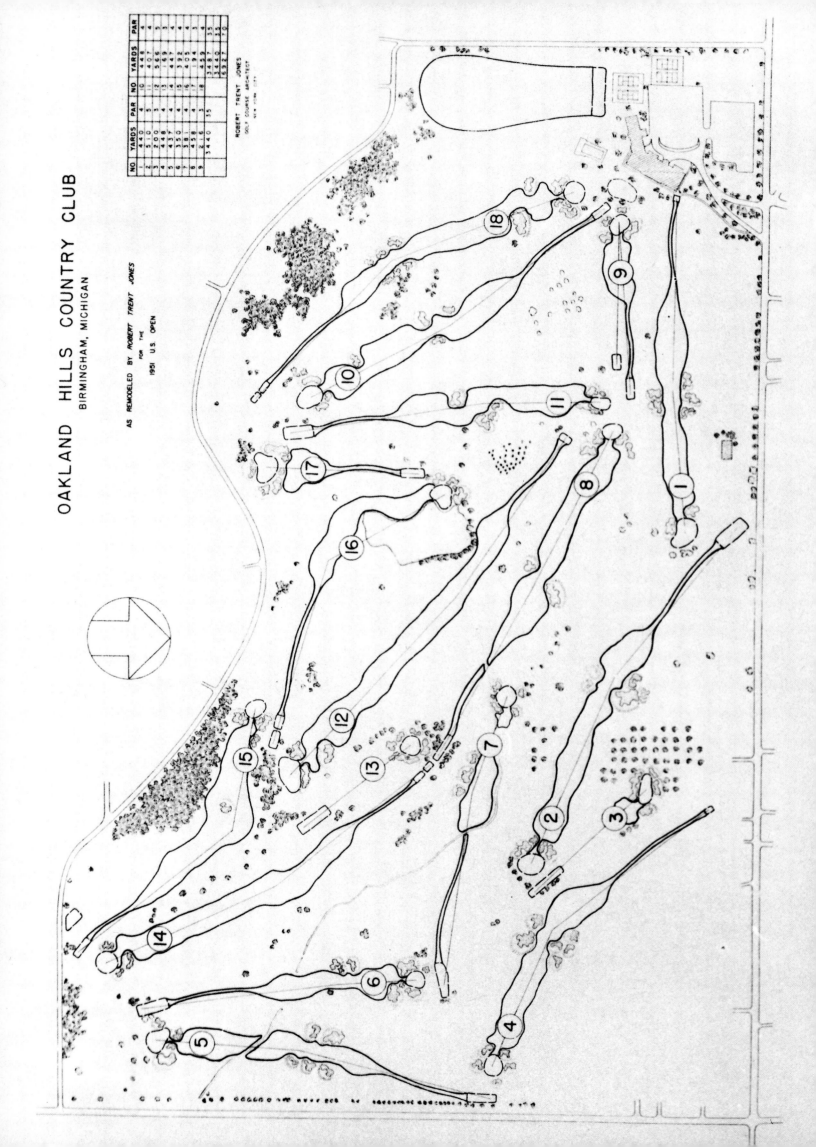

OAKLAND HILLS COUNTRY CLUB
BIRMINGHAM, MICHIGAN

AS REMODELED BY *ROBERT TRENT JONES*
FOR THE
1951 U.S. OPEN

ROBERT TRENT JONES
GOLF COURSE ARCHITECT
NEW YORK CITY

NO	YARDS	PAR		NO	YARDS	PAR
1	440	4		10	448	4
2	510	5		11	407	4
3	200	3		12	569	5
4	448	4		13	447	3
5	437	4		14	392	4
6	350	4		15	405	4
7	358	4		16	194	3
8	458	5		17	459	4
9	216	3		18	458	4
	3440	35			3487	35
					3440	35
					6927	70

have to plan your layout, your hole placements and routing, around where the developer wants the housing. My son Rees, along with illustrator Guy L. Rando, wrote a scholarly and influential book for the Urban Land Institute several years ago entitled *Golf Course Developments* in which, among other things, he outlines five basic course layouts for real estate projects. These include the single-fairway 18-hole course with nines that return to the clubhouse or the continuous single fairway course with only the 18th hole returning, in both of which designs the housing can be placed both inside and outside the routing of the holes; the double fairway course with either continuous or returning nines, in which the housing is placed on the perimeters of the course; and the core course, which essentially is an element unto itself surrounded by the housing units.

There can be many variations of these formulas, of course, but in any case the juxtaposition of the holes and their relationship to the housing units becomes a strong, if not primary, consideration.

In any project the number one priority is the kind of golf course that is going to come out of it. If you haven't seen the total plan when you first look at undeveloped property, you could have some problems. You may like the land, but you may find out later that some of the best parts of it aren't going to be the golf course.

Opposite: *A blueprint of Oakland Hills as remodeled by Trent Jones before the 1951 U.S. Open.* Below: *Scale maps showing gradation levels of the greens must be prepared prior to building or remodeling.*

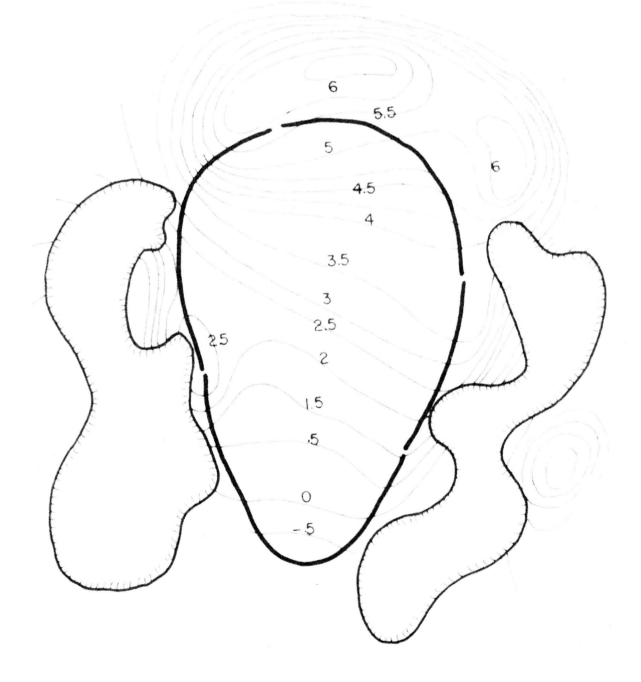

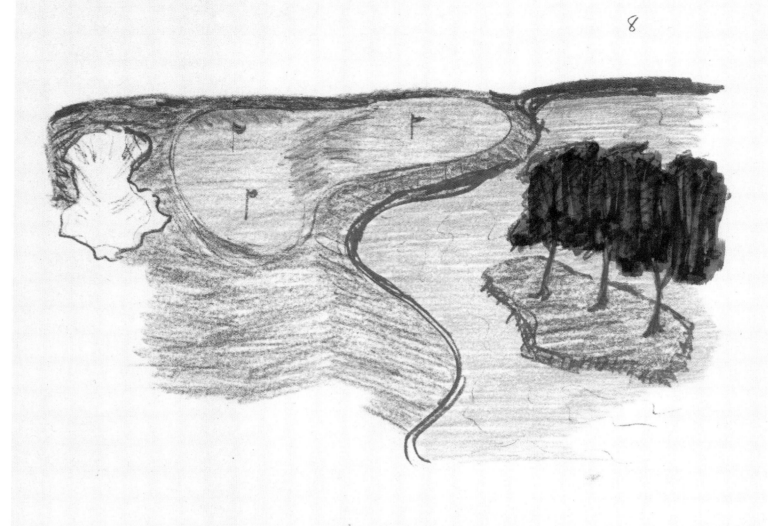

Above: *A Trent Jones rendering of a green at Geneva Golf and Country Club in Switzerland. Opposite: A green, this one the 14th at Burning Tree in Bethesda, Maryland, is conceived with a number of pin placements in mind, as this Trent Jones sketch illustrates.*

We work with developers, of course. Too often, I must say, they want to take the best land for the housing and leave the dregs for the golf course. I suppose that's a natural reaction on their part, and we can adjust and compromise and move things around, give up some things we want and do it some other way. But we have to draw a line somewhere and eventually say, hey, this is as far as you can go. If you do too much of this or that, you're not going to have a quality golf course.

The golf car has been both a boon and a curse to modern golf and golf course architecture. We are allowed more flexibility because car use is more prevalent. You can place tees farther from greens on a course on which you know the players will be riding cars. You can stretch the course and take better advantage of natural hole sites. This is especially helpful on a real estate development course where the developer insists on as many on-fairway housing sites as possible.

Because golf cars are available, you sometimes can build courses on terrain that wouldn't be suitable for golf if the players had to walk. Treetops, our course in Michigan, really is not a walking course, because of problems with the terrain. The connections between holes are long and the hills are steep, and you really would be asking a lot of players to make them walk. It's a gorgeous golf course, but the golfer has to ride it.

The problem, from a purist's viewpoint, is that golf is meant to be a walking game. It's sad that we are getting away from that more and more. Even on

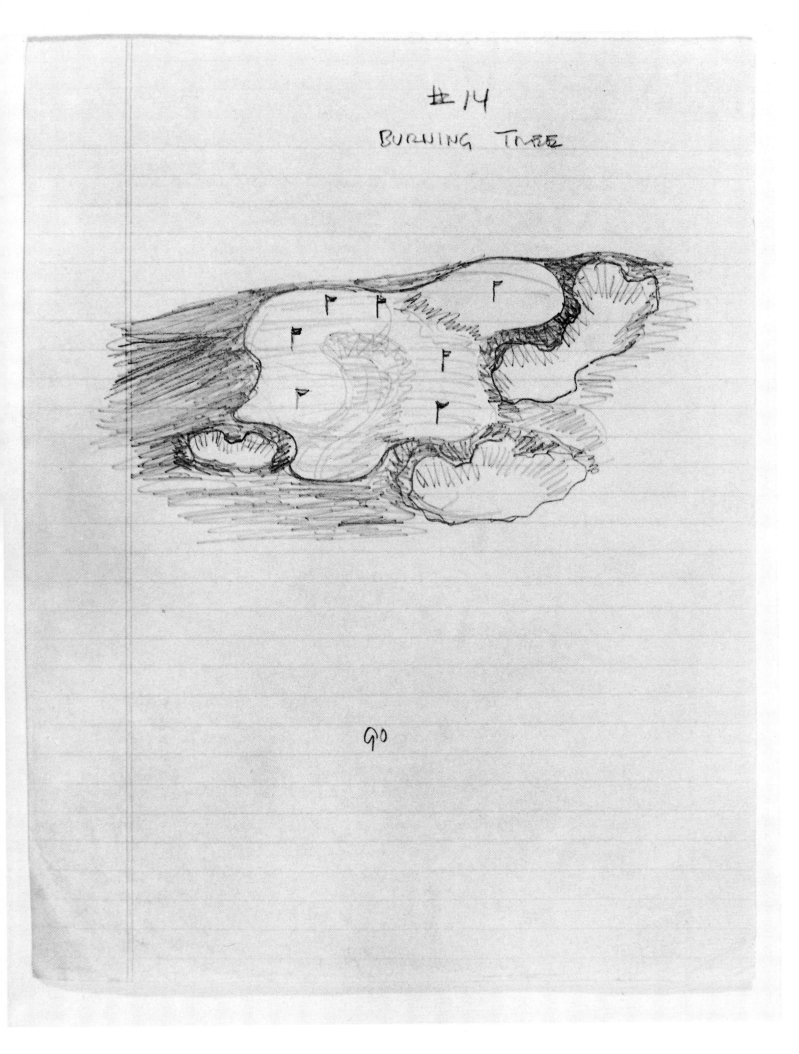

GO

courses that are easily walked, especially resort courses, golf cars often—usually, I guess—have become mandatory. The problem from an architect's standpoint is that it's difficult to design courses to accommodate both foot and car traffic. The older courses, which were intended to be walked, can handle the cars (although some of the better ones do it grudgingly). But a course that is designed to be traveled in a golf car usually is unsuitable for walking. The good architect will compromise as best he can, but on resort/development courses it often is difficult.

Further, you now have to worry about building car paths. If you don't want them scarring the aesthetic value of your course and interfering with play, you must be very careful where you route them, making them as unobtrusive as possible. You also must consider what material to use in building them. Usually we use asphalt, although I have used concrete and red-brick dust and like it a lot with proper curbing around it. Of course, this is a problem that Old Tom Morris never had.

At the point where you get the route plan basically in place, you might not have the individual finished holes well in mind, although you start thinking about that immediately. Once you have the basic layout pretty well set, you have to consider making each trip from tee to green as interesting and challenging as possible. Now you start considering the various elements that go into

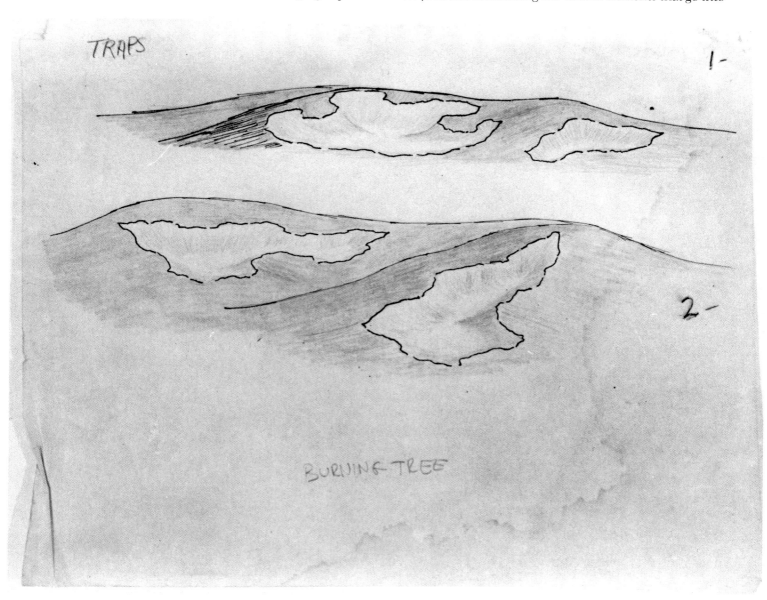

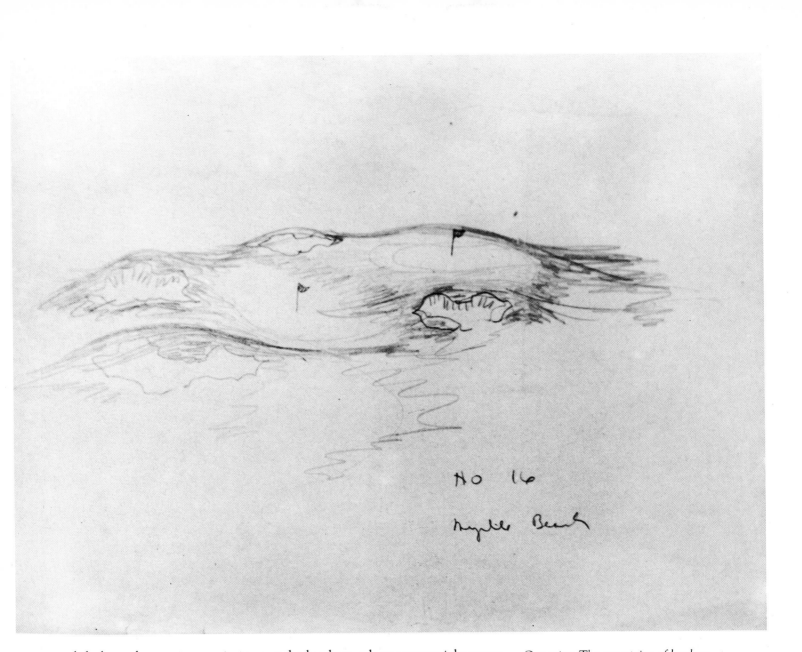

HO 16

Myrtle Beach

each hole—where you are going to put the bunkers, where water might come into play, what tree or trees are important to the strategy of the hole, the contouring of the fairway, the size and shape of the green and the pin positions you want on it.

Again, the architect who can sketch does the preliminary work on paper. I can do two or three green sketches in twenty minutes, always trying to make the green fit the site in as natural a way as possible. So we'll have some alternatives, some different pin positions and contours, to consider before we make the final decision on the design of each green.

Even if the land is good, some holes are harder to design than others. For example, to make a short par-4 hole is something special. You may have allocated 310 yards from tee to green for the hole. But now you need those extra elements to make it a good hole. It's pretty easy to make a 440-yarder tough, but doing the same thing with a little hole requires some ingenuity, some creative work with the bunkering, other hazards, the shape of the hole, the green or whatever.

The characteristics of the land do dictate, to a great degree, the way the holes are designed. You have to adapt what is there to the shot values you want to build into a hole. Where will the landing area be for this drive from a par-4 tee? Where will the second shot be on this par-5? How long should this par-3 hole be to best utilize the land that is here? You have to take advantage of whatever form of defense is there. And a good architect must be able to see these things in the raw land.

If you have planned carefully, when you finally stake out each hole, mark-

Opposite: *The conception of bunkers, like these at Burning Tree, ideally starts with a sketch.* Above: *This sketch of the two-tiered 16th green at the Dunes in Myrtle Bearch shows bunker placement and pin locations.*

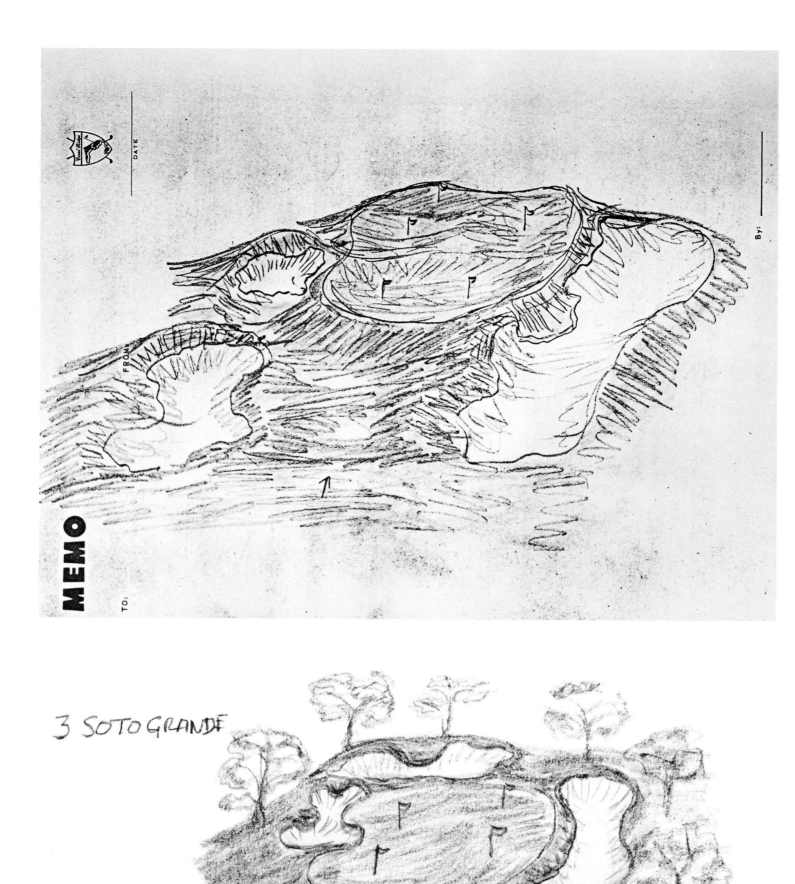

MEMO

TO:

FROM

DATE

By:

3 SOTO GRANDE

ing tees, bunkers, greensites and other features, you should not have to make many changes—perhaps move a stake fifty feet one way or the other, but nothing drastic unless unforeseen problems crop up.

I have always liked to start with the tee area and design the hole from there, but that does not obviate the fact that the greensite probably is the most important element in the hole. Once you find that site, somewhere within the range of the intended length of the hole, everything starts to fall into place. Of course, the greensite often determines the length of the hole. As you can see, making golf holes often is more art than science.

Occasionally you must create a greensite or make other alterations to accommodate the length and type of hole you want to put in a particular location, but you try to hold that sort of thing to a minimum. I don't believe in moving a lot of dirt unless it is absolutely necessary.

At the New Course at Ballybunion in Ireland, for example, my associate in Europe, Cabell Robinson, was having difficulty with the routing, especially with the 15th hole. He said, "We've been looking around here for two days and don't know what to do." I went out to the area and right away saw a greensite. And it made the hole. That's a gift, perhaps, but it's a gift that comes from knowledge and experience, what you've learned during a lifetime of doing that sort of thing. You also must have imagination.

There are many elements that go into the making of a good golf course but, as I indicated earlier, probably the prime consideration is that it be a course that everybody, at all levels, can play and enjoy. Especially important is that the regular clientele, whether club members or public course customers, can enjoy playing it day after day and year after year.

Of course, that's not as easy as it sounds. Under any conditions and for any client we're probably going to build a golf course that is challenging to the professional and the low-handicap player. In the first place, the client wants that. The task then is to make that same course manageable for other players. We're going to do that, too, even if we're not directed to do it by the client.

There are members at clubs, or at resorts, or wherever golf courses are built, who object to so-called championship courses. They don't want length, they don't want "tricked-up hazards" and so forth. Sometimes we have the opposite problem, getting flack from the club champions or the better players who figure we're putting the bunkers in the wrong places, usually not far enough out

Trent Jones's sketches of the 3rd at Sotogrande and the 2nd again showing location of the traps and the ideal pin positions.

SOTO GRANDE   #2

to challenge them. These folks almost always figure they hit the ball as far as the professionals, and they don't. Which, incidentally, is one of the problems with amateur players. Few of them know how far they actually hit each club, from the driver to the wedge, which makes it very difficult for them to score as well as they might. The answer is to go to the range or a fairway in the evening with a caddie and accurately measure the average distance the ball flies and rolls with each. But not very many take the time to do that.

At any rate, to be callous about it, a golf course probably is going to be around a lot longer than the people now playing it, and circumstances change over the years. It doesn't cost any more to make a flexible course, one that all levels of golfers can find a way to play and enjoy. So that's what we're going to try to do.

It is easy to make a hole *too* difficult simply by building in trouble around the green that is too treacherous for the shot required, and the good architect will avoid that. The Road Hole, the 17th at St. Andrews, is an example. It is a par-4 that is 461 yards long. The tee shot must be directed over a corner of the Old Course Hotel, where the old railway sheds used to sit. That is not necessarily the problem, although the drive must be accurately placed to have any chance at the green.

The trouble lies with the second shot, usually with a long iron for the professionals and a wood for everybody else. It must avoid the dangerous Road Bunker nestled into the left side of the green, and into which the green slopes. But a shot that strays to the right will encounter the road and the wall that borders it, both of which are in play. Those hazards, which probably wouldn't be allowed anywhere in the world except at St. Andrews, have cost many a competitor the British Open Championship, including Tom Watson in 1984.

Occasionally they can be overcome. Francis Ouimet, with his ball lying a foot from the wall, once played a carom shot to within three feet of the hole to win a Walker Cup match. But normally only disaster awaits.

Originally the hole was a par-5, so a player would be comfortable laying up short and pitching for his par. If he went for the birdie with his second shot, it was at his own risk. Now that the hole is a par-4, he feels compelled to go for it, even though the risk is probably greater than the reward.

Tee placement combined with fairway design can make a hole flexible enough that players at all levels of strength and ability have a chance to play the hole approximately the same way. Let's take a par-4 of, say, 425 yards. That's not a particularly long hole for the professional or top amateur, who probably can reach it with a medium or short iron on his second shot. So in his drive zone, which would be 250 to 280 yards from the back tee, we might pinch in the fairway. Perhaps we would trap it on both sides, giving him the option of trying to drive the ball long and straight or laying up short of the bunkers with a fairway wood or long iron. This is not necessarily good design for most golfers, nor should it be done constantly even for the better player. Occasionally, though, it gives him something to think about.

Now we set up two or three more tee placements—one at 400 yards for the members' back tees, another at 375 yards for the members' front tees, and perhaps one at 350 or 325 yards for the front tees that can be used either by women or senior players. Now, just short of the professional's target zone, the fairway is widened to give everybody else a bigger area in which to hit the tee shot. There still may be bunkers, at least on one side—probably on the left, where they are more likely to catch the player who hooks the ball. On the right, where the slicer is more apt to go, we might put a grassy hollow instead of a sand bunker. Certainly there will be rough bordering the fairway, but there will be more margin for error. The average player should have a challenge, but it should not be as demanding as that given the professional.

Opposite: *Greensites sometimes are hard to find, as was the case with the 15th hole at Ballybunion New, a short par-5 that tumbles through the dunes. But once discovered, this site made the hole a marvelous one.*

Opposite top: *The placement of the cup on the 15th at Sotogrande, a difficult 426-yard par-4, can provide many different options for the player because of the four bunkers strategically surrounding the green. Opposite bottom: The fairway on the 15th at Pine Valley (bottom), a 603-yard par-5 from the back tees, narrows as it gets farther from the tee, posing added difficulty for the longer hitter.*

The same design will be applied to the second shot. The green itself should be well-guarded, but the fairway will open up short of the green to provide a layup area for those who don't want to risk bunkers or other hazards in a try for the putting surface. For everybody, then, the hole becomes a difficult par but an easy bogey.

With this type of design, the architect does two things—he defends par against the better player and he gives the poorer player a chance to enjoy himself too. The bogey golfer has a comfortable chance to make his "par" on the hole and, with an exceptionally good shot perhaps can make "birdie."

It's not all that cut-and-dried, of course. There are many higher handicap golfers who can hit the ball a long way. Their high handicaps are a result of other deficiencies, wildness usually, or a bad short game or whatever. So, within the confines of the land and the money available, you can't come up within a design that's going to fit every type of game. The golfer has to make some adaptations of his own to fit the course, which is what golf is all about.

One of the major problems for an architect is making a course completely flexible—that is, a challenge to the long-hitting professional or amateur and still playable, and challenging, for the player who does not hit the ball far at all. Sometimes this is the senior player, but in most cases it is the woman.

Alice Dye, the wife of Pete Dye, is a fine player and an architect in her own right. She has long contended that women deserve a better break on tee placement than they get. She has researched the subject extensively, and she says that the average woman has a handicap of 31 and can carry the ball about 130 yards off the tee. This might not have been so bad in the days before fairways were so heavily watered. Then the ball would roll 33 percent of the shot, which means a 150-yard carry would roll to 200 yards. Now, with the softer conditions that extensive irrigation systems have brought, that same drive would roll zero to 13 percent, meaning it would go a maximum of 165 yards. (That same statistic, Alice points out, also applies to men.) Thus the holes that might once have been fair for the average woman now are unreachable.

Basically, within the guidelines for par established by the USGA, it is difficult if not impossible for most women to play a hole in regulation. A par-4 hole can be up to 400 yards long for women. If Alice is right, and I'm sure she is, the majority of women cannot get home in two on a hole that long.

The answer, Alice says, is to move the women's tees drastically forward. Let the average woman drive the ball to a point farther down the fairway than the good male player would drive it. She suggests that par-3 holes for women be 90 to 150 yards in length (the latter only if there is an entrance through which the ball can be rolled onto the green), that par-4s be 240 to 340 yards and par-5s 420 to 500, which can be reached in no more than four shots by most women. This would seem to be the simplest solution. At that point, however, other problems can arise. Bunkers or water meant for the better player could cut into play for the woman, for instance.

Unfortunately, the trapping on many of the older golf courses has been outmoded today by the increased length of the ball, better club technology and the increased strength and skill of the better player, so it is badly placed. The location of many bunkers makes them much more punishing for the average to high handicap player, and especially for the woman, than for the professional or top amateur. So the distance from the tee at which fairway bunkers are located becomes a critical factor.

It's easy to set up a golf hole and a golf course for the professionals in this manner. But setting it up for the professional, the average club member, the senior player and the woman player at the same time is another matter. Flexibility in the tee placement would seem to solve the problem, but it really doesn't. Place the bunkers for strong players and sometimes the women can't get over

them on their second shots. String multiple bunkers along the fairway's edge and the women then are playing the same hole as the better men. Often there is no total solution, no way to accommodate all classes of golfers. But the conscientious architect will devote careful attention to achieving the best possible compromise.

Another problem is that—although I have no research to verify this—there probably is a greater disparity in distance among women of different abilities than there is among men at comparable levels. So if you drastically reduce the length of the course for all women, you probably will be making it too short and uninteresting for the better player who might be able to drive the ball 200 yards or more and hit her other clubs comparable distances.

One answer to the dilemma is multiple tees for women. Build at least two, as we do for men, or make one tee long enough to serve more classes of golfers. This means the club or developer must be willing to bear the cost of construction and the architect must take pains to properly design the placement of the additional tees. That can be done, with some care, in planning a new course. Remodeling or adding tees to an existing layout and making them fit the design could be a lot more difficult.

At this point, however, we run into an interesting phenomenon. Many women, maybe most of them, like their golf courses just the way they are. They don't necessarily want the course made easier or fairer for them. Maybe it's because hitting a green in regulation is foreign to most women players. It's an occasion when they do it, and they enjoy that. They don't mind that they don't do it regularly. If you make it physically possible for them to do it all the time, some of them don't really want it.

Maybe they don't want to change what they're used to. Or maybe it's just the challenge, the same reason, subconscious or not, that we all play the game. If you made it easier, it wouldn't be as much fun.

Architects have different philosophies on how courses should be designed and the game should be played. That's good. If they didn't, every course certainly would play the same even if it didn't look the same. But any philosophy can be carried to extreme. Jack Nicklaus believes, or at least he did at one stage of his design career, that all courses should play downhill, or appear as if they did. Ben Hogan felt the same way. When he and Joe Lee designed the Trophy Club outside of Fort Worth, Ben's his only serious attempt at golf course architecture, he tried to get every green below the elevation of the tee or the drive zone.

You can't do that. Invariably, when you go downhill you must, at some point, go back uphill. As I said earlier, MacKenzie did a marvelous job of this at Augusta. Ideally you would like to see the green and even be able to see where the flag is on the green, although that doesn't always work either. But I think uphill shots and shots to elevated greens are wonderful, an integral part of the game and its variety.

There has been an ongoing argument, through the centuries, I guess, on whether golf is an air or a ground game. In truth, it is both, depending a lot on a player's skill and especially on the nature of the course on which he is playing.

I don't believe there should always be an opening to the green so the ball can be rolled on. Variety is the key. Some holes, especially the shorter ones, should require a carry over water or sand or to an elevated green. And on the holes on which the ball can be rolled onto the green, you must create problems with the contours on the putting surface. That was done on the old links courses—the player might be able to bounce or roll a shot onto the green, but getting it close to the cup with that method often was extremely difficult. Tillinghast did that on most of his courses—Winged Foot is an excellent exam-

Opposite: *Multiple tees on the 13th at Medinah, a par-3 over water, make it testing but playable for the longest and shortest hitters.*

ple. There are openings to most greens through which you can roll the ball, but because of the placement of the openings and the contouring of the greens, getting it close is a problem.

That's why the theory that golf is an air game in the United States and a ground game on the links courses is semi-myth. Even on the links, and even in the old days, the better golfer played the ball in the air a lot of the time. He had to because of the uncertainty of the bounces and, in many cases, to have any chance at all of getting the ball close enough for a one-putt.

There is no question that American golf is *more* of an air game. It has to be because of the heavier watering and subsequently softer fairways in the U.S. Bouncing and rolling the ball onto the green, even if there is an opening, is very chancy under those conditions. In Britain and other parts of the world, because the turf is dryer, firmer and faster, that method works better, especially for the less-skilled player. Sometimes it's even preferable for the expert, because the firmness of the greens makes it difficult to stop a pitch shot.

The advancements in equipment and changes in the golf swing also have contributed to golf being played more in the air everywhere in the world than in the early centuries. The original wooden-shafted clubs, combined with the flatter swings and the body sway employed back then, tended to sweep the ball away low with a lot of roll. Now, with stiffer shafts of steel, titanium, graphite and God knows what else, combined with high-tech balls, the shots go higher. The so-called modern, more upright swing contributes further to this. So now the ball is in the air longer and doesn't roll as far.

All of this, of course, means that the architect has to tailor the design of his courses to better accommodate—or better confound—the players who are doing it differently than Old Tom Morris and that gang.

Another ongoing debate is over the use of deception on a course. I happen to be firmly in favor of it, as long as it is not overused and as long as it is fair. I don't like blind shots, although as I said earlier, the fact that you can't see the green from the tee does not necessarily make it a blind hole.

Deception is not an undesirable quality in a golf courses. It creates another element of trouble for the player, without which the game would not be very challenging. The architect designs trouble into a hole for a specific purpose, to force the player to make decisions based on his ability, his frame of mind at the time and perhaps the status of his round or match. The options may be subtle, not easily seen or perceived. But the choices are there if the player takes a moment to ponder them. If there aren't decisions to be made on a hole, it isn't a very good hole.

Dogleg holes, those that bend to the right or left, are important in the overall strategic design of a course and also offer the architect a grand opportunity to practice deception. They can be either par-4s or par-5s. In either case, they force the golfer to think, to take either the strategic route, which makes him plan the best place to place his tee shot, or the heroic route over a bunker or lake or trees at the corner of the dogleg. In the latter case, the element of risk versus reward now comes strongly into play.

By skillfully designing the turn of the hole, the architect can make it appear that the shot must go in a certain direction—closely skirting the corner or bending it around the corner, for example—when in reality a straight shot down the fairway would get the ball just as close to the green.

That kind of deception, of course, is eliminated by knowledge. The second time you play the hole you should know better. Deception in general has been eliminated to a great extent by the modern practice of installing yardage markers every fifty yards. The architect still can create illusions by contours and swales in fairways and by the placement of his bunkers—a "greenside" bunker

Opposite: *The 17th at The Country Club, doglegging around two bunkers, provides options for players of various strengths.*

175

that actually is thirty yards in front of the putting surface can fool the player. But if the golfer knows exactly how many yards he has to the center of the green, the illusions are easier to overcome in his mind and lose much of their effectiveness. It's too bad, too, because I think that has taken some of the charm out of the game. "Eyeballing" the distance used to be a skill at which the Ben Hogans and Byron Nelsons and Sam Sneads of the world were adept. Now all the player has to do is look at his yardage book.

Yardage markers do, however, speed up play for the average golfer, so maybe in this day and age of crowded courses you have to give up something to gain something else.

Which, of course, brings up another couple of design elements that *should* be strongly considered but often are ignored by architects bent on building holes and courses that photograph beautifully but can be extremely difficult if not unplayable for most golfers. Difficult or unplayable translates into *time-consuming*. It also often translates into much higher maintenance costs.

Frankly, we don't think much about future maintenance costs when we're designing, because we normally shape and grade a course as naturally as possible, which makes maintenance easier. It seems the more artificial a course is, the more mounds and cones and sharp edges there are, the more difficult and costly it is to maintain.

These same factors, plus the incursion of too much water in too many areas of play, also contribute greatly to slow play. This is especially true at resort courses, where the players almost always are unfamiliar with the layout and quite often are higher handicappers. At many of these around the country the player spends six hours or so losing balls in the water, hacking out of grass-covered mounds and generally having a tough time. Somehow I can't envision spending that much time under those conditions and enjoying it much.

I'm not saying courses should not be difficult or beautiful or strikingly different. You want the player to feel that he or she is on a golf course, not playing through a bunch of housing lots. But a course can be all those things and playable, in brisk fashion, at the same time.

I have been accused of making all my courses look alike. I guess that's a compliment of sorts—Tillinghast, Ross and a lot of others all have readily identifiable styles. But the fact is, all of their courses do not look alike, nor do mine. If people want to criticize, that's their right. But if that's all they can say, they'd better study up on golf course design. Does Spyglass Hill look like Firestone? Does Peachtree look like Ballybunion New? Does Mauna Kea look like Sotogrande or The Dunes? Do any of them look like any other? The answer, of course, is no. My courses do have certain characteristics, which is true of any architect. But, as I have said repeatedly, the land dictates the holes and the look of a course. If the land is different, the course is going to look different.

I'm a great believer in variety, in not copying or mimicking in the design of holes and courses. Naturally we all are influenced by great holes and great courses, and consciously or subconsciously we incorporate some of their features into our designs. But that doesn't mean we turn out cookie-cutter courses.

All kinds of tools are available to the architect to produce varied designs— the green itself with its many variations in size, elevation, pockets and folds; the different kinds of bunkers and their location; water or the absence of water; trees or the lack of trees; the length of the hole, the lengths of the different shots; the terrain itself, of course. It's especially easy for me and any architect who can sketch to take advantage of these tools. I can do hundreds of sketches during the preliminary stages, turning a green one way, angling it slightly another way, changing the contours, altering the hole routing, fiddling with the bunkering. All of this can and does result in great variety and a lot of different looks without the expense of first building, then tearing down or making costly alterations.

Climatic conditions, especially prevailing winds, must be considered in laying out a course and determining the length of the holes. If the wind blows fairly consistently from one direction, for example, you certainly don't want to build a 460-yard par-4 into the teeth of it, unless you provide a great deal of tee flexibility. Nor do you want to build a 340-yard hole downwind that might be easily driven by the bigger hitters.

Elevation and the density of the air also are factors to be accounted for. The ball goes farther in Chicago than it does at sea level, and it goes even farther in the Rocky Mountains. The typical firmness and dryness of the indigenous turf also is a factor, as are the prevailing winds. It makes it tricky for the architect. In Denver or higher, a 7,400-yard course will play like one of 6,700 or 6,800 at sea level.

In designing courses in the mountains, especially the Rockies and other lofty areas, the architect also must consider the effect of the thin air on the player. I learned that in remodeling the Broadmoor courses in Colorado, one nine in 1954 and another in 1965. I became a good friend to Bud Maytag of the Maytag Company and a long-time Iowa champion, and we played a lot at the Broadmoor. I remember that the walk up to the sixth tee just puffed us out. I guess people don't walk so much anymore, but you have to remember not to make any long, steep climbs in the rarefied mountain atmosphere. In fact, recalling my experience with Thomas Watson on the IBM course, I guess you shouldn't do it anywhere.

In general, holes that play uphill should be held to a minimum in mountainous terrain. That's another reason, other than construction considerations, to build mountain courses in valleys whenever possible. Steep slopes and large rock formations are less of a factor there.

Kananaskis in Alberta, Canada, provides an example of the care that must be taken in choosing the site for a mountain course. When we first discussed doing the course, the province officials already had decided where they wanted it—basically on the side of a mountain. I pointed out that, in the first place, if it were located there nobody could play until 10 in the morning because there would be frost on the greens and the sun wouldn't get to it until then. Secondly, it was very rocky terrain. I suggested instead moving the site to a nearby river valley, where we could build two courses instead of one. They agreed, and we did, producing two scenic layouts with great shot values as well. That move also gave them a plateau some 200 or 300 feet up on which they could build a hotel, looking right down on the courses and ideally located for an adjacent ski area.

Ingenuity is a major requirement in building courses in the mountains. This is where the inept architect often is found out. The architect's plan must suggest the ruggedness of the setting, but in a passive rather than an active sense. Blind holes should be avoided. One bonus that is almost always found in mountains is water, usually in the form of rushing streams. These give the architect a natural hazard, beautiful, interesting and a challenge to the player, that can be incorporated into the design.

Incline Village, which we built at Lake Tahoe in California, is an example of the ideal mountain course. It is a beautiful layout cut through Ponderosa pines on mountain slopes 500 feet above Lake Tahoe, which itself is a mile high. Except for the doglegs, there isn't a hole that can't be seen from tee to green. Three of the first five holes on the back nine run slightly uphill, but the rest of the course is downhill or level. And there is a fast-moving stream that poses a strategic hazard on a dozen holes.

Water running all along the left of the 5th at Mid-Ocean in Bermuda and the slight dogleg shape of the hole give the player an opportunity to bite off as much as he chooses, the reward being a shorter shot to the green and the risk being a wet ball.

The ultimate test of a mountain course should be its shotmaking requirements, not the physical demands it imposes on a player, no matter how hard the architect has to work to achieve this.

Of course, that's a yardstick that can be applied to any course, regardless of location.

On interesting terrain, such as mountains and valleys, designing is fun, difficult though it may be. It's on flat, ugly land that the creativity of an architect comes out. Almost anybody can design a course on flat land, but designing a good one is another matter. Now the architect has to work hard at it. That happens a lot, especially in Florida. At Coral Ridge, our course in Fort Lauderdale that I designed in 1956, I was working with dead-flat land. I created lakes, digging them out and using the material to elevate the tees and the greens. By doing that, and by properly mounding and shaping the bunkers, I created the impression that the course is rolling, even though it really isn't.

And after you finish working at the task and produce what you feel is an interesting and challenging course, that becomes fun, too.

Remodeling a golf course can be a tough business. There are a lot of holes and a lot of courses that should be preserved, because they are indeed classics. Cypress Point, for example, might be one of them. Yet even Alister MacKenzie changed the course plan drastically even before he built it. The fabled 16th, the 233-yard par-3, originally was sketched as a par-4, and who is to say it perhaps should not be that now with some tee alteration?

I have some qualms about changing the work of great architects who are dead and unable to defend themselves. In my opinion, the greens Bobby Jones worked on personally at Augusta should not have been changed without his permission and acceptance. Maybe I feel this way because I wouldn't want any of my courses changed after I'm gone.

Still, as a practical matter, I know that eventually some of my courses that I consider masterpieces (we all think of our work that way) will be remodeled in the years to come, just as I have spent a good part of my career remodeling the works of other architects, some of them great ones. There is very little done in this world that can't be improved. Advancements in technology (which made it necessary to remodel Donald Ross's Oakland Hills course and many others), new ideas and techniques, the passage of time itself eventually dictate change in almost everything. The Mona Lisa will never be altered, of course, but she wouldn't win the Miss America contest today.

Sometimes the architect simply must go in and redo a bad course, plowing it up if need be and starting over if that is the client's wish. But this has seldom been the case with the remodeling work I have done. Since I worked on Oakland Hills, I have been called on to touch up great courses, usually those that have been chosen as major championship sites. Obviously they are great courses to begin with. The key in these cases, then, is to preserve the architectural philosophy of the original designer, the shot values he intended for the hole, while bringing the course up to modern standards. Of course I did not alter the basic design of Donald Ross's greens. I hope I improved some of them, but I would not for a moment have changed the character of them, because they were uniquely his and uniquely great. Nor have I tried to change the character of any great course I have been asked to remodel.

In that regard, however, there often are problems. The desire of the client, or the members, or whomever, to "preserve the character" of a course or a hole can create controversy and cause problems for the architect when there isn't much character there to begin with.

As Ross himself admitted, too many courses were built under his name that didn't exactly emulate his style. But if it's a "Ross course," most members or owners are adamantly against too-drastic changes, even if they are much for the better.

An equally ticklish situation often occurs when changes have been made over the years. Trees have been planted, bunkers have been removed or added, and the character of design has been gradually but substantially altered. Now the members or owners want to preserve the character of a course that little resembles what the architect originally built.

My work at Oakland Hills for the 1951 Open is an example of how a course can be remodeled to accommodate all types of players and still maintain the integrity of the original architect's design. Designed by Ross in 1917, the course had played host to the Open twice before. In 1924 Cyril Walker won with a score of 297, nine over par. In 1937, playing relatively the same course, Ralph Guldahl was the winner at 281, seven under par and, at the time, an Open record.

The difference is indicative of the great improvement made during that thirteen-year span in the skills of the players and, perhaps more important, the technological advantages stemming from the change from Walker's wooden shafts to the steel ones employed by Guldahl. The invention of the sand wedge by Gene Sarazen and the change to the larger, easier-to-control ball in the interim also contributed greatly to improved scoring.

As a result, a great golf course lay virtually defenseless. Oakland Hills' fairway bunkers were deployed 200 to 220 yards off the tee. Studies I had done in previous Opens told me that the better golfers now were carrying the ball an average of 236 yards with a driver and were getting rolls of up to thirty-five yards more. Obviously, the bunkers posed no threat to these players.

My changes were simply to relocate the fairway bunkers, installing new ones in the 230- to 270-yard range. Some of these were steep-faced clusters that bracketed the fairways on holes other than the par-3s, forcing the player to be accurate off the tee or suffer the consequences. I also increased the number of greenside bunkers to restrict unprotected entrance areas and to provide a variety of hole locations that would pose a true championship examination.

Fortunately, Ross's great greens, with their crowns, swales, terraces and slopes, were large enough and needed little revamping, except for the installation of a tongue area here and there.

The biggest change came at the 16th hole, heretofore a straightaway 350-yard par-4 where the second shot had to carry about seventy-five yards over a pond. I changed the fairway routing and built a new green, transforming the hole into a right-angle dogleg of 409 yards that required a carry of 140 yards over the pond to a peninsula green, the right half of which jutted into the water. In 1965 the 16th was selected by *Sports Illustrated* magazine as one of the best eighteen holes in America. In 1972 the hole was the scene of Gary Player's "miracle" second shot from the rough, over trees to within three feet of the hole. He made the putt for birdie and won the PGA Championship. It was a historic shot, fittingly made on a great hole.

The result in 1951 was a course of 6,927, playing to a realistic par of 70. But there was no "tricking up" of the golf course. My changes simply forced the professional to make decisions. If he used the driver off the tee, thus gaining a shorter and easier shot to the green, he had to hit it straight. If he laid up short of the bunkers, he was faced with a longer, much more difficult shot into a tough target area.

And did the pros howl! Only two players broke par during the championship—Ben Hogan shot 67 and Clayton Heafner 69 during the final round on Saturday afternoon. Hogan, who had played cautiously in the three previous rounds, went out and attacked the course for the final eighteen. As a result, he won the Open with a seven-over-par total of 287 and promptly issued his famous remark that he had "brought this monster to its knees." It has remained "The Monster" ever since, an appellation that may or may not be justified.

That also led to the remark that Hogan made to my wife, Ione, that is recounted in Peter Dobereiner's foreword to this book—that if I had to play my own courses for a living, I would be in the bread line.

Well, I haven't yet had to resort to the bread line, and Hogan never did concede that it was a good course, but he later admitted that he might have won more Opens had he been able to play them on more Trent Jones courses. To me, that's the ultimate compliment. Hogan's victory at Oakland Hills confirmed my opinion that only a great player can win on a great golf course . . . and I suspect that deep in his heart Hogan feels the same way.

There is no better example of how an ordinary par-4 can be made into a great one than at Augusta National, where I remodeled the 11th hole in 1950. At the time, it was a drive-and-pitch hole. The tee was just above the 10th green and the hole doglegged to the right. A big hitter could slice the ball around the corner and get it almost to the green. It was really an inadequate hole for the length the professionals were driving the ball.

So I went down into the woods on the other side of the 10th green and immediately saw how I could make the hole better. Set the tee back forty or fifty yards into the woods and make the player drive uphill through a chute of trees. Then dam the creek that ran by the left side of the green to make a small lake. Then it would be a great hole. So that's what we did, and we came up with a hole that scares the hell out of the pros during the Masters. It now plays to 445 yards and usually requires a medium- to long-iron second to the green. When the pin is set on the left side, nobody goes for it. Ben Hogan once remarked that if you ever saw him any place other than the right side, you'd know he missed the shot.

The remodeling job wasn't without problems, incidentally. Bob Jones didn't want to do it. But Clifford Roberts did, not only because it would dramatically improve the hole but also because it would relieve the gallery congestion around the 10th green and old 11th tee. And Roberts won out. Then he and I got into a brouhaha, because I wanted to take out a big tree about thirty yards in front of the new tee and he didn't want to. He was madder than hell, but I won that one.

Equally effective in creating a dramatic hole was our redesign of the par-3 16th in 1947. Originally the hole required simply a short-iron shot across a creek, played from alternate tees on either side of the 15th green. Bob Jones wanted a long par-3 that required a carry over a pond, so that's what we did. We dammed the creek to create the pond, which runs from the front of the tee all the way to the front and left of the green. We abandoned the old green and built a new, bean-shaped green, terraced at the back and right and sloping from right to left toward the water. The right-hand tee was eliminated. The left tee was moved and extended so the new hole would play at about 190 yards from the back. Two bunkers were built on the right side of the green, and the next year a bunker was added on the left and the green was extended behind it to provide another pin placement.

There is room to bail out on the right side of the hole, but any player going for the green must risk finding the water if the shot is just slightly short or left. The combination of the water and the green contours has provided some of the Masters' most thrilling moments in the years since.

We also had some trouble building this one, although this time the cause was nature, not Clifford Roberts. One day, as we were excavating to create the lake, using the fill to build and shape the green, it started to rain. The bulldozer operator left his machine in the hole he was digging, and we all went into the woods and got in the car to stay dry. Well, it rained hard for about an hour, and when we returned the lake had filled up right over the bulldozer. We had to wait until the water went down before we could get the machine out of there.

My trouble with Roberts came after the hole was finished. He told the public that Bob Jones, not Trent, had done the remodeling, that I had nothing to do with it. Well, Bob certainly had input, but the design was mine. It wasn't until Roberts wrote his book that he conceded my contribution.

Sometimes remodeling a course takes the form of a restoration. My son Rees was involved in such a project at The Country Club in Brookline, Massachusetts, prior to the 1988 U.S. Open. The course came into being in 1893 and represents an amalgam of architectural input since then. As with most old courses, the characteristics had been altered over the decades. The green sizes and outlines had changed, a not-uncommon occurrence with any course, and three of the greens had been totally rebuilt and were out of character with the rest of the course. This is one of the serious problems that happen when redesign is done by club committee rather than a professional architect.

Rees used old photographs to rebuild those greens and to expand other greens and alter their positions so they would look and play as they had in the early part of the century. He restored and rebuilt old bunkers, eliminated other bunkers, recontoured fairways and added the old chocolate drop moundings. All of this was designed to re-establish the original character of the course as nearly as he could determine it.

Rees also did extensive testing to insure that the soil mix in the new greens was the same as in the others, so that all would have the same feel and firmness.

Much other work was done on tees, rough and fairways, of course, but the basic principle remained the same. In Rees's words, "We took it back in style, not in design."

The result was that the competitors in the '88 Open loved the golf course, proclaiming it one of the best and fairest they had ever played in that championship. They all seemed to enjoy it, and fairness and the quality of enjoyment, as I said earlier, is one of the trademarks of a Rees Jones work.

It is an example of a remodeling, or restoration, if you will, that was done with integrity and without an architect's ego getting in the way.

As with anyone else whose work goes on public display, an architect is subject to criticism. Sometimes it is deserved. But critics of golf courses too often make snap judgments. This, more than anything else, upsets architects. Few people realize what goes into the designing and building of a golf course—all the money that was spent, all the work that was done, the blood, sweat and tears, if you will, all the people involved with it trying to do the best they could. Then some 6-handicapper who sells insurance for a living comes out and spends four hours on the course and pronounces it a piece of junk.

If you look hard enough, you can find something wrong with almost any course. Cypress Point has a relatively weak finishing hole. So does Royal Portrush. Royal County Down finishes with ordinary holes, including the 17th with a stupid pond right in the middle of it. Prestwick has some crazy holes, including a blind par-3 and a nothing finishing hole. At Yale, it appears C. B. Macdonald got caught out on the course after finishing seventeen holes and had to get back to the clubhouse. The 18th is a long and, shall we say, rather unusual finisher, a par-5 that demands a second-shot carry over a small mountain. In defense of Macdonald, however, I must say that his work was done before the days of bulldozers that could level every obstacle in site. Besides, as my son Bobby says, it was a great hole on which to settle matches.

Yet nobody calls any of these bad courses. Indeed, they all are considered great courses. And they are fun to play, which is the most important consideration of all.

Length often becomes a criterion in judging the worth of a course. I've been as guilty, if that's the word, as anybody of building long courses. I guess that's because I usually have the professionals in mind, and there must be length in a course to properly test them. But I also feel I build flexibility into my courses by effectively shortening them with multiple tee placements.

The point is, many great courses are overlooked and suffer by comparison because they are "too short to hold the U.S. Open." What nonsense! I can name dozens of marvelous courses in the 6,400- to 6,600-yard range—Maidstone on Long Island, San Francisco Golf, Somerset Hills in New Jersey, Pine Valley, Harbour Town on Hilton Head Island, Chicago Golf, Baltimore Country Club at Five Farms, Cascades in Virginia, Kittansett in Massachusetts come quickly to mind.

Maidstone, down the road from National Golf Links and Shinnecock Hills (site of the 1986 U.S. Open), measures slightly more than 6,300 yards, yet it may be the best of the three if pure enjoyment is the criterion. And it should be for everybody who never competes in a U.S. Open. And even for those who do.

Perhaps there should be less emphasis on lists of "great courses" and on "toughness." Challenge is one thing. Extreme difficulty is quite another. Unfortunately, nobody likes to think his course can be taken apart by anybody, and that too often becomes the measuring stick by which courses are designed.

It becomes a matter of perspective, or at least it should, which is why the mature architect can shrug off criticism. Those who criticize a course for whatever reason should remember the one wonderful thing about golf and every golf course in the world—whatever the shortcomings of a course, a lot of folks are out there playing it and having a good time.

PART
2

Chapter 5
Off the Tee and Beyond

All roads lead to the green. But just as every journey has a beginning, a middle and an end, so does every golf hole. The green may be the most important element, but getting there is certainly more than half the fun and half the battle if the architect has done his job. The way he designs the teeing areas and the fairways and their surroundings determines the playability and flexibility of the hole and the course, as well as a great deal of its beauty. In this chapter, let's look at those elements—the tee, the fairway, the surrounding rough and trees. Water and bunkers will be examined in the following chapter.

Throughout history one of the most overlooked elements of the golf course has been the tee. In the very early days of golf players simply moved the ball a club length from the hole they had just finished, teed it up and went on. Even when tees became formal components of the course, architects traditionally built them square or rectangular and usually quite small, so the hole basically played to one distance and one way. Only in recent years has that practice changed perceptibly. I like to think I contributed to that change, which has added a great deal of flexibility to courses.

When we were designing Peachtree in Atlanta just after the war, I said to Bob Jones, "Look, the only way you can have a championship golf course and a course that is still comfortable for the membership is to create flexibility in the tees. That way the average golfer will arrive in the same target area as the better player or even ahead of him. He may still have to use a longer club than the better player, but at least he now has a chance to reach the green with his second shot. From the championship tee, he wouldn't have a prayer."

So we built tees at Peachtree that average almost ninety yards in length, with four sets of markers. And we have continued to follow that principle ever since, with some modifications.

Shortly after Peachtree had opened, Bob Woodruff, then the president of Coca Cola, approached me in the locker room and asked, "Trent, how many more shots would I take if I played one day from the front of the tees and the next day from the back?"

I knew that he normally shot between 95 and 100, and I knew he was talking about a difference in overall length from 5,700 to 7,400 yards, so I told him twenty-five shots. I was back at Peachtree about three weeks later and Woodruff came up to me in the locker room and said, "You were right. I took twenty-six more shots from the back of the tees than I did from the front."

That's an example of how tee placement can change the difficulty and playability of a golf course.

Early on I discovered one problem with the concept of extremely long tees. After building them at Peachtree, we did the same at Coral Ridge, my course in Fort Lauderdale, Florida, and at Dorado Beach in Puerto Rico for Laurance Rockefeller. One long tee makes sense from a maintenance standpoint, because it can be cut very easily by a man on a mower. But it does some damage to a player's psyche.

I was playing one day at Dorado Beach with Rockefeller, who went to the front of a tee, put his ball on a peg and said to me, "Trent, why do you make these tees so long? I get up here at the front and I feel like a sissy."

I knew immediately I had to do something, so at most of our courses after

Opposite: *Castle Pines Golf Club, home of The International, is a strong and spectacular course carved out of the mountains and valleys near Denver, Colorado, by Jack Nicklaus. The first hole here is a heroic 644-yard par-5 starting from an elevated tee.*

that, instead of having one long tee, I broke it up into four or five separate tees. Then the player who wants to play from the front or middle tee doesn't even know the tiger tees are back there.

Breaking up a tee into individual areas has the added advantage of increasing both the flexibility of a hole and the beauty of a teeing ground. Obviously you want to position the tees back to front to change the length of the hole for the different classes of golfers. You also can position them from side to side to change the angle of the hole and the way it plays. For example, moving a tee just ten or fifteen yards to one side or the other can change a hole from straightaway to a dogleg. You can bring a fairway bunker more directly into play for the better player using the back tee, or you can take it more out of line for the higher handicapper playing from the shorter tees. And if there happen to be existing trees in the teeing area, the architect can take advantage of them to change the playability of the hole even further.

Instead of the square or rectangle, now we try for free-form designs wherever possible. This adds to the interest and beauty of the teeing area and increases the flexibility of the hole from any given tee. By moving the markers from one side to the other, front and back, the look of a hole and sometimes even the way it plays can be changed.

This also avoids the problem of square or rectangular tees that are built askew to the line of play, a common occurrence in the past. Too often players would use the front and sides of the tee to help them line up their shots without realizing that the tee actually was pointing them into the woods.

A free-form tee seldom provides an alignment aid, but its very nature makes the thoughtful player aware that he must be more careful with his aim and be sure not to use the tee markers for that same purpose. Often the man setting the blocks is careless in aligning them correctly.

Considering the increase in play on golf courses today, the architect must give considerable thought to the size of his tees. The forward tees, because they get so much use, must be made bigger, especially wider, so they can be maintained properly. The back tees, used only by the better players who are fewer in number, can be smaller. But they should not be so small as to be uninteresting or to inhibit the flexibility I mentioned earlier.

Elevation of the teeing areas can be critical in the design of a hole, although this usually depends on the nature of the land. On dead-flat ground we build up the tees slightly to provide better visibility, although we seldom change the elevation dramatically because of the additional expense.

Where the land allows it, however, varying the placement and thus the relative elevation of the tees can do much to enhance the beauty and excitement of the hole. Especially on rugged terrain, the more elevated the tee the more beautiful the hole becomes. There is a par-3 at Treetops Golf Club, the course we built in Gaylord, Michigan, that is only about 140 yards long but has a 120-foot drop from tee to green. From the tee you can see thousands of trees in the background, and in the fall the foliage is gorgeous. My son Bob designed a hole like that at Beaver Creek in Vail, Colorado, and one similar but longer at Sugarloaf in Carrabassett Valley, Maine. The views are spectacular, and that kind of beauty is important to a golf course.

The differences in elevation also are critical to the play of a hole. Playing a 140-yard shot from 120 feet up is a lot different than playing it from green level, especially if you are seeing the hole for the first time. Firing the ball into the air and waiting to see where it will come down is . . . well, interesting. Even if you know what club to hit after several trips around the course, the wind from that height can affect a shot quite dramatically.

Where water, especially large lakes or the ocean, is involved, astute placement of the tee areas can greatly enhance the appeal of the course and can dramatically influence the playability of a hole. This is particularly true at seaside, where the wind comes more strongly into play.

Fairways should range from perhaps forty yards in width, which is wide, to thirty yards or maybe slightly less in the case of short holes. The terrain, hole routing and the amount of penalty you want to place on an errant shot all have to do with determining width.

Like greens, fairways should have contour—they should have tilts and slopes and undulations, mounds and swales. In the first place, like a green, a dead-flat fairway would be terribly uninteresting, both from an aesthetic and a playing standpoint. The good architect not only will give his fairways curve—there are no straight lines in nature—but he will make them flow and roll. Here again, we are imitating the original links, where the dunesland provides natural undulations that are appealing to the eye.

Further, contours in the fairways put an additional premium on a player's skills. It is much easier to strike a good shot from a level lie than from a slope. So you can create problems for players by the way you contour the fairways, and you can do it selectively. In the normal target area for the better player you might install undulations that seldom if ever give him a flat lie. In the zone where the higher handicap player would be likely to end up, you can soften your contours, although again you won't make it flat, because that level of player wants and should have some challenge too.

It is important, of course, that you don't repeat your contouring and the problems you are creating on the various holes. That becomes boring. The skillful architect will use his imagination to vary his contouring, enhancing the attractiveness of the course and multiplying the trouble for the player, thus requiring him to use a greater range of shotmaking skills.

Oakland Hills is a rolling course with marvelous contours and few flat spots to be found. There is a story that in the 1951 U.S. Open Ben Hogan's fellow competitor in the first two rounds said, "The first day I thought Hogan was the luckiest man I'd ever seen. I'm playing uphill, downhill and sidehill shots all day, and every one of his second shots is from a level lie. On the second day, I realized he was playing his shots from exactly the same spots as the day before." The story is perhaps apocryphal, but it is indicative of Hogan's ability to map out a course and his skill at making shots. It is difficult for the architect to defend against that kind of ability, nor should he want to. That's what the game is all about.

If the land available is flat and uninteresting, then you must create contours with a bulldozer. That's where Pete Dye is so good and imaginative. He moves a lot of dirt, but he turns wastelands into art.

On the other hand, if you are working with rolling or hilly or even mountainous terrain, your slopes are usually there for you. Some modifying and contouring might have to be done, but the major task is to route the holes to take advantage of the terrain. Slopes and rolls always have a major impact on shot values, so this must be taken into consideration in the design of each hole and in determining the overall playing value of the course. It adds another dimension, a good one, to the game. The architect simply must be able to incorporate that dimension into his plan. It gives the course that elusive quality called character.

The architect can and should direct the way a hole is played by where and how he utilizes slopes, swales and mounds, but he should always be fair about it. For example, if a hole doglegs to the right, with a lake or creek on the right side, a fairway that slopes steeply from left to right could be unfair. One answer might be to soften the slope a little and install a trough down the right side of the fairway that would catch balls rolling toward the water. The hole would still be challenging but not unplayable.

There might be other answers to that same problem. There is really no formula for dealing with or creating undulations. We don't always slope a fairway with or against a dogleg, for example. We do it different ways at different times, for different reasons. It's part of the variety we're trying to build into a course. We're trying to force the player to stand on the tee and make a judgment, devise a strategy for playing that particular hole. And we want that strategy to have to be different on as many holes as possible through the round.

Sometimes mounding and contouring can be overdone. I am not particularly in favor of "chocolate drops" or mounds that are supposedly built for aesthetic reasons. They usually look artificial and often they unfairly interfere with play. Nor do I like mounds or bumps in places that tend to kick a fairly struck shot off line and into trouble. I believe in deceiving the player, but that's the cheap and easy way to do it.

Natural slopes also can be unfair, or can be unfairly used. An excellent example is the 17th hole at The Olympic Club as it was played in the 1987 U.S. Open. The hole was a 428-yard par-4 with an uphill tee shot to a landing area that sloped sharply from left to right. The hill was so steep and the fairway grass was cut so short that virtually every drive, even those hit to the left side, would roll down the slope and into the right-hand rough. That made a long, difficult second shot even harder. This is a trick design and unfair to the player who strikes a good tee shot.

The trouble with the hole is that it was never designed as a par-4. The membership plays it as a 522-yard par-5 from a tee almost 100 yards back in the woods. For them the drive is to a flatter, more receptive area, and they have two shots left to get home. Played like that, it is an excellent hole.

This is an example of man messing with nature. Man rarely wins when he tries to fight the natural flow instead of using it correctly.

Rough is the most ubiquitous hazard because it lies almost everywhere off the fairway. And while rough is cursed throughout the world, few players realize that it also is tremendously important in adding an element of beauty to most courses. Rough frames the fairways and the green areas, and the result is like a beautiful painting.

How rough should the rough be? How high should it be? That depends, of course, on what's happening at a particular golf course. If the U.S. Open is being conducted there that week, you know the primary rough is going to be four inches high with a secondary cut just off the fairway at probably two inches. If instead this is a busy public course where it is important to get the players around in good time, the rough should be cut relatively short—high enough to create some difficulty for the player but not so high that it is hard to find balls hit into it.

Most courses, during most of the year, fall somewhere between those two extremes, so the rough should be cut accordingly. The USGA feels that, ideally, rough should invoke a half-stroke penalty on the player who finds it. He should be able to get out of it but should have difficulty controlling the ball. I basically agree with that philosophy, although I'm not sure how you determine half a stroke. I think rough should allow you to get the ball close to the green but not necessarily on it. Rough should prevent you from putting enough spin on the ball that you can fly it to the green and have it hold when it lands. Rough should be of a consistency that will allow the strong player who makes a super shot to get the ball on or around the green. It also should allow the ordinary player to get the ball out and close enough that he has a *chance* to recover for his par.

There can be no cut-and-dried standards for the height of rough. The type of grass on the course dictates how high it realistically should be allowed to grow.

Bluegrass rough is ideal. The blades do not intertwine and so are relatively easy to cut through with a club, yet the stalks are firm enough to keep a ball from falling all the way to the bottom. Bluegrass rough provides a definite hazard, yet it gives the player a reasonable chance to escape.

If the rough happens to be fine-bladed bentgrass, as is the case on some northern courses, the ball will bury in it. Two inches of bentgrass rough is extremely difficult to recover from, and anything higher than that can be impossible.

The same is true of Bermuda, a tough, thick-bladed, knotty grass that will entrap a ball and is hard to cut through. With Bermuda, the height of the rough becomes critical. At the 1987 PGA Championship, played on the Champions course at PGA National in Palm Beach Gardens, Florida, the Bermuda rough was allowed to grow to four inches. That was asinine. It absolutely took the clubs out of the players' hands and eliminated any opportunity for good shotmaking out of the rough. That removes an element of skill essential to good play and good competition, in major championships or anywhere else.

The same thing happened at the old World Open at Pinehurst in 1974. It was during the period in which some misguided new owners were messing with the design of Donald Ross's wonderful No. 2 course. Among their decisions was to replace the sand and pine needles off the fairway with Bermuda rough, which they let grow to a height of four inches or more for the tournament. Once in the rough, the best players in the world simply reached for a wedge and tried to get back to the fairway. It was brutal and totally unfair, but it did lead to one of the great lines I've heard.

In the second round Johnny Miller, who went on to win the tournament, shot a then-record 63. Afterward, a writer said to him, "John, you're not supposed to shoot 63 on this course. That's why they let the rough grow."

To which Miller replied, "I know, but when you're shooting 63 you're not in the rough."

True enough. But that change, which since has been reversed, is an example of how rough can be misused to alter the characteristics and playability that an architect intended in a course. Pinehurst No. 2 does not need heavy Bermuda rough, because it has thick stands of trees. The natural covering of sand and pine needles outside the fairways requires a skillful shot to recover from the trees. But, unlike heavy grass, it affords the opportunity to make that shot, and that's how Ross intended it when he designed the course.

Rough, whether it be grass, desert growth, heather and gorse or sand and pine needles, can and should be native to the area. The skilled and perceptive architect will design his course accordingly, as Ross did. Seldom, if ever, should the concept be tampered with.

Pine Valley, that wonderful course in New Jersey, adds another dimension to rough. It is perhaps the most intimidating course in the United States because of its sandy waste areas, many of which are difficult to carry for the average golfer. The sand is unkempt and spotted with wild vegetation throughout. Yet these areas are really only a form of rough and actually are easier to escape than most heavy grass rough.

The Players Club, designed by Pete Dye in Jacksonville, Florida, home of the PGA Tour and the Players Championship, also has sandy waste areas of a somewhat different nature bordering many of its fairways. At first glance, they frighten most players, but they can be played from and actually serve to effectively widen the driving area.

Sometimes rough is not needed at all. Augusta National has none to speak of. There are trees, of course, because the property is heavily wooded. But the trees are used more as individual barriers than collective hazards. The fairways are generous. If you find yourself in dense woods at Augusta, you have hit a truly bad shot. And the lack of rough does not detract from the quality or difficulty of the course. It was designed that way. The problems lie in other areas.

The use of trees and rough together requires a judicious touch on the part of the architect and the course superintendent to maintain a fair balance for the player.

Bobby Nichols, a former PGA champion and one of the fine players in the annals of the Tour, was contemplating playing the 1975 U.S. Open at Medinah No. 3, a heavily wooded course on the outskirts of Chicago.

"You can play from rough and you can play from trees," he said, "but you can't play from both of them at the same time."

I quite agree. Rough is penal enough. Add trees and you produce situations from which it is impossible to recover, not only for the average player but for the best players in the world. I suppose my affinity for linksland courses is showing here, but I think the combination of trees and rough should be avoided whenever possible, fully realizing that it is *not* always possible.

Pine Valley has trees, thick and sometimes impenetrable in places, along with all its other trouble. But the driving areas are generous and the thickest stands of trees usually are far from the playing area, seldom intruding into it. As at Augusta National, if you are wild enough to find the dense woods at Pine Valley, you deserve whatever problems you get.

Many great courses—Medinah, Winged Foot, Hazeltine, Oak Hill, Point O'Woods, Southern Hills, to name just a few—have both trees and rough that sometimes come into play, even for shots that are not far off target. In these cases it is up to the course superintendent to make sure the areas are reasonably playable for the members. And it is up to the USGA or other governing bodies to be judicious when the courses are used for championship competition.

Trees are a fact of life on parkland courses. And they are a thing of beauty, adding to the appeal of the course. For that reason trees are important components of course design. In general, however, I do not think trees are acceptable hazards. Thick stands of trees, especially at fairway's edge, are unfair from the player's standpoint. Too often they set up a wall. Too much is left to chance. The penalty range is too great. You and I might drive into virtually the same spot in the woods. I might be stymied against a tree and likely will make double-bogey or worse. You might be a few feet away and have an opening that gives you a chance for birdie. I know that golf is not meant to be a fair game, but that's carrying it too far. I have no problem with a truly wild shot winding up in jail. But it bothers me when a shot that misses the target by only a few yards suffers the same severe penalty.

Besides, the recovery shot is one of the attractive aspects of the game. I know of nothing more exciting than to see somebody hit a shot through a hole in the trees and wind up on the green. But first there has to be a hole in the forest. So the canny architect selectively clears trees from areas near the fairways to make the holes more playable for the golfer, at the same time trying to figure out what to do with the rest of the forest.

Trees can and should be used around the teeing ground and to frame target areas, especially around the greens. Sometimes trees are even planted for that purpose. This both defines and beautifies a hole and course, although the architect must be careful not to group trees too close to a green or tee. Too much shade can make it difficult to grow and maintain grass.

We've done that with The International outside of Washington, D.C. Almost every hole is heavily wooded, but we decided to use the trees as a framework and rely on other design factors to give the course its character and playability. We cleared out a lot of trees, in some cases to provide a better view of the adjacent water. Some of the thickly wooded areas are used to hide nearby housing. That's a problem that most modern designers face, as I've discussed, but it has nothing to do with the playability of the course.

Ideally, from the standpoint of playing values, a single tree can be utilized within the strategic design of a hole. Make the golfer play around or over it. If the shot is mis-hit and the tree gets in the way, the penalty is not as severe. A single tree still can be nicely avoided on the next shot.

The problem here is that trees can die. They become diseased, get hit by lightning, are blown down by wind or just naturally expire. If you design playing characteristics around a tree or two or three and they disappear in a few years, the character of the hole is lost. We have done that and have learned the folly of those ways.

It is especially dangerous to isolate a single tree from a dense wooded area and design a hole around it. When you isolate it, you have changed its environment dramatically. It has grown up with the protection of other trees around it. Its root structure may have been affected by the other trees. Now the wind gets at it, the sun gets at it, and it may get burned. You have changed all the conditions in which the tree survived. Now you are telling it to do something else, and a lot of them don't want to.

If you do want to work trees into the hole design, it is much better to do it with a grouping. But you are still taking a chance. Invariably, when we clear a fairway area out of dense woods, we lose a lot of the trees along the edges for the same reasons I've mentioned, and those are the very trees you usually are trying to incorporate into your design.

For example, when we built Kananaskis in the mountains near Alberta, Canada, in 1983 and 1984, we cleared out a lot of large, full pines in routing the fairways. We tried to isolate some of them, and of course we had them all along the edges of the fairways. These are heavy-topped trees that grow very tightly together and grow very high to get light. They virtually support each other in the heavy forest against the winds and other elements.

Well, some freak winds, virtually gales, swept through the valley, and we lost a lot of trees. Some as big as four feet around at the base went down, not uprooted but simply snapped by the wind. If they had still been growing in the forest, that would not have happened.

We had saved a group of five or six big trees in trying to tighten one hole, a short par-4. Four of them went down in the wind, making the hole play very different than we had intended.

If the architect is lucky enough to find a tree that has been standing under the same conditions for its lifetime, or a group of them in the same situation, he should employ them in the design of the hole if he can. Or he can always plant trees where he wants and wait years for them to grow. Otherwise, trees are wonderful for aesthetic purposes but chancy as hazards. Bunkers are safer, because they will be there as long as you want them.

A final word on trees. The deciduous variety are best on a golf course. Oaks, maples and the others are beautiful—too bad the lovely elm is gone from most parts of the country—and they are more acceptable from the standpoint of playability. Their branches do not grow close to the ground, and those that do can be easily trimmed. Conifers—the pines, firs and spruces—are beautiful, and since they are endemic to many areas of the country you often see them on golf courses. But because firs and spruces grow so close to the ground, they represent an unfair hazard, often creating unplayable lies. So if they are to come into play, at least they ought to be trimmed up a few feet off the ground to give the player a chance to escape without a two-stroke penalty.

There are too many other hazards to worry about on the way to the green to be dealt with so harshly by a tree.

Following pages: Page 193: *Multiple tees on the downhill 11th at Mauna Kea make it a par-3 that ranges from 247 to 166 yards, a hole that is reachable for players at all skill levels.* Pages 194-195: *The 17th at Debordieu near Myrtle Beach, South Carolina, is a 449-yard par-4 with multiple tees and a serpentine fairway flanked by water, sand and trees.* Page 196: *The rolling dunes at Lahinch in Ireland (shown here are the 10th and 13th holes) demand accuracy. . . and sometimes pop up in unexpected places to trap even the best tee shots.* Page 197 top: *A free-form tee on the par-5 9th at Melrose on Daufuskie Island, South Carolina, provides options for the drive.* Page 197 bottom: *An elevated tee, the highest point on the course, and bunkers down the left side add excitement to the drive on the 456-yard par-4 13th at Skyland near Crested Butte, Colorado.* Page 198: *A lone dead cypress pine borders the 17th fairway at Cypress Point on the Monterey Peninsula.* Page 199: *The par-5 10th at Wee Burn in Darien, Connecticut, is only 509 yards long, and plays downhill but bunkers and a creek crossing the fairway—the "wee burn"—must be avoided to make par or better.* Pages 200-201: *The 14th fairway at Desert Highlands in Scottsdale, Arizona, presents subtle undulations and pot bunkers in the Scottish tradition on a par-4 hole that is 417 yards long.* Page 202 top: *The back-tee placement on the par-3 13th at Samoset in Rockport, Maine, turns the hole into a terror that requires a 216-yard shot across this chasm along the Atlantic coast.* Page 202 bottom left: *The*

dunes at Royal Portrush in Northern Ireland are beautiful to the eye of the camera but terrorifying to the eye of the golfer. Page 202 bottom right: *The 5th at Oakland Hills near Detroit is a par-4 that can play as long as 457 yards and requires a precisely placed drive for the best shot into the green.* Page 203: *Spyglass Hill's par-3 third hole, 150 yards long from the back, plays differently from each of its tees, each on a different level.* Pages 204-205: *From the elevated tee on the par-4 10th at Sugarloaf in the Carrabassett Valley, Maine, the bunker-guarded fairway looms as a spectacular target below.* Page 206 top: *The 184-yard 7th at San Francisco Golf Club, considered by A. W. Tillinghast to be his best par-3 hole, illustrates how tee elevation can greatly increase the drama.* Page 206 bottom: *The 420-yard par-4 10th at Oak Hill in Rochester, New York, presents an intriguing downhill view from the tee.* Page 207 top: *The fairway on Shinnecock Hills' 412-yard, par-4 10th slopes down and to the right, then upward to the green, making both the drive and the second shot demanding.* Page 207 bottom: *The 2nd fairway at Coto de Caza, a Robert Trent Jones, Jr., course near Mission Viejo in California, winds treacherously among bunkers.* Page 208 top: *From the tee on the par-3 5th hole of the West Course at the Broadmoor in Colorado Springs, Colorado, the golfer's eye is lured from the green to the Rocky Mountains beyond.* Page 208 bottom: *The green hills of Ireland's County Clare rise in the background as the golfer tees off on the 9th hole at Lahinch, a 348-yard par-4.*

Mauna Kea, #11
Following pages: Debordieu, #17

◁ Lahinch, #10, #13   △ Melrose, #9

                                                                        ▽ Skyland, #13

Cypress Point, #17

Following pages: *Desert Highlands, #14*

Samoset, #6

Royal Portrush, Dunes

Oakland Hills, #5
Following pages: *Sugarloaf, #10*

San Francisco Golf Club, #7

Oak Hill, #10

206

Shinnecock, #10

Coto de Caza, #2

Broadmoor, #5 West

Lahinch, #9

208

Chapter 6

The Major Hazards

Through the centuries, hazards have spawned the legends that make the lore and literature of golf the most fascinating of any game. More money has changed hands, more hopes have died, more championships have been lost—and won—because of hazards than any other element of the game.

Hazards are the bane of the common golfer's life. Hazards are cursed, reviled and almost always feared. To those who have never faced the challenge, it is difficult to comprehend the terror that strikes the player facing a forced carry over a gaping bunker or, worse, over water.

As Bob Jones once said, "The great value of a hazard is not that it catches a shot that has been missed but that it forces a miss upon the timid player; its psychological worth is greater than its penal value."

When the shot fails, the pain is agonizing. Yet what golfer, however many times he has been wounded by failure, would give up the euphoria that washes over him when the shot comes off successfully?

Hazards make golf what it is, a game full of uncertainties, of risks and rewards and consequences, of peaks and valleys, of victories and defeats. They also add immensely to the beauty, to the work of art that is a golf course. Without hazards, golf would be little more than an extended game of croquet.

While actual hazards take many forms—trees, rough, shrubs, wasteland, even the elements—only two types, bunkers and water, are recognized by the Rules of Golf. A bunker is defined as "an area of bare ground, often a depression, which is usually covered with sand."

A water hazard is "any sea, lake, pond, river, ditch, surface drainage ditch or other open water course (regardless of whether or not it contains water), and anything of a similar nature."

While bunkers are certainly the most common hazard, water is by far the most feared, for good reason.

When we were designing Peachtree, Bob Jones said to me one evening, "You know, Trent, getting in a water hazard is like being in a plane crash—the result is final. Landing in a bunker is similar to an automobile accident—there is a chance for recovery."

And so it is. Too many golfers just get up and whale away, seldom considering the consequences. The best advice I can give is this: When confronted with multiple hazards, steer away from the most dangerous. You can play out of sand. You can play out of trees and rough. Seldom can you play out of water. Other than the out-of-bounds stakes, water is the ultimate penalty.

On Bunkers

As with the golf course itself, or at least the land it lies on, it is quite likely that God created the first bunker. The common theory is that, at St. Andrews, the hollows that were created by the receding sea, or burrowing animals, or sheep hunkering down against the cold nights became the bunkers, strewn everywhere across the fairways and around the greens, visible and hidden. Usually they are hidden, deep depressions or "pot bunkers" that often trap even the best shots. We don't build many like that now, but bunkers still bedevil golfers to this day, not only on the Old Course but everywhere. They have come to have almost a life of their own.

Trees are trees and rough is rough, but bunkers have personalities. Bunkers have reputations. They even have names! The Church Pews and Big Mouth at Oakmont, the Sahara Desert at Baltusrol, the Vardon Bunker at The Country Club, the White Faces of Merion, Hell's Half Acre at Pine Valley, which is not really a bunker but a wasteland, or Hell's Half Acre at Baltimore's Five Farms, which is indeed a series of penal bunkers—all are the stuff of legends.

Nowhere are the legends more alive than at St. Andrews, where almost all the bunkers have names—Hell Bunker, The Principal's Nose, Road Bunker, Hill Bunker, the Beardies, Coffin, Cat's Trap, Lion's Mouth, Grave Bunker, Ginger Beer Bunkers.

There are reasons for all the marvelous names of bunkers, and all have marvelous tales to tell. They are usually tales of horror, but not always.

Many major championships have been lost in bunkers. In 1939, at Philadelphia Country Club's Spring Mill course, Sam Snead needed only a five, par on the final hole, to win the U.S. Open Championship. Instead, his second shot landed in a bunker. He failed to get out with his first attempt and flew the green with his next. He made eight on the hole and never was to win the world's most important championship.

In 1961, Arnold Palmer needed only to par the last hole at Augusta National to win the Masters. But he found the right-hand bunker with his second shot, hit his recovery shot over the green and made double-bogey six to lose by a stroke to Gary Player.

St. Andrews' bunkers have taken their toll on many contenders. In 1933 Gene Sarazen took three swings to get out of Hill Bunker on the short 11th, then two more to escape Hell Bunker on the 14th. He lost the British Open by a stroke.

In 1939 Bobby Locke was five under par in the first round coming to the 14th. He drove into one of the Beardies and failed to get out after unwisely choosing a 7-iron. When he did emerge, he hit his next shot into Hell Bunker and took eight on the hole, ruining his championship hopes.

In 1978 Tommy Nakajima, the Japanese star, made history of sorts when he hit his second shot in the third round onto the 17th, the Road Hole. Three under par and very much in contention at the time, Nakajima then putted off the green into the Road Bunker, a deep, steep-faced pit that requires the most delicately played shot to escape. It took him four tries to do it. He made a nine on the hole and vanished from sight.

On the other hand, bunkers have provided winning drama. Who can forget Bob Tway holing from the front bunker on the 72nd hole at Inverness in Toledo for a birdie that won the 1985 PGA Championship? Or Sandy Lyle's great 7-iron shot from the fairway bunker on the 18th at Augusta that led to a birdie and the 1988 Masters title? Or Curtis Strange's explosion from the front bunker to within a foot of the cup on the 18th hole of The Country Club that saved a tie for the 1988 U.S. Open title, which he won the next day?

So bunkers provide excitement at both ends of the spectrum. They remain critical in the design and construction of a course, although their difficulty for the professional and better amateur undoubtedly is less than it once was.

In this modern era bunkers are an anomaly. Before Gene Sarazen invented the sand wedge in the middle 1930s, bunkers were penal hazards for everybody, including the best players. It required extreme skill to get the ball close from a bunker then. I've seen Walter Hagen, Bob Jones and the best of them miss shots from a bunker.

Now the professionals and the better amateurs have no fear of the sand. They have developed the skill and confidence to make what is essentially one of the easier shots in golf, even though 90 percent of the people who play the game would not agree with that. The best sand players on the PGA Tour get the ball up and down in two shots from bunkers about 70 percent of the time or better. Even the worst recover about half the time. So the impact of the bunker has been lessened for the better player.

Actually, the grass trap illustrates the difference between the professional level of play and all the rest of the golfers. The higher handicappers would much rather be in a grass trap around the green than in sand. They feel they can chop the ball out, which they can. They rarely can get it close, but they probably can get it on the green. Their innate fear of the sand and their lack of technique in playing out of it causes them to make bad swings, which of course results in bad shots. The professional, on the other hand, cannot control the ball out of the grass bunker nearly as well. He cannot put spin on it and stop it where he wants. He can do that out of sand.

The United States Golf Association, in setting up its U.S. Open courses, caught onto the fact that rough is the real hazard for the professionals. Water they can avoid and sand they can play out of, but long grass kills them, taking away their control of the ball.

Still, because of the trouble most amateurs have with it, sand remains a viable hazard for most of the golfers in the world, those for whom we really are building golf courses, as long as the bunkers are fair and fairly placed.

Over the years, the trend among modern architects actually has been toward fewer bunkers.

Donald Ross and A. W Tillinghast and others of that era, having taken their design philosophies from the links concept, usually built their courses with a great many bunkers, often more than two hundred. They figured that if that was the way of the links, that was the way it should be. One of the problems there has been that as the years went by, and especially during the Depression, it became too expensive to maintain all those bunkers and many of them were filled in on a lot of courses. That changes the playability of the hole and the course. The shot values are no longer as the architect intended.

Of course, in some cases, the shot values might not have been correct in the first place. In his later years Tillinghast went around the country redesigning courses and removing bunkers, including many he had built himself. He became aware, as many of us have, that a multitude of bunkers on a course usually requires a lot of long bunker shots, perhaps the hardest stroke in golf, especially for the higher handicappers, women and seniors. Oakmont is considered one of the world's hardest and most penal courses, and its almost two hundred bunkers are certainly one of the main reasons.

Then along came Bob Jones and Alister MacKenzie and built Augusta National, a parkland course that had relatively few traps in the beginning. There are only forty-four or so now. But Jones and MacKenzie introduced the elevated and contoured greens to offset the lack of bunkers. This was a stroke of genius. Not only did it make it more difficult for the professional, who has more trouble with greens than sand, it made it easier for the average golfer, whose problems are the opposite.

So a great course doesn't have to have a lot of sand, but it must be designed accordingly so that the playing values and the challenges are maintained.

What is the purpose of a bunker? A bunker should pose a penalty for an errant shot, a punishment of up to one stroke, but no more than that if you can manage a halfway decent shot out of the sand. It should be a less stringent hazard than water, which is an automatic one-stroke penalty when you hit into it and often is more.

Most of the bunkers in the fairways on the Old Course have steep faces and require a lofted club just to escape. Making headway is difficult if not impossible. Many of them are deep pot bunkers, from which you extricate yourself simply by wedging out, sometimes sideways or backwards. Similar bunkers have been built into other links courses in England, Scotland and Ireland that were patterned after St. Andrews, and traces of them can still be found in the earlier courses in America.

In any event, if you get in one, the penalty is a full stroke and maybe more if you don't execute the shot satisfactorily. Penal, perhaps, but that's the way the game began. Who is to say it is wrong?

Still, the philosophy today—at least my philosophy—is that you should have a chance to recover, either from a greenside or a fairway bunker. I don't believe in steep-faced bunkers that often prohibit the player from escaping in the direction he wants to go. That is too penal a design, especially for most amateurs. In other words, the greenside bunker should not be so severe that the shot from sand cannot be gotten close with a skillfully played shot. Nor should the fairway bunker be so deep that there is absolutely no chance of getting a good shot to the green. The architect controls that with the height of the lip, which controls the club that must be used from the bunker. So by carefully placing the bunker a certain distance from the tee and the green and by making the lip a certain height, the architect forces the better player to choose a club of a certain loft and then play the shot precisely to get the ball just over the lip if it is to get anywhere close to the green. The same philosophy holds true for the higher handicapper. In other words, the farther the bunker is from the green, the flatter it should be and the lower the lip should be. The golfer still must play a good shot, but he should have a chance to get it close.

So, while it should be fair, the fairway bunker never should be easy and should never afford the player an opportunity to get the ball close to the hole without a superlative effort.

The 10th hole at Muirfield Village, the Jack Nicklaus-designed course in Dublin, Ohio, is a long par-4, a slight dogleg left that requires an uphill tee shot. A flat bunker with very little lip, along with a sentinel tree and rough, guards the left corner of the dogleg. During foursomes competition in the 1987 Ryder Cup Match, José-Maria Olazabal and Severiano Ballesteros were paired for the European team. On the 10th, Olazabal pulled his tee shot left, heading for the bunker or the rough. As the ball was in the air, Ballesteros was yelling, "Get in the bunker." The ball did bounce into the sand, leaving Seve with a smooth lie, and he laced a medium-iron shot a few feet past the hole. The Americans, just ten feet away but in the rough, could not get the ball on the green.

That is not equity. Without a lip and a slope to the bunker, a player of Ballesteros's skill might as well be in the middle of the fairway. There was no penalty for hitting an errant shot.

Bunkers are guards. They guard the driving area of the fairway and they guard the pin positions on the green. So the architect must determine the latitude he is going to give players at the various skill levels. He must estimate how far the ball will be struck off the tee, and he must decide how wide or narrow to make the target before an errant drive finds the sand.

As guards, bunkers also influence and direct play. By skillful placement of his fairway bunkers, the architect literally can "tell" the player how he wants the tee shot played. If, then, he has properly contoured the fairway, the approach to the green and the green itself, as well as correctly placing the other bunkers and hazards on the hole, he dictates the most judicious route the player should take to get to the cup. At the same time, he leaves some options for the player who wants to gamble and can be rewarded if he does so successfully.

That's why I don't usually like to see trapping down both sides of the fairway. I have done it at certain times, usually to force the professional to make a decision on whether he should drive the ball long and super-straight or lay up short of the trouble, as I did at Oakland Hills. And it can be done for variety or special purposes. But it should not be a routine practice, because it gives the player no options. It says to him, "You have to hit the ball right *here*, right between the bunkers. There is no other place to go." It's better to tighten the hole by placing a bunker at the dogleg, for example. That makes it effective for the entire hole. Move the hole around the trap, so you put a premium on driving as close to the bunker as possible. But if you don't, your penalty is simply a longer next shot.

For the reason that bunkers should direct play and should be hazards that can be fairly avoided, I don't like to hide them, although I have on occasion. Bobby Locke blamed a bunker hidden over a hill on the fifth hole at Oakland Hills for his loss in the Open in 1951. He drove into it twice on Saturday to ruin his chances of catching Ben Hogan. In defense of the architect who worked that evil, however, I must say that the bunker was 240 yards from the tee, unreachable by most golfers other than the professionals. And since this was the final day after a week of practicing and competition, Locke surely knew the bunker was there.

The bunker, in addition to being a hazard, is indeed a thing of beauty that can do much to enhance a course. The cloverleaf or free-form bunker is an example. I've been credited with originating the cloverleaf bunker, but I really think Alister MacKenzie was the first to use that form. He didn't like square bunkers, nor do they appeal to me. MacKenzie's first courses, such as Moortown in England, lacked some artistic quality, but later he began to soften his lines. Flashing, the practice of building sand up the front of the bunker, accentuates the artistry, because now you can see the sand, see the outline of the bunker. The picture is there for you to admire . . . and to fear.

Flashing echoes the linksland, the way nature shaped the dunes. All we are doing is copying, and there is no better model.

Variety throughout the course also enhances the beauty and enjoyment. Bunker variety is achieved by size and design. For example, if you build one big bunker on a hole, on the next hole you break it into three bunkers. The penalty is the same, but the visual effect is vastly different.

Bunkers on golf courses today must be carefully designed because of maintenance costs. We do not particularly design bunkers with that in mind. We will not destroy the design, the appeal of a course, for the sake of easier maintenance. Most attractive, well-designed bunkers will require a certain amount of hand mowing around the edges. But bunker construction can be carried to the extreme. You see them with hard edges, terraces and steep slopes, sometimes almost vertical turf slopes leading down into a deep trap. Some slopes are so steep the sod has to be pegged on so it will take root. It's difficult to understand how the grass can be cut, other than by getting a barber in there with his scissors.

Roger Rulewich once was asked if we built "shadow bunkers." At the time he didn't know what those were. Obviously, the prospective client had been talking to other architects. Shadow bunkers, as it turns out, are those with hard edges and very severe slopes that cast a strong shadow when the sun gets low. You see it as a very dark line. It's obviously done to create a visual effect . . . and often to make it impossible to mow or to play a shot.

On Water

Like the bunker, the water hazard also originated at St. Andrews in the form of the Swilcan Burn, a narrow stream that wanders, apparently benignly, directly in front of the first green and across the 18th fairway. I say "apparently benignly" because the pitch over it to a close-set flag has caught many a competitor foolishly trying for an easy birdie and has ruined many a round at the outset.

And like bunkers, water also has created its own lore, usually more terrible than that of the sand. In the 1938 U.S. Open, Ray Ainsley stubbornly took 15 strokes to escape Little Dry Creek on the 16th hole at Cherry Hills in Denver, eventually scoring 19. In the 1980 Masters Tom Weiskopf made a 13 on the 12th at Augusta, pumping his tee shot and four more pitches into Rae's Creek, trying all the while. That is the highest Masters score on any hole, matching the 13 recorded by the unfortunate Nakajima when he ran afoul of the same creek on the 13th in 1978, just three months before his losing battle with the Road Bunker.

In 1985, with the Masters title well in hand, Curtis Strange found water on the 13th and 15th holes and lost the chance for his first major championship. The following year, Seve Ballesteros, looking like a winner, found water with his second shot on the 15th and promptly expired. Ben Crenshaw lost his chance at the 1975 U.S. Open Championship when he dunked his tee shot on the 17th at Medinah.

Water also provides excitement just by being there—Jerry Pate's 5-iron over water on the 72nd hole to win the 1976 U.S. Open at Atlantic Athletic Club; Gary Player's 150-yard 9-iron over trees and water on the 16th at Oakland Hills in the last round that set up a birdie to clinch the 1972 PGA Championship. Without the water, the drama would not have been nearly so great in either case.

In the 1979 World Series of Golf at Firestone Country Club's South Course, Lon Hinkle, trapped in the woods to the right of the fairway after his second shot, deliberately skipped a shot off the pond guarding the front of the green, made his par and went on to win the tournament. That is not, however, the recommended procedure for circumventing water.

Water is my favorite hazard, for several reasons. It is the most penal hazard, and it certainly is the most dramatic hazard. It adds beauty and it often is useful in the maintenance of the course.

I've found that water holes, because of their beauty and challenge, are the most popular among the majority of golfers. They get excited about water. It is a hazard that is immediately recognizable, and it appeals to them, even if in a perverse way. They are intimidated by it, but they are fascinated by it.

And why shouldn't they be? There is no more glorious challenge than to stand on the 16th tee at Cypress Point or on the third tee at Mauna Kea and be faced with a full carry over the surf pounding below, the ocean breezes whipping around you. Nor are there any more beautiful sights.

From the roaring oceans to the majestic lakes, the rushing streams and quiet ponds and burns, water adds a beauty and a test to golf that entrances. The player may quake and he may curse. But he also knows that secret joy that comes from facing a worthy foe and, at least some of the time, overcoming him.

Water in its many forms comes into play on the world's great holes, a subject I will discuss further in the next chapter. A burn guards the first green at St. Andrews; small ponds flank the 12th green at Southern Hills; Baffling Brook threatens constantly on the 11th at Merion; Salt Creek, which is really a river, puts the golfer in danger on the seventh and eighth holes at Butler National; Lake Kadijah poses a hazard on no less than four holes at Medinah; Turtle Spawning Bay awaits the shot that misses the third at Mauna Kea; the ocean comes into play on the 15th, 16th and 17th at Cypress Point, transforming them from very good to marvelous holes.

It has been said that if Pebble Beach were located in Omaha, Nebraska, it would be just another ordinary golf course. Perhaps, but it is *not* in Omaha. It sits on Carmel Bay, a beautiful inlet of the Pacific that comes directly into play on six of its holes and makes them stern and wonderful tests.

The 17th at The Players Club in Ponte Vedra, Florida, the controversial island hole, would be an ordinary and relatively uninteresting par-3 if it were surrounded by grass. Instead it is surrounded by water and poses a chilling hurdle, even to the world's best players.

Any architect, when he sets about planning a course, will look for whatever natural water is available and try to incorporate it directly into his design. If he is lucky enough to be working with a seaside or lakeside tract of land, the job usually is easy. If he is unlucky and has little or no water available, he must do what he can to create some, whether it be by damming streams or actually making artificial lakes.

Water is especially important on courses where there are no other natural hazards, no contours or trees, where the terrain is uninteresting. That's why you see so much water on Florida's flat courses. If the architect didn't use water, he would have to create a lot of other artificial hazards. Water, even when it is created, never quite seems artificial.

Water should be used judiciously, of course. Water hazards on every hole would cease to be beautiful and challenging and instead would become annoying and wearisome. Water should be brought into play on five or six holes at the most. I like to use all the different hole combinations—the 3s, 4s and 5s—utilizing all the shot values. There might be a carry over a water from the tee, a pitch over water, a fairly long shot to the green over water, maybe a par-5 with water off the tee and near the green. And sometimes I've used water just for its scenic value without bringing it into play.

Nor should water be placed where it cannot be circumvented, or at least carried by a player at any level who hits a moderately good shot. Seldom would you have a hole with water running all the way down one side, for example, unless it were a lakeside or seaside hole specifically designed with that in mind. If that were the case, there certainly would be alternate routes away from the water, enough width to the fairway with few or no severe hazards to the other side. Otherwise it would not be any kind of a fair hole.

Never, ever, should water be hidden. The penalty for a surprise is too severe. If it looms over the hill on a path the player deems correct, the architect is carrying deception too far.

Water is a hazard that fits the heroic concept perfectly. On a well-designed hole—the 13th at Dorado Beach again comes to mind—it offers the bold player a chance to make a long carry or carries, with the ultimate consequences if the shot fails. But it also affords the more cautious or less skilled player the opportunity to play away from it and take a safer route to the green.

The par-5 sixth hole at Bay Hill, a Dick Wilson course outside Orlando, Florida, is a wonderful example of a hole that curves around a lake, offering the daring player a chance to play as close to the water as he wants or bite off part of the lake if he wants to try to make it home in two shots. And there is plenty of room to the right for the fainthearted. The long par-4 18th at Doral, the famed Blue Monster, is another Wilson masterpiece. A lake borders almost the entire left side of the hole. There is really no need to cut off any part of it, but the closer you play to the lake off the tee, the shorter the second shot will be. If you bail out to the right, the shot is longer and you might find trees. But at least your ball will be dry.

As magnificent as the 16th at Cypress Point is, it really is not a par-3 for many players, at least not a fair one. Unless he wants to go to the women's tee, any man is faced with a carry of 218 yards over water from even the front of the tee. Many players, maybe most of them, cannot carry a shot that far. He can lay up to the left with an iron, of course, but that makes par extremely difficult and birdie unlikely.

On the other hand, the third hole on my course at Mauna Kea requires a similar carry over water, although a bit shorter—178 yards to the front of the green, 210 to the middle. With the wind in force, that's a heroic carry for any player. But there are three other sets of tees that offer carries of 167, 158 and 113 yards respectively to the front. The latter shot must carry over only a tip of the water. Thus the player has the option of playing the tee that best suits his ability, and he or she still will be able to make the shot. As it should be.

These are situations in which the player can, indeed must, swing full-out. Water can be even more dangerous on delicate pitch shots, such as over the burn on the first at St. Andrews or the third shot over the small pond on the 16th at Firestone, when the nerves can wreak even more havoc on a precise swing.

Wherever it lies, water lures us to a supreme triumph or a painful death.

Following pages: Page 217: *The second shot on the par-5 14th at Baltimore Country Club's East Course must clear a mine field of bunkers, making it easy to understand why the hole, 608 yards long from the back tee, is called Hell's Half Acre. Pages 218-219: The 14th on the Dunluce Course at Royal Portrush measures 205 yards from the medal tees and is one of the world's most frightening par-3s. There are no bunkers or water, but the deep abyss ready to swallow any shot hit to the right is a fearsome hazard. The hole is aptly called Calamity. Page 219: Sand bunkers and areas of unraked sand provide the protection for the 14th green at Kingston Heath in Cheltenham, Australia. Pages 220-221: These huge, multi-fingered fairway bunkers and an equally imposing greenside trap on the 438-yard, par-4 18th at Metedeconk in Lakewood, New Jersey, are ready to grab the player who shies away from the woods on the left. Page 222 top: An off-line shot on the 8th on the Ailsa Course at Turnberry in Scotland, a 440-yard par-4, will find one of these deep pot bunkers. Page 222 bottom: The short 15th at the Olympic Club in San Francisco is circled by deep bunkers that make the tee shot, only 149 yards at its longest, an exciting one. Page 223 top: The 13th at Pine Tree in Boynton Beach, Florida, only 152 yards long, is enhanced—and protected—by this beautiful "garden" of sand. Page 223 bottom left: The par-4 12th on the Old Course at St. Andrews is only 316 yards long, but don't land in one of these sod-walled pot bunkers, typical of Scotland's famous links courses. Page 223 bottom right: Finding one of these deep pot bunkers on the 542-yard, par-5 17th at Muirfield in Scotland makes it impossible to get home in regulation. Pages 224-225: Water far below on the left and the intervening terrain, with the Atlantic in the background, makes the 205-yard carry on the par-3 13th at Port Royal in Bermuda beautiful but exceptionally terrifying. Page 226 top: Water adds beauty and danger to the par-4 2nd hole on* the North Course at La Costa in Carlsbad, California. *Page 226 bottom: Both water and sand protect the par-4 9th on the Stadium Course at PGA West in La Quinta, California. It is a 450-yarder that provides a heroic opportunity for the player who thinks he can avoid disaster. Page 227: The par-3 2nd at Medinah demands a carry of 169 yards over water from the back tee. The huge trap on the left is a saving bunker that keeps many shots from drowning. Pages 228-229: The second shot on the 16th at Oakland Hills' South Course, a dogleg-right par-4 of 409 yards from the back, must fly all the way over water to a well-bunkered green. In the foreground are the branches of the willow tree over which Gary Player slashed a 9-iron to within three feet for a birdie that won the 1972 PGA Championship. Page 229 top: Carmel Bay on the left threatens the golfer at Pebble Beach's par-5 18th. The intimidating tee shot can be played boldly or safely on the 540-yard hole, but a fairway bunker and a bothersome lone tree protect the right side of the driving zone. In the foreground is the 17th green and its guardian bunkers. Page 229 bottom: The 9th on the Blue Course at Doral in Miami, Florida, measures only 169 yards at its longest, but the carry is completely over water to a sloping green protected by bunkers front and left. Here it is sand that sometimes saves a ball from watery death. Pages 230-231: One of the finest sequences of golf—and hazards—anywhere is Cypress Point's par-3 15th, whose bunker-surrounded green is at lower left, the spectacular 233-yard 16th over water and, at the top of the picture, the 375-yard par-4 17th, a dogleg with the ocean threatening on the right. Page 232 top: The 12th on the South Course at Frenchman's Creek in North Palm Beach, Florida, poses both watery and sandy challenges on the way to the green. Page 232 bottom: The Atlantic Ocean and the winds that whip off it make the 216-yard 15th at Ballybunion Old in Ireland an especially difficult and nerve-tingling par-3.*

Royal Portrush, #14

Kingston Heath, #14

Following pages: *Metedconk, #18*

Turnberry, #8

Olympic, #15

Pine Tree, #13

St. Andrews, #12

Muirfield, #11   Following pages: *Port Royal, #16*

La Costa, #2 North

PGA West, #14

Medinah, #

Oakland Hills, #16

Pebble Beach, #18

Doral, #9 Blue   Following pages: *Cypress Point, #16*

△ Frenchman's Creek, #12

▽ Ballybunion, #15 Old

Chapter 7
Threes, Fours and Fives

A golf course is a collection of holes. No matter the terrain, the surroundings and the intent, the purpose of the course, as a whole it is no better than the sum of those holes. By "modern" standards, established four hundred or so years ago, the course numbers eighteen holes. The "par," an arbitrary figure, will be somewhere in the neighborhood of 72. On a few courses, and usually for the women golfers of the world, it can be more than that. Often it is less than that. But the very designation, along with historical precedent, makes it incumbent upon the architect to provide a mix of holes with different individual pars. Generally this means par-3, par-4 and par-5 holes. There are par-6 holes in existence. Legend has it that architect Tom Bendelow, having staked out seventeen holes of a course he was doing and finding himself nine hundred yards from the clubhouse site, designated the final hole as a par-8!

The United States Golf Association sets some guidelines for the lengths of holes to which the various pars shall be prescribed—for men, a par-3 hole is up to 250 yards, a par-4 is 251 to 470, a par-5 anything longer than that. A par-6 is not specified for men. For women, a par-3 is up to 210 yards, a par-4 is 211 to 400, a par-5 is 401-475, a par-6 is 476 and up. Allowances can and should be made for topography, essentially whether the holes run uphill or down.

Within those guidelines the architect is free to design whatever challenges, hazards and horrors he sees fit. The good architect, of course, will do it right, presenting a panoply of intriguing shotmaking examinations within a balance of one-, two- and three-shot holes.

The good and careful—and intelligent—player will face these examinations and, by becoming aware of the choices the architect has designed into the hole, will be able to pass each test by assaying his capabilities and then playing the shot that best fits the situation and his ability to deal with it.

A look at each of these categories follows, beginning with the most common.

Par 4s

It is relatively easy to design striking par-3 and par-5 holes and put them in balance with the golf course. Designing par-4 holes is the toughest task the architect faces.

You can use many more hazards on par-3s and par-5s, testing the player to find some way to overcome them. On the par-3 hole, no matter what you do with bunkers or water, the target is the green. If you make it the right size for the shot and with the correct contours, you can embellish it with hazards in a number of different ways and make a strong hole out of it.

The same is true of par-5s. There are a lot of elements on the three-shot holes that allow for interesting creativity and variety. You can miss a shot on a par-5, for example, and par is still within your grasp. Because the par-5 is much like the par-3 in that it provides for a relatively shorter shot to the green, you can be more creative with the hazards. There is always the element of the heroic carry to reach a par-5 in two shots. All of this makes the par-5 more exciting to design.

You have to work a little harder to conceive par-4 holes. For one thing, there are more of them—ten compared to four each for the other holes on a so-called standard course. You have no opportunity to create a layup position for the second shot on a par-4, at least not for the golfer who is trying to get home in two and make par or birdie.

Because of the number of them, it's more difficult to create a variety, so the lengths of the par-4s must vary more drastically than on the 3s or 5s. Everybody is enamored of long, strong par-4s, but once the architect falls in love with them it's easy to end up with a string of holes that look alike. When you are putting together a sequence of strong holes, you can overdo it. It's like a rich diet. If you eat too much of it, it makes you sick. Each long, tough hole may be great in itself, but the overall balance of the course is destroyed.

A good hole isn't always a tough hole, at least in terms of length. There is nothing wrong with a drive-and-pitch hole. They're the most overlooked holes in the design of a golf course. And they can be some of the best, really something special, if they are properly designed, if some spice is built into them by the way the hole is configured, the way the hazards are set.

The 10th at Riviera in Los Angeles, for example, is right in the middle of a long, strong golf course, one of the hardest and best in the world. It measures only 311 yards, yet it is one of the greatest holes on the course, doglegging to the right around a series of gaping bunkers to a smallish green that pitches severely from right to left. A strong player can attempt to drive the green, or at least take a huge bite out of the dogleg, but if he misses he can be caught in a bunker or rough with the almost impossible chance of getting his next shot close . . . or even on the green. Even if a layup shot is played off the tee into the proper position, the pitch to the green must be precise.

Another marvelous short par-4 is the fourth at The Country Club in Brookline, Massachusetts, site of three U.S. Opens. The fourth, whose green and surroundings were redesigned by my son Rees for the 1988 Open, is only 338 yards long. The stronger player will lay up with an iron and has but a short iron or a pitch left, but the target is downhill to a small, heavily bunkered green that tilts sharply from back to front. From the bunker recovery is difficult and unlikely. The hole, which doglegs around three pot bunkers in the left corner of the landing area, also offers the option of going for the green, one of the joys of the short par-4. But potential disaster awaits the errant drive, especially on the left.

Another, even shorter, is the 288-yard seventh at The Olympic Club, which I redesigned for the 1955 U.S. Open. The hole is straightforward except for bunkers and rough guarding the opening to the green. It can be driven, but laying up is the wisest choice even for the big hitter. Awaiting him is a tiered green that can befuddle the best putters if they wind up on the wrong tier. The green is the "spice" in this case, and it makes a little hole a giant.

Even beyond the drive-and-pitch category, a par-4 does not have to be overly long to be great. The sixth at Seminole measures 390 yards, far from a monster, yet it is considered one of the best par-4s in the world, mainly because it does exquisitely well what a good hole is supposed to do—it rewards the well-played shot and penalizes one that is loosely played. A string of four bunkers, one of them a monster, guards the left side of the driving area. Playing close to the bunkers affords a better shot into a long, narrow green, but the risk there is obvious. If the bunkers are widely avoided with a tee shot more toward the center or right, the second shot must come in at an awkward angle over another line of bunkers along the right side of the green and stretching well in front of it. The sixth is one of Ben Hogan's favorites, and few ever appreciated a well-designed hole more than he.

Cypress Point's 17th, only 375 yards long, is another medium-length hole that provides a stringent test of the player's skill. The drive is from an elevated tee to a wide fairway, not difficult in itself, but it must be placed far enough and accurately enough to get past a large pine that can catch the second shot. With a tee shot that is short, the player must direct his second shot over the bordering ocean cliff and try to hook it back into a green that is guarded by massive bunkers, cypress to the back and the ocean to the right.

A single element can go into the making of a great hole. The 13th on my New Course at Ballybunion on the west coast of Ireland measures just 374 yards and requires only a simple but straight drive to the top of the ridge. But the green lies in one of the most natural and beautiful sites in the world, a cliff towering to the left and a sharp dropoff into trouble on the right. The green itself is long and relatively narrow, and the shot, gorgeous though the scene may be, is intimidating.

Long par-4s can rely on their length alone to test the golfer, but the great holes provide other examinations as well. The 458-yard 12th at Southern Hills, once called by Ben Hogan "the greatest par-4 12th hole in the United States," sweeps grandly around a bunker on the left of the driving area, turning left and down to a green protected by bunkers front, left and back and by two flanking ponds. The view for the second shot is spectacular and frightening at the same time.

The 10th at Augusta is one of golf's more majestic holes. It measures 485 yards, but because it is downhill most of the way it does not play that long. A daring shot that curves left around the corner is required to get close enough for a middle or short iron, but it must escape the woods that blanket that side. A drive that goes right, or short, leaves a long second to a difficult green, with a bunker awaiting on the right and those thick woods on the left.

Merion, one of the shortest championship courses at just over 6,500 yards, finishes with one of the longest and hardest par-4 holes anywhere, the 458-yard 18th that demands a 200-yard carry over wasteland through a narrow gap, then a long downhill second shot to a green well-fortified by bunkers.

One of the marvelous unknown long par-4 holes, probably because the course is not played that much by world travelers, is the fourth on the Dunluce Links at Royal Portrush in Northern Ireland. At 463 yards it poses every challenge that a great hole should. The drive from an elevated tee to a rolling fairway must avoid gaping bunkers on the left and heavy, mounded rough on the right. The second shot is to a longish green nestled among mounds and set at somewhat of a diagonal to the approach. Once on the undulating green the problems have just begun. The hole is called Primrose Dell, but the path is hardly that.

Having survived there, if he has, the golfer goes to the fifth, where he faces a sharp dogleg right of 392 yards, the tee shot downhill from an elevated tee across impenetrable rough. Bite off as much as you dare, but if you miss, simply play your provisional. The second, then, is back uphill to a green perched on a gorgeous seaside cliff.

There is no record of such a survey, but these may be the two most spectacular back-to-back par-4 holes in the world.

Par 5s

The par-5 might be the favorite hole for most players. As I said earlier, it gives them a chance to miss a shot and still make par. It also offers the most variety in options, club selections, target and so forth. Certainly it can be an intriguing hole for the architect because of those same factors. He has a great deal of creative license in determining the routing of the fairway, the placing of the hazards and the size and contour of the green. There also is a grandeur to the par-5 hole, because of its length, which the good architect can use to his advantage and which all players appreciate, whether from an aesthetic or technical standpoint.

The par-5 certainly is, or should be, the favorite of the better player. The concept of a par-5 hole has changed considerably over the years with the improvements in technology and the strength and skill of the better players. The original long par-5 was designed to be played with a driver, a brassie, a niblick and two putts. Nobody was supposed to get home in two. Now even a 600-yard hole is not inviolate. Some bomber will be able to reach it in two shots.

For some players nowadays there is no such thing as a par-5 hole. On many courses the stronger hitters can reach all of them in two. I chuckle sometimes at the designation of "eagle." They don't make eagles. They make two shots and a putt. The par-5s have become simply long par-4s.

I'm not opposed to a par-5 being reachable in two shots, if the hole forces the player to make two very good shots and if there is a strong risk/reward factor involved. If a player wants to try to make a three-shot hole in two, he must be willing to pay the price if he fails. That's why water has been introduced and is now so prevalent on par-5s, especially around the green. There wasn't any on the old links course, but it wasn't needed. Now it is necessary, to penalize the player who gambles and misses.

The difficulty in designing a good par-5 lies in the very element that makes it attractive. How long or short do you make it? A 500-yard par-5 can be handled nicely by the majority of male players, at least as far as distance is concerned. That's a drive of 210 yards, a wood shot of 190 and a short iron of 100. Unfortunately, that's little more than a good par-4 for the stronger player. Yet a 600-yard par-5 is one that most amateurs will find difficult to reach in three shots. The placement of different tees obviously can help solve the problem, although that makes the placement of the bunkers and other hazards even more critical.

That aside, the architect must strive to achieve in his par-5 holes what he does in all the others—variety. Par-5 holes should vary in length and characteristics. A long par-5, probably one that is unreachable in two shots by most players, a short par-5 that can be reached but has trouble everywhere, and two medium-length par-5s that incorporate different hazards—water, sand, elevated greens, whatever—might be the ideal mix. But that's simply a formula, and as I've said elsewhere, we don't build our golf courses that way. Usually the available land dictates the nature of the holes, but a good architect can use his imagination to come up with four testing holes, each of which plays differently.

The 13th at Augusta National, for example, is one of the world's classic par-5 holes, perhaps the best short par-5 ever built. It measures just 485 yards, barely longer than many par-4 holes on championship courses and in fact the same length as the par-4 10th hole at Augusta. It is easily reachable in two shots for the longer hitters, yet danger lurks with every swing. It is a superb example of a strategic hole that does not require great length to be intimidating, penal and rewarding at the same time. Thus it has been the scene of many memorable moments, both triumphs and disasters, in the Masters.

The 13th doglegs sharply left. Trees line the right side in the driving zone. Deep woods and a creek run all along the left, and the creek winds across the front of the green, which is set on the diagonal to the line of the second shot, slopes from back to front and is particularly severe toward the front portion. Bunkers and swales guard the back and sides of the green.

A tee shot hit straight leaves a much longer shot into the green, and if it is hit too far it will find the trees on the right. In either case a layup in front of the creek probably will be necessary. The hole can be shortened considerably if the drive is drawn around the corner. For the professionals, only an iron shot is left to the green. But if the draw turns into a hook, the ball can find the woods or creek. Even from good position in the fairway, the second shot must be precise—slightly pushed, it will find the creek in front of the green; if it is pulled or hooked, the natural reaction under the circumstances, it can go left or over, and the player is left with a treacherous shot down the slope.

The hole thus becomes the perfect model of the risk-versus- reward philosophy. If the player takes the risk and executes the shots well, the reward is there. If he fails in the execution, severe trouble awaits.

The 15th hole at Augusta National and the 16th at Firestone South, which I designed when I remodeled the course in 1959, are examples of par-5 holes that are more heroic and less strategic. In a way, they're close to being penal.

The 15th at Augusta, now stretched to 522 yards, is a straightaway hole that is marvelous because it offers the opportunity to gamble. After the drive the hole rolls downhill to a pond that fronts an elevated green, wide but shallow and crowned. A second shot to the green almost always has to be played with a fairway wood or a long iron, and it has to be a near-perfect effort. Slightly short and the ball is likely to roll back into the water. Slightly long and it will bound over the green into rough beyond, from which recovery is difficult because the crowned green at that point falls away from the player.

If the player chooses to lay up short of the pond on his second shot, he still must carry the water with a difficult pitch that usually must be struck from a downhill lie. There really is no alternate route to the putting surface.

All of this makes it a hole on which thinking is extremely important and shot execution even more so.

Firestone's 16th is a massive hole of 625 yards, although it plays shorter than that because it is all downhill. Woods border the fairway on both sides, and a large bunker on the left could catch a mis-hit second shot. And mishitting that shot is a definite possibility, because it is played from a downhill lie. A small pond guards almost the entire front of the green. There is a narrow opening to the left through which a skillfully played shot could be bounced onto the green. But even if it avoids the bunkers on the left, there is no chance to get the ball close to a hole cut on the right side, where it usually is for championship competition. In most cases, then, the third shot must be a precisely struck pitch to a green that slopes sharply from back to front, with even a plateau area on the right side. If the shot is slightly short, it likely will find water. If it is too long, a near-impossible putt or pitch from the surrounding rough awaits. So the hole requires that wonderful combination of power and length with an exquisite touch on the shorter shots to be successfully negotiated.

The 13th hole at the Dunes in Myrtle Beach, 576 yards from the back, 522 yards from the regular tees and angling sharply to the right around a large lake, is an archetypical heroic dogleg. The tee shot is straightaway, and the player has the option of hitting anything from a driver to an iron. The iron is the safer play, but it leaves a longer carry across the lake on the second shot. On the second shot the player can bite off as much as he wants—the more he bites off, the closer he is to the green for his third shot, providing he clears the water. The second shot has to be with a fairway wood or a long iron for the bigger hitter if he wants to get within short-iron range of the green. If the golfer chooses to play safe with an iron and carry just the corner of the lake, he usually is unable to get home with his third shot.

The 18th at Pebble Beach, 540 yards long with Carmel Bay hard by the entire left side, poses another strategic option, this time off the tee. The player can shorten his route almost as much as he wants by directing his drive at whatever angle over the water and rocks below. Just make sure it doesn't go left. To the right lies safety, although a bunker and trees lurk in the landing zone. But now the rest of the route is longer, and it's best to approach the tilted, heavily bunkered green with the shortest shot possible.

For sheer brutishness it is hard to top the 17th at Baltusrol. At 623 yards it is the longest par-5 ever to be played in a U.S. Open. About 375 yards from the tee the fairway is split by the Sahara Desert, a vast area of sand and rough-covered mounds. This poses no problem for the professional who can direct a drive through towering trees, then strike a crisp second shot. But it can cause much trouble for the amateur who might not play with such precision. Providing the Sahara is successfully negotiated, the third shot is uphill to one of A. W. Tillinghast's insidiously subtle greens.

The 17th is the first of back-to-back finishing par-5s at Baltusrol, another daring Tillinghast touch. The 18th is shorter at 542 yards, a stream traversing it at a point designed to catch the player who slightly misses either his drive or second shot. The green is again elevated from the fairway, guarded front and side by bunkers. And again the putting surface, while not severe, is difficult to judge. But not by Jack Nicklaus in 1980, who birdied both the 17th and 18th in the final round to win his fourth U.S. Open Championship.

Par 3s

A par-3 hole is, of course, a one-shot hole. It's been said to me that, because of this, these must be the most boring to design. On the contrary, the par-3s can be the most charming holes on a course to design and to play. They also can be the most difficult, from both perspectives.

To begin with, the par-3s can be the most beautiful and spectacular holes on a golf course. Each is a whole, a self-contained entity encompassing the tee, the hazards and the green, all visible and within reach. Unlike the par-4s and par-5s, which climb and fall and turn, the green not always in sight, the par-3 is an arena, a stage.

The element of one shot enhances the drama. If the player is seeking a birdie or a two-putt par, there are no options, no strategies here, other than choosing which portion of the green to aim for. Unlike the par-5, where a miss can be overcome, a miss on a par-3 means the next shot must be a brilliant recovery. That puts added pressure on the player.

In the normal allotment of four par-3s there again should be balance and variety—long, short and in-between. There must be that change of pace to make the par-3s exciting. The variety in design can be infinite—the Redan, the punch bowl, the water hole, the sand holes. All these concepts combined with the difference in lengths make the variations inexhaustible.

Some architects believe no par-3 should require a wood for most players, that none should be longer than about 190 yards. I disagree. I think one par-3 hole should be longer than 200 yards, stretching to 250 if need be, so that, with the use of flexible teeing areas, players from high handicappers to professionals must use a wooden club—or a metal fairway club, as the trend seems to be these days.

Oakmont has two of these, the 244-yard eighth hole, where the shot must avoid a huge bunker on the left and a string of bunkers down the right-hand side, and the 16th, a 230-yarder over a swale to a green guarded by a deep bunker on the right and a huge one on the left. This is where Larry Nelson, playing his first hole after an overnight rain delay, won the 1982 U.S. Open with a wood shot to the green and a lengthy putt for a birdie.

Two of these semi-monsters may be too many on a course—the shortest of Oakmont's par-3 holes is 185 yards, in fact—but it's in keeping with its reputation as perhaps the hardest course in the world.

Perhaps the most talked-about par-3 hole in the world is the 16th at Cypress Point. It plays 233 yards from the back tees, usually into the wind, almost always requires a wood, often a full driver, and the carry to the green is all over water and rocks. As I discussed earlier, there is a bail-out area for the timid, which makes the 16th a fine strategic hole but not necessarily a good par-3 for the majority of players, who must seek that relief. The lovely 15th, at only 139 yards and also requiring a carry over water and bunkers as well, probably is a better hole.

In fact, some of the best par-3s, perhaps *the* best in overall shotmaking requirements, are the shortest. The second most talked-about par-3 among golfers, undoubtedly because it is on television every year during the Masters, may be the 12th at Augusta. It measures only 155 yards, but the green, while wide, is shallow, with a swale on the back left, a crown on the back right, two bunkers at the back, a small bunker at the front and Rae's Creek guarding the whole thing. And the winds, constantly swirling, protect it all, creating continual confusion in the mind of the player trying to select a club. It is the essence of the short but treacherous par-3.

So, too, is the seventh at Pebble Beach, a mere 120 yards and steeply downhill, its tiny green sitting on a promontory that juts into the ocean and surrounded by bunkers. On a calm day it is a mere flick with a wedge. When the wind is howling, as it often does, professionals have been known to launch 3-irons into the elements.

Without the water and the ferocious gales, the 10th at Pine Valley still can hold its own. Just 145 yards long from the championship tee, it requires a precise placement of the tee shot to a sloping, undulating green. If the shot falls a bit short—and even if it lands on the front edge with backspin—it may end up in a deep pot bunker known as the Devil's Asshole, a vulgar but totally appropriate sobriquet. Once in it, the best escape may be to pick up and trudge to the next tee.

Certainly the most famous par-3 design is the Redan, which originated on the 15th hole at North Berwick in Scotland. It is usually a longish hole— 192 yards at North Berwick—where the green sits on the diagonal, sloping from front to back or right to left and protected by a huge bunker on the left. A play to the right front is the safe one, but if the hole is cut left the putt can be impossible. If the shot is directed at that pin position, it must be unerring. There is little chance of recovery if the green is missed. At this point the player must marshal his senses, using the most objective analysis of his abilities at the moment to decide which route he is going to take. Having made that decision, he then must be in complete control of his emotions in order to pull off the shot. This is the essence of what golf is all about.

The Redan design has been copied innumerable times, most notably by Charles Macdonald at the National Golf Links and by Tillinghast on the second hole at Somerset Hills in New Jersey. Both the seventh and 17th at Shinnecock Hills bear marked resemblances. So does the 17th at Pebble Beach, although the hole runs upward rather than downward from front to back.

If they depend on the natural conditions, as so many holes do, there need be nothing tricky about a great par-3. The 15th at Portmarnock outside Dublin, Ireland, is an example. It plays to 192 yards from an elevated tee. The narrow green is protected on the front by devilish pot bunkers, one on either side, but the real problem is the wind that whips off the sea lying off the right side. Arnold Palmer has called it the greatest par-3 in the world.

I'll leave that judgment to others, just as I would leave to you your choice of the greatest holes. To paraphrase a bit, greatness is certainly in the eye of the beholder.

Following pages: Page 241: A parkland flavor, as close as you can come to it in Scotland, shows up here on the 433-yard 13th on the Queen's Course at Gleneagles, where water, rough and an elevated green make for a testing par-4. Page 242: Water, sand and marshland combine to threaten the golfer on the 539-yard par-5 6th hole at Old Trail near Boynton Beach, Florida. Page 243 top: The par-5 15th at Lake Nona outside Orlando, Florida, is 578 yards long from the back and requires the golfer to avoid this huge bunker on the left both off the tee and on the second shot. Lake Nona itself also threatens to the left of the sand. Page 243 bottom: The 10th at the Greenbrier in White Sulphur Springs, West Virginia, site of the 1979 Ryder Cup Matches, is a short par-4 that requires a dangerous carry over water on the shot to the green. Page 244 top: One of the most famous and testing par-5s in the world is the 625-yard 16th at Firestone South in Akron, Ohio, requiring a delicate pitch over water for the third shot. Page 244 bottom: The par-4 11th on the Valley Course at Royal Portrush is flanked by dunes and pocked by bunkers. Page 245 top: The 5th on The Bear at Grand Traverse in Acme, Michigan, a 243-yard par-4, winds through dunelike mounds that will swallow the errant shot. Page 245 bottom: The par-4 3rd at Carnoustie in Scotland, a difficult and fabled British Open Course, typically takes advantage of the natural dunes and undulations. Page 246 top: The 4th at Portmarnock outside Dublin, Ireland, swings left through rugged dunes and, at 460 yards from the back, is a strong par-4 that demands length and accuracy. Page 246 bottom: The 14th green at Tralee sits at the top of the Dingle Peninsula overlooking Tralee Bay and one of the gold world's most beautiful views. Most of Ryan's Daughter was filmed on the beach below the course. Page 247: The 17th on the Old Course at St. Andrews, the famous Road Hole, was once a par-5 but now is a 461-yard par-4 whose green is guarded by the Road Bunker on the left and the notorious road and wall behind and to the right. Page 248 top: One of the world's most famous and most-copied par-3s is the 12th at Augusta National, a 155-yarder to a wide but shallow green, bedeviled by swirling winds that make guesswork of the tee shot. Page 248 bottom: The 7th (now called the 8th) on the Queen's Course at Gleneagles is a downhill par-5, doglegging 491 yards through some of Scotland's notorious bunkers. Page 249 top: The par-4 16th at Jupiter Hills is a stern 335-yarder that heads straight uphill, with a rank of bunkers pro-

tecting the left side and trees threatening on the right. Page 249 bottom: The 17th at National Golf Links on Long Island is a medium-length par-4 of 386 yards that requires a tee shot over wasteland, then a shot to the green that must miss these menacing bunkers. Page 250-251: The beguiling and bedeviling 7th at Pebble Beach is perhaps the world's most feared short hole. At only 120 yards from the back tee, with bunkers surrounding and the ocean encroaching on three sides, the shot from the elevated tee can be benign on a windless day. But it can entail horrifying guesswork when the breezes blow, which they usually do. Page 252: The 6th at Treetops in Gaylord, Michigan, is a spectacular 185-yard par-3 with a 125-foot drop from tee to green. This view inspired the course's name, for obvious reasons. Page 253 top: The par-3 3rd at the Boulders in Carefree, Arizona, is a 187-yard beauty set in a spectacular setting that exemplifies the course name. Page 253 bottom: Perhaps the greatest short par-5 in the world, the 485-yard 13th at Augusta National doglegs left and offers the better player a relatively easy chance to get home in two shots, provided he can avoid the creek in front and the bunkers at the rear. Then he must negotiate a green that slopes perilously toward the water. Page 254 top: The 3rd at Mauna Kea on the Island of Hawaii, one of the world's most spectacular par-3 holes, requires a 210-yard carry from the back tees over Turtle Spawning Bay to this huge green that offers several exacting pin positions. Robert Trent Jones considers it perhaps his best par-3. Page 254 bottom: The 2nd at National Golf Links is only 271 yards long, but once the player has negotiated the 200-yard carry demanded off the tee and the short pitch, he must contend with a severely contoured green that tests putting skills to the utmost. Page 255 top: The 17th on the Calibogue nine at Haig Point on Daufuskie Island, South Carolina, is a par-3 that calls for a 179-yard carry and shows an adroit use of wetlands. Page 255 bottom: The 7th at La Grande Motte, a Trent Jones seaside resort course in France. Page 256 top: The 9th at Yale in New Haven, Connecticut, a C. B. Macdonald design, is a good-sized par-3 with a deep swale dividing a huge green. If the tee shot ends up on the wrong portion, or in the swale, two-putting is a task. Page 256 bottom: Immediately preceding the famed 16th at Cypress Point is another and perhaps better, par-3, the beautiful 15th that requires a 139-yard tee shot over an inlet to a treacherous green surrounded by bunkers.

Lake Nona, #15

Greenbrier, #10

Firestone, #16 South

Royal Portrush, #5

Grand Traverse, #11 The Bear

Carnoustie, #3

Tralee, #14

Portmarnock, #4

Augusta, #12

Gleneagles, #7 Queen's

Jupiter Hills, #16

National Golf Links, #17

Following pages: *Pebble Beach, #7*

Boulders, #3

Augusta, #13

Mauna Kea, #3

National Golf Links, #2

Haig Point, #17

La Grande Motte, #7

Yale, #9

Cypress Point, #15

Chapter 8
Greens, the Ultimate Defense

The marvelous appeal of golf lies in its infinite variety. The tees, fairways, rough, hazards and all that we have examined to this point require an unlimited number of decisions and the execution of many different skills on the part of the player to be successfully negotiated. Yet perhaps the best and most challenging aspect of all is left for last on every hole.

The green is the ultimate target. Nothing is more enjoyable than to play a shot to a beautifully designed green, placed in proper perspective to the overall hole, where the adjacent bunkers are in harmony with the contours of the putting surface and where the pin positions are so subtle as to demand of the golfer the greatest possible planning and skill to put his ball where he has the best chance to make his putt.

The variety of green design is infinite. There are elevated greens, greens at fairway level, terraced greens, greens tilted toward or away from the player, dished-in greens that collect the ball, mounded greens that reject all but the most precise shots . . . or various combinations of all these characteristics. There are greens protected by trapping on the sides or by trapping in front. There are greens guarded by creeks or ponds that demand the ball be carried to the proper position. All these various and varied designs contribute to the joy of playing a golf course . . . or to the frustration of golf when the player fails to meet their demands.

The great golf courses of the world are that because of their green contours. The routing must be good, of course, and the holes must be challenging to a player's shotmaking skills. But many not-so-great courses have well-designed holes that fall short in the long run because they have ordinary greens that fail to put a premium on placing the ball in the right place on the putting surface, on making the player think out the approach shot and then executing it properly if he is to get it close. Thus there is less premium on making shots from the tee and the fairway.

The good architect creates strategy, as I have said. He dictates the way the hole is played by the various classes of golfers by the placement of his tees and hazards and the configuration of his fairway. But the strategic demands are greatly diminished if he fails to properly design the ultimate target.

For example, The International that we built outside of Washington, D.C., has a green that sits very close to an embankment falling off into water on the left. There is a tongue area on the left, protected by a bunker in front, and a pin position there is challenging for the better player but extremely penal for most golfers. So you provide a large area to the right, put a grass bunker in front, give the player a chance to run the ball on the green, and you have a hole with a lot of latitude, one that most players can enjoy. At the same time, you have a green that offers championship pin positions.

MacKenzie's greens, for example, are strongly contoured—sometimes to the extreme, as I have said—and often are hemmed in with mounds. The mounds serve a dual purpose—they impose shotmaking hazards near a green that require an extremely deft touch from unusual and awkward stances in playing chips and delicate pitches, and they become an integral part of the characteristic of the adjoining green. The slope or ridge in a green is designed to be a continuation of the slope of a mound, and the hollows between the mounds flow into similar swales or depressions in the green. His greens and the areas surrounding them are sophisticated creations that beautifully integrate the mounds and the bunkers with the putting surface.

I have often followed the practice of framing greens with mounds, usually in conjunction with bunkers. Among other benefits, mounding penalizes in direct proportion to the seriousness of the error. If a shot is badly missed, the next shot will be a hazardous one over a mound or trap. The golfer who makes only a slight error and thus ends up closer to the putting surface will have an easier recovery shot.

Mounding creates a termination to each hole that can be aesthetically pleasing. It also can give the hole a sense of isolation from the other holes, since the mounds tend to block part of the view beyond the green.

On the green itself MacKenzie was a master of what I like to call "the reverse curve," a slightly convex sector that gradually descends to an adjoining area that is concave in its configuration. The well-designed green is made up of a series of these curves, one perhaps shorter than the next, one longer, all blending into each other so that the green has a rhythm of line, a beautiful flow that gives the entire putting surface a lovely look, all the while tending to confound the putter. There is nothing harsh about it. It is the look we take from the curvature and flow of the dunes. There are no straight lines there.

MacKenzie abhorred straight lines, so all his greens had a free-flowing sweep and grandeur to them. Both he and Bob Jones believed, as I do, that there should be hazards to putting, so it is no surprise that the greens at Augusta National manifest this philosophy. Many of the putting surfaces there have been redone, but within the concept of MacKenzie's original design, and the contours, swales, slopes, crowns, tiers and terraces make them, collectively, the most unusual group of putting surfaces in the world. The challenges are sometimes severe, but they are tests that the amateur, who cannot strike the ball as long or as well as the professional, has a chance to handle as well as the best players in the world.

The architect's job in designing a great green is to deceive the player if he can. Certainly he should develop contours that require the player to have a fine sense of touch to negotiate the rolls properly, to find the right combination of line and speed. It's amazing how much touch, how much feel, the really good putters have. If you give them a flat surface, or one with very little contour, you're giving away a lot of easy birdies. It's the job of the architect to make sure that no birdie comes easily. MacKenzie certainly achieved that.

So did Donald Ross and A. W. Tillinghast, both of whom had specific if different philosophies regarding greens, as I have indicated. Ross's greens generally were crowned, falling away at the sides, making it especially difficult to get an approach shot close to the hole and putting an emphasis on chipping and pitching. Tillinghast liked to dish in his greens so they would "collect" an approach shot. But his greens are smaller, for the most part, and once on them the putting problems often are excruciating.

Tillinghast especially was a master in creating deception with his putting surfaces, some of which seem innocuous at first glance. His dished-in greens often tilt sharply from back to front with the slopes running from each side toward the middle. This means that in the confluences where the slopes meet it is extremely difficult to determine which way a putt will break.

Tillie, of course, was not limited to one style. He designed many marvelous and varied greens. One in particular is on the long par-3 10th hole at Winged Foot West. It is a triple-level green that is only slightly dished in, sloping from back to front, wider at the back and narrow at the opening in front. A bunker, rough and trees left and a huge, deep bunker on the right pose trouble for the shot that misses. The green becomes easier to hit the farther back the ball is played, but a putt from above the cup on any level is treacherous.

Even more diabolical is the 18th green on the same course. The general slope of the putting surface is sharp from back to front and left to right. There is a shelf on the front third of the green, falling off sharply to the front. A swale runs through the back third. The combination provides all kinds of pin positions, and all of them are difficult to read.

There are many ways to practice deception. Tillinghast knew most of them, as does any good architect. It is up to the golfer, then, to cut through that deception and figure out the best position in which to put his ball for the best possible putt at the hole. Almost always that is somewhere below the hole and as close as possible, unless other considerations intervene. Getting there demands a perceptive look at the particular green, then the skill to execute the shot. Both are required for the ultimate satisfaction.

Selecting a green site is critical, because if you want the green and the hole to look natural, the location of the green has to be correct. Sometimes this is difficult and sometimes it is easy, depending on the land with which the architect has to work. The New course at Ballybunion had probably five hundred natural greensites. I told them I could build the greatest golf course in the world there, simply because God gave me the land. But we always try to design to a site. In other words, if the area we have chosen for a green tilts a certain way, we design the green to accommodate that tilt. The green must "fit." It must look as if it belongs. The good architect doesn't simply blow off the top of a hill because he thinks it would be a good site for an elevated green. Bad architects sometimes do, I must admit. When at all possible, and I can think of very few times when it is not, the green must be worked into the topography. While God didn't design it, the good architect will make it look as if He did.

This is not to say we don't look for unusual greensites. In fact, we must if we are to create variety, making each hole and each course different from the rest. For example, in 1938 I built what I believe is the first island green, one surrounded by water. It was part of nine holes I built for Doris Duke on her preserve near Somerville, New Jersey. The island was in the center of a lake, about 110 yards from shore. The players had to get to and from the green by rowboat. I also put a tee on the island so players had to drive over the lake to reach the next fairway.

I was accused of building the hole only for its attractiveness, but it really was an extremely playable hole, and the water made it dangerous, at least in the minds of the golfers. The green had 6,300 feet of putting surface, which would seem easy to hit, but the psychological pressure of the water often did funny things to golf swings.

Today there are many island greens of one type or another, but this was the first I had ever seen.

Greensites come in many forms. They can be nestled in a valley or a hillside to form a "punch bowl" effect. They can be set against a hill or cliff on one side with a sharp dropoff on the other. They can be elevated on a natural plateau. They can be set into woods or built on treeless plains, guarded by natural water formations or protected by bunkers built specifically for the purpose.

Equally as important as the site itself is the manner in which the green is set into the site, the angle at which it is built in relation to the approach shot that must be played and the shape of the green. The much-copied Redan Hole at North Berwick in Scotland is an example of the importance of angle. The hole and the green would be good under any circumstance, but the diagonal angling of the green makes it great because of the options it offers and the severe test it provides in getting close to certain pin positions.

Similarly, the angle and sloping of the par-5 13th green at Augusta makes the hole what it is. If the second shot is laid up, what is left is an ordinary pitch into a wide and reasonably deep green that slopes toward the player. But if the second shot is aimed at the green, the target becomes much narrower, sloping treacherously toward the water in front.

The width and depth of a green, along with its shape, also can be critical. Both the par-3 12th at Augusta, another hole that has been extensively copied, and the par-5 15th, have greens that are comfortably wide but relatively shallow from back to front. Both have water in front and trouble behind. Therefore the player is required to strike his shot a precise distance.

The shape and size of the green are especially critical in making a short par-3 or par-4 hole challenging. A pear-shaped or kidney-shaped green often is applicable here. The front area can be used for any occasion on which you want the hole to play easier. For tournament competition the back area of any green shaped like this will provide a more difficult target, especially if it is guarded by bunkers or water. And it almost always should be.

These are but a few examples of how an imaginative architect can force the player to think through his shots and to decide carefully on any venture that poses risk versus reward.

The green itself should be designed to provide a variety of options for different circumstances. It should be divided into areas, each with a different problem that requires a controlled stroke to overcome. Yet each area should be such that the cup can be located in a fair position where, if the shot is properly executed, the chance to make the putt is a good one. Each green should offer a challenge, yet it also must offer players of all ability levels the opportunity to conquer it with a properly conceived plan and a correct stroke. If the green is suitably designed, there will be enough variety in possible hole locations that, coupled with changes in the tee placement, the hole can and must be played in an infinite number of ways.

Variety is important not only within an individual green but among all the greens on a course. Each green should have a slightly different mold than the others. There are unlimited ways you can do this by varying the slope in individual portions of the green, the tilt of the whole green, the pockets and swales you build into greens. The general concept might be the same, but the look should vary, one sweeping one way, one another, the contours subtly or sharply different, each blending in the most natural way into the site chosen for the green. The great courses—Augusta, Cypress Point, Peachtree, Pine Valley (especially Pine Valley)—all have greens that vary from hole to hole, as do the great links courses around the world.

The one thing I don't want is a dead flat green. That's a nothing. The only time a green should be even relatively flat is when the player must cross a creek or a lake to get there.

The difficulty of the respective pin positions should be determined by the shots that are going to be played into them. Remember, no birdie should come easily. So if there is a tournament on the course and the professional or good amateur is going to be playing a short iron into a particular green, I want there to be some places to put the hole that will require an extremely precise shot to get the ball close. And there should be a great deal of risk, a great potential for trouble, if the player doesn't pull it off. A shot hit to the wrong side of the hole should have a very good chance of winding up in a bunker or water. And if the player bails out on the shot to the safe portion of the green, the birdie putt will have to travel over contours, through folds and swales, and will be difficult to make.

At the same time, the green must allow hole locations that are reachable for the higher handicap players who will be playing from greater distances with longer clubs. They should be given a chance to get the ball reasonably close without undue risk, providing they strike a good shot.

I'm fond of building bays or tongue areas into a green. These are simply areas that protrude from the green proper, generally fronted by bunkers or rough and usually relatively small, in which you can "hide" the cup. They call for an extremely precise shot if the player is after a birdie, or if he is called on to recover after missing his approach shot to the green. At the same time, placing the hole in a tongue allows the less skillful or less daring player to aim for the center of the green, where he doesn't have to contend with the hazards. If he makes it, he won't be close to the hole, but he will have a reasonable two-putt opportunity.

That's why I've always preferred big greens. I've been criticized for this, but mainly by professionals and the better players who have the ability to play shots to a smaller target.

Henry Longhurst, the late British writer and television commentator, used to kid me about the size of my greens. One day we were walking around Royal St. George's in England, one of the stops on the British Open rota, and I said, "Henry, you criticize the size of my greens, yet look at these. They're a lot bigger than any green I ever built." Henry replied, "They have to be, because the shots don't hold as well here and you have to allow room to let the ball run." Which is true.

My philosophy *has* changed some, and over the years we've incorporated more small and medium-sized greens into our designs. One reason for this is that maintenance procedures have become more refined and the ball holds better now. Certainly the size of the green should be commensurate with the length of the hole and the shot being played into it, as well as the prevailing turf and weather conditions. Still, the bigger green provides more pin positions and gives you more flexibility in setting up the course for all levels of players. The bigger green also helps the higher handicapper. The flagstick is the target for the better player. The green is the target for everybody else, and the bigger the target, the easier it is to hit, of course.

Putting is the great equalizer. The green, more than any other area, is the leveler for all golfers. Once a golfer moves out of the duffer stage, he or she is likely to be able to handle putting better than any other facet of the game. The professional or very good amateur can make the long chip shot or the tricky pitch as easily as a long putt. Most other golfers cannot. Therefore, the bigger the putting surface, the better chance they have of making their par or bogey, assuming the hole is located in an area of the green that is fair for them.

For example, many architects used to install bunkers ten or twenty yards in front of the putting surface, or just to the side of the line of play. That was deceptive, and I have no problem with deception. But the player who got just over the bunker often found himself short of the green, facing the task of playing a skillful pitch to get close. We might install a bunker in the same relative place on the hole, but we would simply extend the putting surface forward to meet it. Thus the player who was deceived still would have a chance to recover by getting a long putt close, something more within his ability than a delicate pitch or chip. He makes a better score and has more fun, which is supposed to be the object of golf. The better player, meanwhile, usually knows exactly where the pin is and how far he must hit his shot. He likely won't miss short, and if he misses right or left he is still faced with an exacting recovery shot.

So a big green, properly designed, is really just a connected series of smaller greens. If the player misses his target area, he is likely to end up on "another" green. He still has a chance to get his putt close with a skillful stroke, but he has greatly diminished his opportunity to make the first putt.

Incidentally, every big green I've ever designed pales in comparison with the one I did at Aventura Country Club in Miami, now called Turnberry Isle, back in the 1970s. I was asked to give the club "something spectacular," so I built the biggest green in the world. It had 47,936 square feet—more than an acre—of putting surface. It actually was a triple green, serving the ninth hole of the North Course and the sixth and ninth holes of the South Course. That makes it bigger than the double greens at St. Andrews, bigger than the sixth green at the International Golf Club in Bolton, Massachusetts, which has 30,000 square feet of surface, and bigger than the 27,500-square foot double green we built at the Golf Club de Geneve in Geneva, Switzerland.

The back of the green is 491 feet wide. How wide is that? Julius Boros, the Hall of Fame player who represented the club on Tour, tried to hit a 6-iron across the green and repeatedly failed by about five yards.

Even so, the player doesn't get the impression of a massive green. The putting area is broken into three broad fingers, ranging in depth from 138 to 120 feet. Each is separated by expansive areas of sand that define the green area for each hole. So the club got its "something spectacular," but there is no hint of the grotesque and the playing values of the courses were not diminished.

The ability to sketch becomes invaluable in designing greens. I can sketch a green and a variety of pin positions. On paper I can see how all of those positions should be defended, whether it's with a shoulder, a pocket, a crown, a swale, nearby water or some other means. At the same time, because I was a good player, I can attach a shot value to each position. I can get a good idea of how great the shot has to be or how much error is allowed. So I can modify a green or change it dramatically as many times as I want on paper. I may make a hundred sketches before I come up with eighteen greens, which is an awful lot cheaper than having to redo a green once it's built.

Peachtree and Augusta National exemplify the best principles of modern golf course architecture. The difference between the two courses lies basically in the design of their greens. Each green on each course has five or six definite pin positions, of which at least four are ideal for tournament play. These positions are the target areas for the better golfer, whereas the whole green is the target for the handicap player.

The greens at Peachtree are undulating, but they are not as severe, the slopes are not as continuous and tilted, nor are the crowns as severe as they are at Augusta. The undulations at Peachtree are folds between the various pin positions, and the greens there are larger in keeping with this principle.

The greens on both courses are of the plateau type for the most part. But the greens at Augusta generally fall from back to front, while the various pin areas at Peachtree fall in no general direction but take the nearest obvious outlet to all sides of the green.

This plenitude of possible locations for the cup, coupled with the extreme length of its tees, gives Peachtree its tremendous flexibility and the possibility for infinite variety. This, of course, is the mark of a course that can be great for players at all levels of skill and strength.

In some cases, especially with some of the older courses, the greens are the total defense of the course. The Olympic Club is an example. The course measured only 6,714 yards as set up for the 1987 Open. It plays longer than that, but if those greens were flat, the professionals today would tear it apart. Instead, they are treacherously sloped and contoured, for the most part, so even though the course is short, the shot to the pin is usually one that must be carefully negotiated.

The 18th green is a prime example. Guarded by a bunker in front, the green slopes severely from the back. If the hole is cut on the front portion and your shot winds up on the back plateau, getting down in two putts definitely requires God to be on your side.

It is possible, of course, to design greens that are sloped too severely. If the player, no matter how skillful, cannot apply his sense of feel to a putt and stop it somewhere near the hole, if the ball basically moves of its own momentum, then the slope is too steep or the hole is placed unfairly. If you just start the ball moving and it rolls off the green, or unfairly far past the hole, then the element of touch has been removed from putting and luck takes over.

Even if the green has been skillfully designed, there has been a tendency in recent years, especially in the major championships, to make the putting surfaces so fast it's like playing on linoleum. Even the greens for normal club play are super-fast compared to forty or fifty years ago. This has had two impacts on golf courses. New courses cannot be designed with as much green contour as in the old days, at least if the putting surfaces are to be generally fair. And some greens on some of the great old courses are close to being outmoded. When MacKenzie, Tillinghast, Ross, Flynn and the other great architects were designing their courses during the first half of the century, neither grasses nor mowing equipment were as sophisticated as they are today. The grass was not cut as short and the putting surfaces could not be made nearly as fast as they can be today.

Tillinghast, in particular, has a lot of greens around the country that are unplayable if they are cut to a speed that is considered normal for championship play. The ninth green on the East Course at Baltimore Country Club, for example, is tilted so severely that from above the cup there is usually no way to stop a putt close, even at normal speeds. On the first green at Winged Foot West, which is not even the most severe green on the course, competitors putting from above the cup during the first round of the 1974 U.S. Open often were chipping back with the next stroke.

In the 1981 Open at Merion East, designed by Hugh Wilson in 1912, the upper portion of the 12th green became so fast that nobody could keep a ball on the putting surface from above the cup. It was difficult enough to make it stop when putting from below.

Those were not badly designed slopes at the time, but they are at modern speeds.

On a very fast green, the ball will continue to move of its own momentum on slopes steeper than three or four degrees. So the faster the green speed, the more difficult it is to find fair hole locations. The USGA and other bodies that set up major championships always try to be fair, and to their credit they target a particular speed for all the greens in a championship based on the severity of the greens. Sometimes they even order certain greens to be made slower than the others if the tilt is too great. But grass and weather are difficult to control, and occasionally they still let the greens get too fast for the slopes. Then the complaints come thick and fast, and rightly so.

That's why the architect must be especially careful in working with greens on which major championships, Tour events or other top tournaments will be played. A good example is the 18th green at Augusta National, which has a shelf at the back and slopes sharply downward toward the front. In 1946 I was watching the finish of the Masters with Bob Jones. Ben Hogan came to the final hole needing par to tie Herman Keiser, and he put his second shot on the plateau at the back of the green. The hole was cut on the lower level. Hogan was only about twelve feet away, but I said, "Bob, he can't stop the ball within ten feet of the cup, and he'll probably miss the putt coming back." That's what happened.

Jones said to me, "Trent, that's not fair. We've got to change that." So I went back to Augusta and worked with Jones, taking some dirt off the top shelf and padding the bottom of the green until we thought it was fair. The next year, faced with the same situation Hogan had been in, a player still could get a sense of the putt and roll the ball reasonably close to the hole with an excellent stroke.

In essence, then, a green is a microcosm of the game itself. It should be beautiful, pleasing to the eye. It should be difficult, challenging to players at all levels of skill. But it should be fair in that it will yield a reward, whether birdie, par or bogey, to the player who thinks out his plan and correctly executes the shot required.

That is golf, the greatest game of all, the game of a lifetime for almost everybody.

Following pages: Page 265: *The 18th green at the Olympic Club is protected by bunkers front, left and rear. From a shallow shelf at the rear, the green slopes sharply toward the front. The hole is short at 343 yards, but the green alone makes it demanding.* Pages 266-267: *The 16th on the East Course at Royal Melbourne is a testing par-3 of 170 yards featuring this treacherous green surrounded by heather and sand.* Page 268 top: *The Postage Stamp hole at Troon in Scotland, the 126-yard par-3 9th, is one of the world's most charming and dangerous short holes. Its tiny, undulating green is perched on a plateau and guarded by deep bunkers. In the 1973 British Open, at the age of seventy-one, Gene Sarazen solved all the problems by planting his tee shot in the cup.* Page 268 bottom: *The 5th hole at Crail near St. Andrews in Scotland features a square green so prevalent in early links architecture.* Page 269 top: *The par-3 17th at Mauna Lani on the Island of Hawaii plays only 136 yards from the elevated back tee, but the sloping, deceptive green is surrounded by sand and black lava walls.* Page 269 bottom: *The green on the 7th hole at Rye in England, a 164-yard par-3, has undulations that test the best of putters.* Page 270 top: *The green shapes and surrounding bunkers offer a multiplicity of pin placements on the 14th and 15th holes at St. Georges in Bermuda.* Page 270 bottom: *A ridge through the middle of the par-3 16th at Spanish Bay on the Monterey Peninsula makes placement of the 200-yard tee shot especially important.* Page 270-271: *The swale in the middle of the 11th green at Skyland tries the patience of all golfers on this 177-yard par-3.* Pages 272-273: *Getting to the par-3 island green on PGA West's 17th hole is only half the battle. The player must then negotiate the pla-*

teaus and swales to complete the journey unless, as Lee Trevino did in the 1987 Skins Game, he holes his shot from the tee. Page 274 top: *The 7th at Echo Lake in Plainfield, New Jersey, is a short par-3 at 147 yards, but the green drops off at the back, which makes the tee shot over water even more exacting.* Page 274 bottom: *The 17th at Medinah, a 151-yard par-3, is one of the Augusta 12th look-alikes, although it plays from an elevated tee. The green slopes perilously from back to front, with the only reasonable flat areas in the forward portion.* Page 275 top: *If your ball ends up on the wrong tier at the par-3, 175-yard 7th on the North Course at Cerromar in Puerto Rico, two-putting becomes a problem.* Page 275 bottom: *The 192-yard par-3 15th hole at North Berwick in Scotland features the original Redan, perhaps the most imitated green in the world. Guarded by bunkers at the front and left, it cants from right to left on a diagnol away from the player.* Pages 276-277: *Protected by water on the left, the tricky green on the par-4 1st hole at Les Terraces de Genève nestles into the woods below the French Alps. It is in Boisy, France, just across the border from Geneva.* Page 278: *Trouble looms on the sloping, undulating green on the par-5 6th hole at Waireki in New Zealand.* Pages 278-279: *Severe ridges and swales make the 5th green at Tamarisk in Rancho Mirage, California, a tricky proposition.* Page 280 top: *The 4th on the third nine at Portmarnock, a 338-yard par-4, features a flattish, almost convex green often seen on links courses.* Page 280 bottom: *Shape, slope and undulation make the green on the 14th at Keystone Ranch, a par-3 of 172 yards, extremely difficult. But its beautiful setting, nestled among the Rockies in Dillon, Colorado, eases the golfer's pain.*

Olympic, #18
Following pages: Royal Melbourne, #16 East

Troon, #9

Crail, #5

Mauna Lani, #17

Rye, #7

Skyland, #11

St. George's, #14, #15

Spanish Bay, #16

270

Echo Lake, #7

Medinah, #17

Cerromar, #7

North Berwick, #15　　　　　　　　　　　　　　　　　Following pages: *Les Terraces de Genève, #1*

Wairakei, #6

Tamarisk, #5

Portmarnock, #4

Keystone, #14

Robert Trent Jones's Favorite Five

Ask any architect what his best course to date is, and I wouldn't be surprised if his answer was his last one. That could very well be true for myself as well. I'm often asked which of my own courses is my favorite, and likely as not, I'll point to my recently completed.

Ask me however, my favorite five, tell me to be honest and to take my time, and I'd be hard put not to pick the five shown here. In alphabetical order they are: Ballybunion (New); Firestone South (my remodel); Mauna Kea; Sottogrande (I'll cheat and say both courses); and Spyglass.

All right, my absolute favorite: Why, I haven't designed it yet.

Valderrama: The greatest golfers in the world have found it a difficult test, yet it is beautiful and playable for the club member.

Above: *Ballybunion New: I think it's the greatest links course in the world, not because I did it but because of the character of the terrain.* Below: *Firestone South: It's a great test of golf, with some great holes. It's penal where it has to be penal and it's strategic where strategy is called for. There is a diversity that provides a different challenge on almost every hole.*

Above: Spyglass Hill: I've had knowledgeable people tell me that Spyglass is the best course on the Monterey Peninsula. That includes Pebble Beach and Cypress Point, and certainly Spyglass has a better change of pace than those courses. Below: Mauna Kea is one of the best in the world, and the 9th and 18th are two of the best finishing holes anywhere. The change between elevation and descent, because of the terrain, make it a magnificent course.

Index

(Page numbers in italics denote photographs)

Photo Credits

All photos are © Tony Roberts with the following exceptions:
© Tom Doak: pgs. 47 top; 83; 256 top.
© David Earle: pg. 255 bottom.
© Faith Echtermeyer: pgs. 12-13; 70-71; 73; 76.
© John Halpern: pg. 274.
© Red Hoffman: pgs. 99; 126; 127; 128; 130 131; 132; 133.
© Robert Trent Jones Jr.: pgs. 108-109; 112; 113; 133; 138.
© Leonard Kamsler: pgs. 55 bottom; 61; 66; 134-135; 229 bottom.
© Landslides/Alex S. MacLean: pgs. 59, 174.
© Life Magazine: pg. 103.
© New York Times/Ken Regan: pg. 74 bottom.
© Ray Pace: pg. 199.
© Ralph W. Miller Golf Library and Museum: pgs. 60 top; 67.
© PGA World Golf Hall of Fame: pg. 68.
© Phil Sheldon: pgs. 94; 96-97; 152, 281.
© Glen Silkes: pg. 90.
© Mike Slear: pg. 82.
© USGA: pgs. 62, 63, 65.

The following photos are courtesy of Golf Digest:
Photo by Paul Barton: pg. 36 bottom.
Photo by Leonard Kamsler: pg. 55 bottom.
Photos by Tony Roberts: pgs. 81 top, 84 top, 249 bottom.

Special thanks to Tom Drew of Phoenix Communications in Durham,
North Carolina, who put the right people together.